# Lutherans On The Yangtze

福音道路德會

## Volume I

### 1912-1952

Missionary Conference at Kuling in 1931

# Lutherans On The Yangtze

## (Jangtzee Lutheraner)
## Tome I

A centenary account of the Missouri Synod
in Greater China
1913-2013

### By David G. Kohl
Concordia University, Portland, Oregon

### In consultation with Dr. Hank Rowold
Concordia Theological Seminary, St. Louis, Missouri

One Spirit Press
Portland, Oregon

ISBN: 978-1-893075-42-9
Library of Congress Number: 2013944055

Cover Design

Book Design One Spirit Press, LLC
Photographic editing Ellen Lewis
Indexing Joe Galvan-Davis

Cartoons used with permissons

One Spirit Press, LLC
Portland, Oregon

*I have fought the good fight, I have finished the race.*
II Tim 4:7


2013

# In Memoriam


Loving father, faithful servant, dedicated layman
Arthur R. Kohl


Servants who have departed since I began this research:
Lorraine Behling Sonnenberg
Ruth Proft
Paul Kreyling
Edward May
Dorothy Riedel Hartle
Paul Heerboth
Paul Tuchardt
Manfred Berndt

# Preface

## Threads in a Tapestry

Mel Kieschnick
Educational Missionary to Hong Kong, 1956-1965

*Lutherans on the Yangtze* needs to be written now because the number of those who are still alive to tell and weave the details is shrinking. This book tells a story and weaves a tapestry of facts worth hearing and reflecting upon. It is a tapestry of women and men who faced challenges mostly forgotten, yet this account provides for us models of vision and commitment, faith and failure, hopes dashed and dreams come true.

In several ways, this is an account of a very different era in world and church history -especially as it relates to contemporary China. Most of the events recalled here took place during the time when the USA was the dominant country on earth and China was in constant conflict and poverty, striving against occupation and oppression by foreign powers. By the time of the events recounted here, China has the world's most rapid developing economic power - and very significantly, the country with arguably the fastest growing Christian population of any in the world.

I suggest that as the reader's eye takes in the full tapestry of a century of work among and with our Chinese sisters and brothers, that you note especially certain colors, patterns, and distinct threads which make up the overall scene.

The first strand running through this book is one not often highlighted in writings related to the history of The Lutheran Church-Missouri Synod, namely the thread of the role of women. This book very appropriately notes the sense of call and service of wives who accompanied their husbands, including, for example, Cornelia Meyer who died within months of arrival in China. It also very explicitly lifts up women in the roles of the professional ministries of nurses, deaconesses, Bible women, and teachers with names like Oelschlager, Gruen, Simon, Rhodenbeck, Boss, Behling, Proft and Winkler. Their ministries extended from China to Hong Kong to Taiwan and are still strongly felt today.

The consistent commitment in the Missouri Synod to "do it alone" is a second set of threads. Some will applaud and others will lament, but from the very early days, it was the official policy of the LCMS to avoid unionism, and to shun participation in public worship, literature production, or evangelistic outreach with other Christians - or even *other* Lutherans. Early on, it was decided to choose a different Chinese name for Lutheran in order to distinguish Missouri Lutherans from the other Chinese missions. When translating the Chinese name for God, it became critical that the term be different not only from the noun used by Roman Catholics but also different from the term used by most other Protestant groups. In this context, it is interesting to reflect upon the reality that the incredible growth of the Christian Church in China today (an estimated 60 to 100 million souls) began to occur only after the Communist authorities made it illegal for churches to identify themselves with the titles of particular denominations.

A third dominant thread worth its own bright colored thread is the stress on schools. From the very first small school established by pioneer missionary Arndt to the multitudes of Lutheran schools in Asia today, it is apparent that schools played a critical role in the life and mission of the Church. From that school of less than 20 primary students to a current enrollment of some 25,000 K-12 students in Hong Kong and Taiwan, the Lutheran schools shine as bright stars in God's sky. Significantly, Lutheran schools in China were never narrow in their focus. The evidence is that they aimed not only for Christian nurture, and evangelistic outreach, but for academic excellence and independent thinking, providing salt for society and preparing competent and committed leaders for church and culture.

Any church history finds its context in the political and geographic realities of the day. You'll note how the LCMS ministry in China was always in a setting of political conflict, marauding war lords, communist take-over, tens of millions of deaths by starvation, natural disasters, and the demise of the Portuguese, Chinese, British and Japanese empires. All these factors provide the background of a people determined to proclaim one who is the Prince of Peace.

Finally, there is a strand which I looked for and regretted not finding prominent enough at first. That is the story of the Chinese people themselves. It was the Chinese who responded to the Spirit's call, who sought baptism despite traditional and cultural barriers, and are now God's strongest voice along the Yangtze, the rim of the South China Sea, and among overseas Chinese all over the world. Fortunately, while this thread may not be prominent in the text, the marvelous collection of photos shows the flesh and blood of these critical players in this drama. This hit me personally. I had heard of one of our Chinese pastors who had been ordained after finishing his work at the Hankow Seminary. The story I heard was that he became a victim of Mao's purge, that he had been hung up by his thumbs and demanded to deny his faith. The rumor was that he remained steadfast and as a result was martyred. The last part of this saga was proved false when ten years ago I visited the Christian congregation in Wanchien on the Yangtze. There he was - with open arms and folded hands to welcome me! We were held together by the thread of God's grace - a rope which permeates this entire book.

Enjoy the scenery.

# Table of Contents

Chapters in Volume II

Hong Kong Beginnings - 1949 – 1950
Hong Kong Expansion - 1951 – 62
Maturity and Diversification - 1962 – 1974
The Hong Kong Synod - 1974 – Current
English and International Enterprises - 1962 – Current
Macau – "Not the Least of These" - 1952 – Current
Taiwan – Planting Seeds - 1951 – 1966
Taiwan Expansion  - 1966 – 1985
The Chinese Evangelical Lutheran Church -1985 – Current
Looking Back; Looking Forward

# Perspective

## Witnessing the Fullness of God's Grace

Andrew Chiu
Emeritus President
Lutheran Church-Hong Kong Synod

This work by David Kohl clearly describes the missionary endeavors of the Lutheran Church-Missouri Synod (LCMS) in mainland China, Hong Kong, Macau, and Taiwan in the past hundred years or so. Surely, this evangelistic undertaking had its share of ups and downs. But the fullness of God's grace has never failed the missionaries or their efforts. I have no hesitation to attest to this as I have been involved in various capacities in the ministry of the same church for more than sixty two years.

Having been an army officer in my younger days with some success, I was looking forward to promotions and prosperity. I ended up, however, as a refugee in the then British Colony of Hong Kong in early 1950 after the Civil War in China. After incessant prayers and tears by Deaconess Gertrude Simon, I was led to Christ our Savior and was baptized by Rev. Wilbert Holt on Pentecost in the same year.

When I examined my former self-seeking being and the Christ-like loving care of the missionaries, I resolved to walk in their path. After having been baptized for a month, I became an assistant to the missionaries and began to study in the Bible institute and later in the seminary. During this time, I had been sent to work in Macau for eighteen months where two congregations were established and some 360 people were led to our Lord.

Upon returning to Hong Kong, I was charged to teach at Concordia Lutheran School where Dr. Melvin Kieschnick was the principal. At the same time, and under the auspices of Rev. George Winkler, we started the ministry of Concordia Lutheran Church in the school hall. Eventually, I was to be called and ordained pastor of the same congregation. Some 1,200 people became believers and were baptized into the church in the next seven years.

Then the church sponsored my theological study in St. Louis, where I went twice for the duration of two years each, leaving my wife and seven children behind in Hong Kong. I earned the Master and Doctor of Theology degrees after those years of study.

Back in Hong Kong, I had variously been elected president of the Synod and served as professor and president of Concordia Theological Seminary. After accepting the appointment as the Old Testament editor of the Chinese Bible Commentary, I went to Israel in 1988 and spent a total of four years there, studying and writing about Jewish customs and practices. In 1992, some family members, friends, and I started the New York Theological Education Center. From the time I returned to Hong Kong in 1999, I have been involved in the translation of selected works by Martin Luther and have served as consulting pastor of True Word Lutheran Church. And for several years now I have been teaching a course per semester at the Concordia Theological Seminary.

Today, the works that I have written, translated, and edited can be found in many Chinese seminaries and some university libraries. What achievements there are by this convert from his sinful and pitiful state speak volumes of God's bountiful grace and results of the missionary endeavors of the LC-MS among the Chinese, just as David Kohl has described in his book.

May all glory and honor be to the Holy Name of God who has saved us all through Jesus Christ. Alleluia! Amen.

# Forward

## What It Means To Be a Missionary

Rev. Paul Kreyling
Missionary to China 1946-1949 and Japan 1949-1971

What compels them to go, these people we call missionaries? It is none other than the love of Christ, as St. Paul says in II Corinthians 5:14, "For Christ's love compels us." He was referring to both himself and his partners in mission accompanying him or back in the "sending" churches, like Antioch. When each individual accepts Christ as their personal Lord and Savior, they have a new vocation - to live their lives for Christ. Each believer seeks the answer for himself. The answers expose the full range of human activity.

Missionaries, single or married, have gone because they have received that precious gift of God we call faith, and the Christ-like love which is engendered in them by that faith. Actually, all of us who have received that gift of faith have also received that command of Jesus to "Go!" Not necessarily go overseas, or even to remote parts of our own country, It is obvious that not all of us are able to heed that call by journeying and living abroad. These Christians would not leave family and friends, get vaccinated, learn new language, disrupt sedentary home life, and risk disease if they aren't convinced that they have been sent, not only by the Church, but most importantly, by God Himself. They go on behalf of Christians who, for various reasons, cannot go, but who can support them in word and deed. Every Christian can live out mission where they live and work and raise families and participate in the life of the Church.

Missionaries go because Jesus himself commands all of His followers; "Therefore go and make disciples of all nations, baptizing them in the name of the Father and of the Son and of the Holy Spirit, and teaching them to obey everything I have commanded you." (Matthew 28:19-20)

Taking St. Paul's words in Romans 10:14-15 to heart, they paraphrase: "How, then, can the Chinese call on the One they have not believed in? And how can the Chinese believe in the one of whom they have not heard? And how can the Chinese hear without someone preaching to them? And how can they preach unless they are sent?" These missionaries go because they are sent! Sent of their own volition, by a Board, or the Church – in this case the Lutheran Church Missouri Synod. The very word *missionary* comes from the Latin word which means *send*.

They go, in spite of the myriad difficulties that face will them, especially those who went out a hundred years ago. The LCMS pioneer missionaries to China were not even sponsored by the Church, but had the backing and support of one mission society. To keep costs down, they traveled in "coach" and "steerage." After a difficult voyage, they were faced by the many unknowns of completely unfamiliar non-romanized tonal language; strange and poorly understood culture and customs; exotic and questionable food; a new world of flavors, smells, and sanitation; and living conditions that were alien to American and European life following World War I. It was a different world!

Yet these Americans adapted and acclimated themselves to the Chinese environment because they were certain that God also loved the people to whom He had sent them, and that Christ was also Savior of all nations. He gave his life on the cross of Calvary to redeem them from the death all humans deserve because of their sin. Newly commissioned pastors and wives felt a fervent and committed drive to share this Good News (*Fu Ling* = Happy Sound; good News) as best they could. They had the message of Life, and were convinced that the Chinese desperately needed the Gospel message. These Americans tried to live their lives according to the pattern set down by the Lord Jesus, for it is eminently true that, as Marshall McLuhan put it, "The medium is the message," or "do as I do, not as I say."

A missionary and his family need to be careful that appearance and life-style are consistent with the message they are trying to proclaim. Missionaries must decide if, and if so, how and to what extent and he should go *native*. Most missionaries feel that they should just live as much as possible commensurate with the lifestyle of their own native land. Others go to the extreme of trying to live as much as possible as the people among whom they live. There are all sorts of variations between these two extremes. Each one must make his/her own decision. There is no *best answer.*

In discussions with the peoples of the land who were brave and kind enough to be honest, this is what was learned: The local people do not expect the missionary and his family to live like the natives; they are Americans (or Europeans), and so should live their usual life-style. Otherwise there is room for the suspicion that they are just piling up funds in their own country, and after a time, will just return and live in luxury. Missionaries are not judged on their life-style but on the basis of their attitude, their warmth, their kindness, their genuineness and consistency. If indigenous folks can feel welcome and comfortable as guests in the home of the missionary, if they feel really accepted as people, regardless of their station in society or in the economic ladder, they are also accepting and happy with the missionary, and feel comfortable in his/her presence. In other words, the missionary must have the same loving, forgiving attitude toward everyone and treat them with respect and dignity as Jesus did.

To be sure, this was not a dour experience. Inconvenient? Yes. Hardship? Probably. Sacrificial? Not in their minds! The joy of sharing the Gospel in China meant witnessing the Christian message in a setting of adventure, discovery, innovation, adaptability, and the opportunity and challenge to raise their families as expatriates, with eduction in home schools or in a one room school setting.

Most LCMS missionaries were raised in German-speaking households and churches that transitioned to English during World War I due to anti-German sentiments throughout America. Those sent to China knew seminary Hebrew, Greek and Latin, but faced learning a complex new written and spoken language.

# Survivors and descendants of the China Mission

Three men born in China in the Lutheran Mission: Joseph Riedel, Richard Klein, James Koehler

Dorothy Riedel, first baby of the mission, born 1916, with the author in 2010

1) Paul Strege, long time Japan missionary and LCMS Area secretary; Karl Boehmke, first called pastor of Church of All nations, Repulse Bay, Hong Kong. 2) Dennis and Donna Oetting in the center, twenty year veterans of Hong Kong work; surrounded by Maxine and Robert Fiala, guest professor in Taiwan.

Seven missionaries with China roots, in 2008. Richard and Lois Meyer; Max Zschiegner (Japan missionary born in the LCMS China mission); Carol and Paul Kreyling, LeRoy and Ruth Hass. All except Max served in Post-war China before 1949, after which they relocated in Japan. Edith and Ardon Albrecht, Taiwan missionary who specialized in the media ministry.

A very apropos definition of a missionary is: "An ambassador who tries to work himself out of a job!" That takes some explanation. The Church, which is the Body of Christ, is universal, and it encompasses people of all sorts and conditions, with various customs and different ways of doing things. The unity of the Church of Christ does not include methodology, organizational forms, or worship styles, etc. The unity of the Church of Christ consists in the oneness of our faith in, and the worship, of Jesus Christ as Savior and Lord, of proclaiming the Triune God: Father, Son, and Holy Spirit as the One and only God. A missionary is not sent to make other people into Americans, or British, or Germans, or anything other than to make them disciples of Jesus Christ. Therefore, the establishment of a body of believers in Jesus Christ is the goal, and new believers, in turn, must be led to accept the challenge and call of Jesus to preach the Gospel and make disciples as soon as possible. A missionary's job is to help others to become missionaries, and to carry on the work of the Church of Jesus Christ so that the missionary can be sent elsewhere. In a sense, it is like the present situation in China, where the People's Republic has insisted that all recognized churches belong to the same Three Self Church. This means self-supporting, self-governing, and self-propagating. When this is achieved, the missionary is out of a job, and can be sent elsewhere, to repeat his God-blessed role of *sentness*.

This book is essentially a record of the story of one group of missionaries and their work in China over one hundred years. It is our prayer that in reading it, you may be inspired to follow these people in their sense of *sentness*, not necessarily to the scope of their work, but to the essence of their vocation: that you, too, may feel the urge of Matthew 28, and realize that you, too, have been sent to those around you to make disciples of as many as you can, and to equip them as well as possible as disciples of Jesus Christ to witness the Good News.

David Kohl, a former educational missionary in Hong Kong, has searched for the answers to these and related questions about practical Christianity. He has spent joyful hours visiting and interviewing *mish kids*; scouring letters, diaries, church documents; and pouring over hundreds of pictures. Piecing together these stories and situations has revealed insightful and experiential narratives of faith in action by individuals in the real world.

In all of this, he has tried to trace the humane elements – the experiences, the emotions, the trials and tribulations, the agonies and the ecstasies, and all the territories in between; the defeats, sorrows, triumphs, and joys encountered by these real people as they carried out what they felt called to do in a place called China.

Kick off your shoes, sink back into your recliner, relax, and enjoy this trip to China! I think you'll be glad you did!

# Introductory Remarks

*"You are the salt of the earth... You are the light of the world"* Matthew 5:13-14

## David G. Kohl
### Educational missionary, Hong Kong, 1973-1980

Four generations have elapsed since the development of Henry Ford's 1912 assembly line and the disastrous sinking of the RMS Titanic. In that same year, a pioneer Lutheran pastor/professor initiated a small independent and determined effort to bring the saving Gospel of Jesus Christ to the "lost heathen" of post-imperial China. You'll find surprises, adventure, dedication, pathos and intensity in the lives of committed Lutheran men and women in a little understood corner of the third world at a vortex of 20th century history.

The ultimate goal of the Lutheran Church Missouri Synod (LCMS) China enterprise was, and is, to share the Gospel of Jesus Christ with souls who don't know, understand or accept the depth and saving power of God's love and forgiveness. This account is not just about missionaries, but includes businessmen, students, teachers, laymen, evangelists, colporteurs, laborers and refugees. In the words of Margaret Mead, "Never doubt that a small group of thoughtful, committed people can change the world. Indeed, it is the only thing that ever has."

Founded with an Saxon-American heritage, and a consistent theology based on Biblical inerrancy, the Missouri Synod, still endeavors to equip today's Christians for tomorrow's opportunities to *Bring Christ to the Nations*.

In many ways, this is a story about family. Christians are the family of God - the fraternity of believers. Loving their Lord, they can unite, but occasionally act out in sibling rivalry. The LCMS has its roots in Germanic family structure, tradition, loyalty, love, and dysfunction. I've used a 𝔉𝔯𝔞𝔨𝔱𝔲𝔯 font to distinguish 𝔊𝔢𝔯𝔪𝔞𝔫 𝔫𝔞𝔪𝔢𝔰 in the text. LCMS pastors, teachers, and deaconesses were almost exclusively educated in the system of Lutheran elementary schools, attending residential preparatory schools, and graduating from the Concordia system of seminaries, teachers colleges, or deaconess and nursing schools. Concordia means "harmony" and is associated with anything Missouri Synod because of LCMS adherence to the 1580 Book of Concord, which defines Lutheran teachings. Classmates became church workers knew each other well, their brothers and sisters, relatives, friends, professors, and scores of married co-workers.

On a personal note, researching this book has put me back in touch with my Missouri roots. As kids, we learned about our missionaries from parochial and Sunday school teachers, read about them in the Messenger and Witness. Foreign missions were fascinating, a far off adventure for others. I never thought I'd be part of the brotherhood. And I'm glad I am.

Here are plenty of factual and philosophic materials for research and introspection. What would we have done in a similar situation? What do I believe? How do I go about representing the story of the "One thing needful?" And to whom, when, and where? What do we know now that the missionaries didn't seem to understand then? How does that matter? What further discoveries and experiences await Christians of this century in sharing Jesus Christ with the peoples of Asia?

Each chapter of Lutherans on the Yangtze deserves to be treated as a full volume. I've been humbled by the research experience and awed by the network of clues, geographies and trails linking God's people in general, and LCMS members in particular. Tracking leads and scouring books, articles, minutes, and monographs; conducting over 200 interviews with missionaries or their families; identifying and studying photos, tables, and maps; and spending hours filtering personal correspondence and diaries, have not been adequate.

My goal is to present balanced information on internal issues, set into the context of local and world history and cultural trends. I hope to act as reporter, not judge. I've found myself more interested in origins than developments - how programs and projects began. Perspective and hindsight are usually 20-20. I'm not about discrediting anyone or judging philosophies, programs or institutions. Hopefully, several points of view have been explored and the results fairly summarized. My goal is to record objectively how well-intentioned (but sometimes ill-informed or inexperienced) individuals and institutions sought to carry out their understanding of God's will. Directors, commissions, boards, auxiliary organizations, and lay people all played their roles.

Throughout this book, Lutheran is synonymous with the Lutheran Church Missouri Synod (LCMS), unless other groups are noted. I have capitalized Mission when referring to the LCMS China Mission, which was the Fu yin dao Lo deh Huei (Good News doctrine Lutheran society) (say: Foo Yin dow Low Dah Way). At least 16 Lutheran Synods have been active in China since 1831. Non LCMS Lutherans are identified by Synod or ethnicity. Non-LCMS Chinese Lutherans identified as Union Lutherans, or the Faith-Righteousness Society Hsien-I-Wei, or Hsin I Hue (say: Shin He Way). Romanized phonetic spellings of those names may vary.

Herein lies the bi-polarity of anticipating eternal salvation in Christ Jesus while celebrating the life God gives us on this planet in these times. What is significant about being a Lutheran Christian in the 21st century? At the centennial of Missouri Synod presence in Greater China, can we:

1) Reconstruct the history of four related Chinese mission geographies?
2) Offer an insight into theological topics between Christianity and Chinese culture?
3) Identify congregations, mission stations, orphanages, medical and social programs?
4) Trace the development of select congregations and successful schools?
5) Learn from significant but forgotten stories of Lutheran life in 20th century China?
6) Give some recognition to the work of individual missionaries, and Chinese workers, identifying individual contributions and accomplishments?

## In Summary

Fifty-eight missionaries, 56 wives, and 8 deaconesses operated seven mainland mission locations along 800 miles of the Yangtze River in south-central China including chapels, schools, clinics, orphanages, and a hospital. Interrupted by civil and international wars, the Mission operated from 1913 until the establishment of the Peoples Republic of China (PRC).

China was an almost constant and continuous war zone during the forty years of the Mainland mission. War-torn, brigands, warlords, bandits, bolsheviks, heathen were all terms associated with 20th Century China.

In 1949, four evacuated missionaries in British Hong Kong began unauthorized efforts among the Chinese refugee diaspora, eventually reaching Macau, Taiwan, and other overseas communities. Their efforts led to the subsequent sending by the Board of Foreign Missions of about 200 men and women since 1951 to "the Chinas". Languages used have changed from German to Mandarin, English, Cantonese, Taiwanese, Hakka, and Vietnamese. Called workers and scores of lay people have founded and guided congregations, carried out educational and social welfare programs, and established local and International schools.

Thirty years of *bamboo curtain* and Cultural Revolution would pass before the thaw and reforms of the late 1970s. Working relationships have developed with contemporary Christians in China.

As the People's Republic is rapidly emerging as a major player on the international stage, most of us still know only a glimpse of what there is to know about the country, the people, and China's historical relationships with the world. I'll try to share what I've found significant, guessing that you may know little about the LCMS, or China (historically also known as Sinim; Cathay; Middle Kindgom; Celestial Empire; Flowery Republic; or the People's Republic (PRC), as distinguished from the Republic of China (Taiwan) on the island that Portuguese explorers named Formosa.

Merchants, militaries, missionaries, and middlemen were the face-to-face personal and commercial links between the people of China and Westerners. In the modern era, these began only after the Treaty of Nanking ended the first Opium War in 1842. One-to-one dealings were mostly between business people or agents of the Christian church, sent to *pagan* China as missionaries. Reams of personal accounts were written by individual missionaries. Tracts were printed by mission and Bible Societies. Denominational efforts intensified between 1880 and 1930. Many well-crafted reports and promotions designed to be read by folks back home were intended to reinforce the need for emotional and monetary support, more staff, more programs, expansion efforts and prayer.

Less often reported are the internal dissentions, accounts of domestic life and child-rearing challenges, theological and denominational rifts, and the physical and mental stress of living as expatriates, outside their homeland. China was miserably hot and humid in the summer; bone-chilling in winter; prone to natural disasters flooding and typhoons.

Smells were foreign and indescribable. Rudyard Kipling wrote: "He who has not smelt that smell has never lived. It is the scent of very clean, new wood, split bamboo, wood smoke, damp earth, and of the things that white people do not eat.It comes down the street saying, 'this is the East where nothing matters and trifles as old as the Tower of Babel matter less than nothing.'"

Stories are legion of how missionaries accomplished what they determined needed to be done and solved nearly every kind of challenge. They were well educated in the years before the Great Depression (1929-1937). But they were helpless from no command of the Chinese language(s). Communications, in German or English, with the Mission Board in St. Louis took months on a ship and telegraph (electric letters) was unreliable and expensive. Many decisions couldn't wait two months for sea or surface mail, and there was no Clipper Mail (airmail) until 1935. There were few roads. The Yangtze was the only avenue of transportation and communication from Shanghai westward 600 miles to Hankow, and the 400 stretch of river connecting all mission stations, except Shihnan/Enshih.

Many fresh seminary graduates, most with new brides, were farm boys or offspring of pastors and teachers. They held high ambitions rooted in their Christian faith. In addition to teaching and living the Gospel, some experimented with short wave or ham radio. Others turned out to be linguistically or artistically gifted, others were organizers. They did whatever needed to be done, running print shops, translating scripture and catechetical materials, installing wiring, milking goats, organizing famine relief, managing orphanages, building clinics and hospitals, and taking precautions to avoid exposure to tropical diseases. They managed mission funds and personal finances with US dollars in at least three currency systems, complicated by fluctuating exchange rates during wars and The Depression. Four buried a spouse or child in China.

Families hired the domestic labor of local Chinese workers, who were often totally unfamiliar with the fashions they were to sew, foods they were to prepare, and household services they were to provide. Most expatriates maintained a modicum of western lifestyle with help from these local workers–amahs, coolies, boatmen, boys, and the like. Communication was a unique matrix of spoken and written languages–mostly German, English, and Chinese – a patois known as colonial or coastal pidgin.

My aim is for you to enjoy the reading, yet not get too confused with Chinese language, geographic and individual names, wartime events or politics. Westerners find oriental names, titles, places, and philosophies difficult to sort out. Yet to overly simplify this study would do a great disservice to China, its people, and its Christians.

I've tried to set these events into perspective with Lutheran practices, secular history, world events and popular culture. For example, that the Great Yangtze flood occurred in the same year (1931) as Franklin D. Roosevelt's first election; or that the LWML was organized (1942) within a year of Pearl Harbor attack staring World War II.

## In Perspective

Admittedly, this is primarily an account from a Westerner's point of view. I'm severely hampered by not being Chinese, not speaking much Chinese, nor having access to many written documents of these events from a Chinese perspective. The majority of LCMS mission work was done with working class adults or students, many just learning to read and write. Chinese language teachers didn't teach to a syllabus and in some cases, didn't even speak English. Secondary students and seminarians were concerned with academics, rarely taking time to journal their personal histories or thoughts. Household servants were faithful and hard working, but they were not literate keepers of personal diaries nor apologists for their growing understanding of the Christian faith. They were common folk living in a unique time and place, but we have so little of their written history.

Sometimes it's difficult for us cradle Lutherans to appreciate the power of the Holy Spirit in changing lives. Converts committed to new lives often estranged themselves, or were shunned, from family or clan. Several post-1949 refugees decided to serve their newfound Lord as a chosen life work, struggling to become pastors, evangelists, or teachers. In their witness, we learn how Christ gives refreshed meaning and fulfillment. Saved from wretchedness, the Good News of salvation lifts all believers to new joy and purpose. They participate in a community of faithful believers. Hope and purpose partially replaced the loss of their former lives in China, missing wives and children, and suddenly rude and meager survival in the streets and gullies of Macau, Hong Kong, and Taiwan. Are we a people because we have a history, or a people with a history?

Contained herein are selected highlights, adventures, networkings, narrow escapes, and wartime experiences of ordinary and extraordinary Christians in very unordinary settings. Most missionary families survived and thrived amidst the chaos of early republican China, the Japanese Wars, and years of local political uncertainty. After 1949, they brought Jesus into the remote refugee camps, resettlement villages, and government housing of the Chinese diaspora.

Missionaries made the best of most situations. Families endured conditions of disease, climate, isolation, low technology, and rarely, if ever, seem to have given up on monumental tasks amidst overwhelming odds. Observers tend to think that the missionaries "sacrificed" to witness for Christ. But missionaries seldom used the term. Rather, they seemed to thrive on the challenges and opportunities, despite hardships, and inconveniences. Most missionaries evaluated what needed doing, and set out to accomplish the task. It's all in one's viewpoint.

These were hard workers, creative thinkers, sensitive innovators, conscientious translators, competitive sportsmen and energetic explorers, Men were committed husbands often more focused on the drive to introduce Christianity than on the daily details of their own family life and personal health. They were mostly strapping young men, fully capable of heavy labor. The unsung wives and single women of the Mission directed their lives and effort to Christ, and what they saw as their life work. Faith makes things possible, not easy.

One may ponder what is propaganda and what's real, what is theoretical and what is practical. What constitutes failure and/or success? When is Christian witness an adventure, a challenge, or a frustration? Many old and new friends have shared insights and observations in this process! My inadequate acknowledgments to them are listed in the bibliography.

How does one evaluate success? That has to be surmised, rather than quantified. No census or compilation of native staff, students, or membership has survived. Little knowledge of remnant Christianity in China existed until its cautious reappearance after Deng Xiaoping's 1979 revisions. Rare are the attendance records of congregations, schools and social programs that have grown in Hong Kong, Macau, and Taiwan since 1949. Compound this with the transitional role of developing national churches and the emergence of independent groups and house churches now in the process of working with the Registered Three-self Protestant Church.

These stories are presented here in the spirit of enjoyment, factual accounting, human interest, and recognition of the blessings of Almighty God for 100 years in this specific case study. This accounting is only a beginning. The subtitle could read: The Missouri Synod's first century in the Chinese Realm.

Has it worked out? What does this mean? Almighty God watches over us, and the enterprise certainly is far from over. We see the miracle of God's presence, intervention, and blessing in emerging links with the Chinese world every day. What have we experienced, and what can we learn about human nature, witness, service, indigenous culture, localized ministry, and Christian lifestyle amongst ethnic groups, in their homelands, in ours, and throughout the world?

My hope is that your interest will be tweaked to think about, read, mark, learn, and inwardly digest this historical case study in the Christian experience.

The Synod's system of seminaries and colleges produced men and women educated in secular and Lutheran tradition and knowledge. As alumni of particular institutions, they often shared similar characteristics. In his book I've tried to identify these institutions, abbreviated, as follows:

Colq    Colloquy (accepted as full LCMS status with non-Synodical coursework or credentials)
CSA     Concordia Seminary, Adelaide, Australia
CSF     Concordia Seminary, Springfield, Illinois; later CFW, Ft. Wayne, IN
CSL     Concordia Seminary, St. Louis, Missouri
CTC-RF Concordia Teachers College, River Forest, Illinois
CTC-S  Concordia Teachers College, Seward, Nebraska
LH-FW  Lutheran Hospital School of Nursing at Ft.Wayne, Indiana
LH-SL  Lutheran Hospital School of Nursing at St. Louis, Missouri
Valpo   Valparaiso University, Indiana

## Chinese language

Romanizing the graphic characters of Chinese writing has always been a bugaboo and stumbling block to Western scholars. With no hints for a phonetic system, the pronunciation of ideograms is different in each of over 300 Chinese dialects, requiring rote memorization. To read a newspaper, a reader needs to know about 5000 characters, often learned by about the fourth grade. The language has only present tense and little grammar. Wordsmiths from East and West have proposed several systems of transliterating pronunciation of the multiple-toned languages into the Roman alphabet.

Rather than unifying one of those historic western systems for this account, I have chosen to follow the precedent of Sinologist John King Fairbank. Chinese words are spelled as they were most commonly romanized by westerners during each time period, in local and best-known forms. Some names will be in the Nanjing, Yale, or Wade-Giles systems, newer ones in pin yin. Where possible, I've put the contemporary [pin yin] form in brackets when a name appears the first time. Written ideographs over the last 100 years have also changed from classical to wen li, bai hwa, and now "simplified" characters.

Enjoy and have fun with Chinese words and names, rather than getting frustrated with unfamiliar spellings and sounds. There will not be a test! This may be simplistic to true China scholars, but here are a few of my own user-friendly "survival" pointers:

1) I suggest that the reader pronounce Chinese names and words out loud. The more you do that as you read, the easier it gets, and will help you sort out words and names. Syllables may be spaced or run together, but usually start with a consonant (Tsim Sha Tsui = Tsim-shatsui = TST) (say: Shim Shaw Suey). Two or more vowels can be a dipthong (ua, ow, ayah, etc.). Two or more consonants together are syllabic clusters (hs, ts, sh, sz, dz, tsz, etc).

2) Two traditional dialects are significant in this study – Cantonese in the south, and Mandarin elsewhere. I've come to feel that one should not be overly concerned with precision (apologies to linguists). I am not being dismissive, because Romanization and regionalism can befuddle all of us. After years of casual Cantonese, I can barely make myself understood in a Chinese cafe (faan deem). Putonghua (say: pooh tong wah) is the official national spoken language in the People's Republic. Pin yin is its contemporary Romanization system. Since I'm using names as historically spelled, the [pinyn equivalent] is the version set in brackets.

3) Be aware that individuals traditionally use their family name or surname first, followed by their given name, i.e. Sun Yat-sen; Deng Shao-ping [Deng Xio peng]. Many well-known individuals are known simply by their surname, i.e. Ch'iang, Mao, etc. When a western or Christian name is chosen, that name comes first, i.e. Titus Lee. In the case of Rev. Lee, there were Cantonese pastors named Titus Lee (or Li), so they were further distinguished as Lee Way-tao and Lee Fu-shing.

4) Knowing the ten numbers, five directions, and some basic geographic features will aid in recognizing and understanding many place names.

5) Realize that Chinese place names may not read the same in English, i.e. Chin Soi Wan means Shallow Water Bay, but it's known in Hong Kong as Repulse Bay (named for the British warship HMS Repulse). Hong Kong Jai is Aberdeen, named for the Scottish Lord, but

literally means "little Hong Kong." Duplicate names exist for many geographic features.

6) Be flexible. Words will be spelled differently, sometimes with phonetic markings, hyphens or an apostrophe. Spellings may be different from different regimes, regions, or translators. Try to approximate sounds, and verbalize aloud.

7) Transliterated words may have the same spelling, but originate in different ideographic characters, from diverse dialects, with widely different pronunciation tones and meanings.

Learning any Chinese language well is not for the insincere! Here are some starters:

| Cantonese | English | simplified | pin yin |
|-----------|---------|------------|---------|
| **Numbers** | | | |
| `yat | 1 | 一 | yi |
| ee | 2 | 二 | er |
| sam | 3 | 三 | san |
| say | 4 | 四 | si |
| ng | 5 | 五 | wu |
| lok | 6 | 六 | liu |
| chat | 7 | 七 | qi |
| bhat | 8 | 八 | ba |
| gow | 9 | 九 | jiu |
| sap | 10 | 十 | shi |
| paak | 100 | (一)百 | (yī) bǎi |
| ts'in | 1000 | (一)千 | (yī) qiān |
| leng | 0 | 零 | líng |
| **Features** | | | |
| shan | mountain | 山 | shān |
| wan | bay | 弯 | wān |
| chau | island | 岛 | dǎo |
| yuan | garden | 花园 | huāyuán |
| kiang;ho | river | 河 / 江 | hé / jiāng |
| hu | lake | 湖 | hú |
| kong | harbor | 港 | gǎng |
| soi | water | 水 | shuǐ |
| chin | shallow | 浅 | qiǎn |
| sum | deep | 深 | shēn |
| jai | little | 小 | xiǎo |
| dai | big | 大 | dà |
| fung | wind | 风 | fēng |
| ling | beautiful | 美, | měi, |

| Cantonese | English | simplified | pin yin |
|-----------|---------|------------|---------|
| **Directions** | | | |
| peh | North | 北 | běi |
| nan | South | 南 | nán |
| dung | East | 东 | dōng |
| si | West | 西 | xī |
| chu | Middle | 中 | zhōng |
| **Christianity**: | | | |
| san4 | spirit | 神 | shén |
| soeng6 dai3 | God | 上帝 | shàngdì |
| zyu2 | Lord | 主 | zhǔ |
| je4 sou1 | Jesus | 耶稣 | Yēsū |
| gei1 duk1 | Christ | 基督 | Jīdū |
| zeoi6 | sin | 罪 | zuì |
| seon3 | faith | 信 | xìn |
| leot6 faat3 | Law | 律法 | Lùfǎ |
| fuk1 jam1 | Gospel | 福音 | Fúyīn |
| gau3 jan1 | Salvation (Saving Grace) | 救恩 | jiù ēn |
| jan1 din2 / | Grace | 恩典 | ēndiǎn |
| jan1 wai6 | Grace | 恩惠 | ēnhuì |
| sing3 jing1 | Holy Bible | 圣经 | Shèng Jīng |
| sai2 lai5 | Baptism | (圣)洗礼 | Xǐ Lǐ |
| sing3 ling4 | Holy Spirit | 圣灵 | Shèng Líng |
| sing3 saam1 jat1 | Trinity | 圣三一 | Shèng Sān Yī |
| gei1 duk1 tou4 | Christian | 基督徒 | Jīdūtú |
| min5 | forgiveness | 赦免 | shèmiǎn |

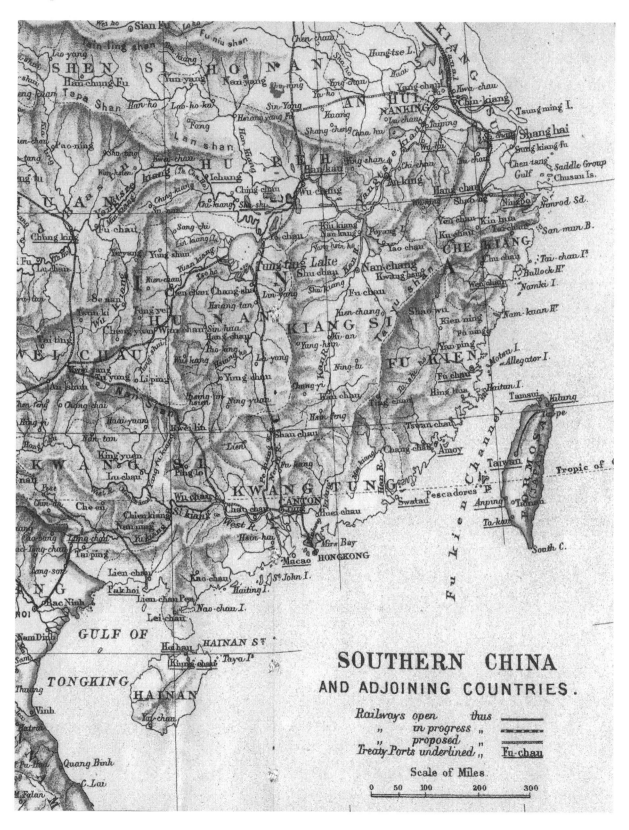

*Then I heard the Lord say 'Whom shall I send? Who will be our messenger? I answered, I will go. Send me.*

Isaiah 6:8

## Chapter One

# Rebel with a Cause

Billowing steam clouds hissed from valves beneath the iron monster resting in the Great Northern depot at St. Paul, Minnesota. Smoke spewed from the glowing flames of its firebox. Grey cinders drizzled onto the crowd. On the frigid evening of January 24, 1913, an emotional drama played out on the trackside platform, amidst steamer trunks, well-packed grips, and the dustings of the gently falling ash. A family of six was leaving behind their home and their three oldest children, bound for undetermined years of overseas absence. Not only were they departing the familiarity of the mid-west and the support their German-American church, they were surrendering most conveniences and comforts of western civilization.

The Edward Arndt family was bound for distant China, the biblical land of Sinim, known as Cathay to Marco Polo and Genghis Kahn. For two thousand years, dynasties had ruled the Celestial Empire or Middle Kingdom, contemporary with the ancient Romans and the European Middle ages. The Arndts would arrive in the new Flowery Republic just 15 months after the 1911 Chinese Revolution replaced 2000 years of medieval imperial rule with nascent representative government. The Middle Kingdom, especially the eastern and coastal provinces, was in turmoil, producing more bloodshed and disorganization than America had experienced during its colonial struggle for independence from Britain.

### Reverend Edward Louis Arndt

A Michigan pastor with 12 years parish experience and 13 more years as a professor, Edward Louis Arndt was a called minister in the Evangelical Lutheran Synod of Missouri, Ohio, and Other States (In 1947, the Synod was re-named The Lutheran Church—Missouri Synod, often abbreviated as LCMS).

Edward Arndt was born December 19, 1864 in Buckowin, Pomerania, a state in the North German Confederation, well before the days of Kaiser Wilhelm and Otto Von Bismarck. His father, Ferdinand, was a shoemaker who migrated to America one year after the close of the Civil War. The Arndt family settled in Chicago, where they found fellowship at Immanuel Lutheran Church among the German-speakers in that Missouri Synod congregation. The site where Ferdinand built their home is now part of the University of Illinois–Chicago campus.

In his youth, Edward obtained work in a print shop, before going to the Synod's residential prep school in St. Paul. Young Arndt was determined to become a Lutheran minister and enrolled at Concordia College in Fort Wayne, Indiana (CFW), on a track that would culminate at Concordia Seminary, in St. Louis (CSL).

Upon graduation in 1885, he was called to serve Trinity Lutheran Church in Saginaw, Michigan, in an area where Franconian Lutherans had settled in the 1840s. Within Saginaw County were several other German-speaking

   Rev. Edward Arndt arrived at East Saginaw in 1885 to found Trinity Lutheran Church, and lived with his bride Marie in the parsonage after 1887. He accepted the Divine Call to teach math, science, and religion at Concordia College in St. Paul in 1897.

   In 1912 he published the monthly Missionsbriefe (Mission Letter) in his living room to raise awareness of China's need for the Gospel. The Evangelical Mission Society for China came into being on July 14, 1912. The Arndt family posed in front of their St. Paul home before selling the house and leaving for China in January, 1913.

congregations at Frankenlust, Frankentrost, Frankenhilf, and Frankenmuth—the latter being an 1847 charter member of the Missouri Synod. Following twelve years of successful parish ministry, and a quadrupling of its membership, Edward received his call to Concordia College in Minnesota.

Arndt accepted his call to be a professor of science and mathematics in 1897 at the two-year college, but insisted that he also could teach religion courses. Very influential on Arndt had been his three years of theological study at the seminary under the Synod's 1847 founder, C. F. W. Walther. The elderly Dr. Walther instilled in seminarians a zeal and ardor for the spread of the gospel of Jesus Christ, the one true God who redeems all believers from eternal condemnation by the consequences of the law—eternal salvation through faith in Christ, without the merit of good works.

After 13 academic seasons, Arndt became disenchanted with his status at the college when the faculty failed to support him in a matter of reprimanding several students who had set off fireworks as a prank in his classroom in 1910. Apparently, the offenders were the sons of several pastors including a top synodical official. The CSP administration intervened on their behalf in the discipline. Arndt resigned in 1911. The episode tainted the professor's reputation.

Concurrently, his awareness of the missionary possibilities in China was growing through the press and periodicals, reports of political turmoil, and through meetings with a furloughing Lutheran missionary and three pastors of other synods. Arndt benefited from connections with Dr. A. W. Edwins of the Augustana Synod; E. W. Landahl and Professor C. Stockstads of the Hauge Synod. In 1910, Arndt also attended an inspirational conference in Minneapolis. Edward became focused on the people of China and the statistic that 99% of them had not heard the saving Christian gospel.

The Chinese Revolution of 1911 re-directed the family's destiny when Arndt became determined to bring Lutheranism to the promising new mission fields of China.

Johanna Marie Solomon Arndt had anticipated a supportive and productive domestic life as a pastor's helpmate when they married in her hometown, Fort Wayne. They had courted while Edward was a student there at Concordia in 1882, and married in 1887, after he spent two years building up his Saginaw congregation. The couple raised six sons and two daughters, thriving on their 11 seasons of ministry together in Saginaw, followed after 1897 by his professorship at CSP. The Arndt's oldest son, Joseph, died suddenly in 1906 at age 18.

As the Great Northern locomotive steamed westward, they passed the wheat fields of the upper Midwest and the dry plains of North Dakota along the route of the Empire Builder. The train had to be re-routed due to severe blizzard conditions.

Awaiting them at the dock was an old NYK liner, *SS Tamba Maru*, preparing for its thirty-fifth Pacific crossing. Boarding the Japanese ship that January 28 meant no turning back. It would take four weeks to cross the Pacific on the Japanese vessel, traveling steerage third class (Chinese first class) to save as much of the Society's money as possible for their work in China. Rough seas and a typhoon added to passenger miseries. During the voyage, Edward hired a Japanese passenger who could tutor him in the Mandarin language. A brief layover in Japan enabled the Arndts to visit with H. Midzuno, a former CSP student who was a professor in Tokyo. Within a day of landing in Shanghai on February 25, the family boarded the smaller Yangtze River steamer *Ta Yi* for the six day upriver float to Hankow, the Chicago of China. Wuhan, the tri-cities of Hankow, Hanyang and Wuchang, was the hub in central Hupeh province where railways from north and south met. There was no bridge. It would be their home for sixteen years.

Edward Arndt would die alone in Hankow in 1929, to be buried in the China he loved. In

Map of Lutheran Mission activity in China, provided by the Christian Continuation Committee for its 468-page "Christian Occupation of China" report in 1922.

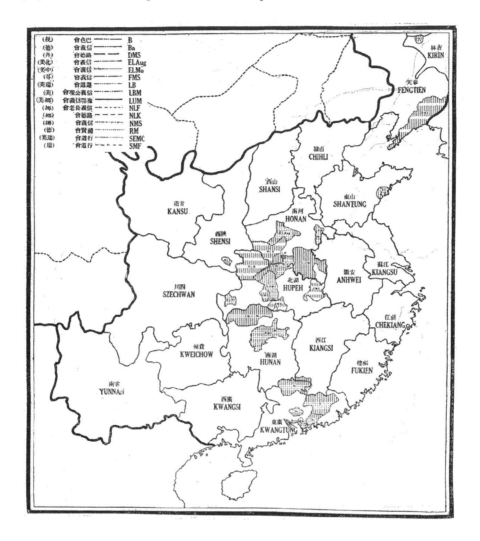

The Missouri Synod (identified as ELMo) operated in Hupeh at Hankow and Shihnan. Longer established Lutheran groups were the Basel (B); Berliner Mission(Bn); Danish Mission Society (DMS); Augustana Synod (ELAug); Finnish Mission Society (FMS); Lutheran Brethren Mission (LB); Lutheran Free Church of the USA (LBM); Lutheran United Mission (LUM); Norwegian Lutheran Free Church (NLF); Norwegian Lutheran Mission (NLK); Norwegian Mission Society (NMS); Rhenish Mission (RM); Swedish Evangelical Mission Covenant of America (SEMC);and Swedish Mission Society (SMF). Altogether there were 400 Lutheran missionaries, 1420 Chinese workers, 23,000 Baptised Communicant members, and 13,000 students in all grades.

the aftermath of his unheralded and unsanctioned arrival, 64 called missionary men and women would eventually carry on his early efforts in the Yangtze valley until 1949. When the mainland was closed off, over a hundred more workers would be sent from The Lutheran Church—Missouri Synod to serve in Hong Kong, Macau, and Taiwan.

## Previous Lutheran Mission Efforts in China

The first German missionary to China was Karl Guetzlaff, arriving from Pomerania in 1827 at age 24. The lone Lutheran had spent 25 years in southern China, first working with pioneer Robert Morrison of the London Missionary Society. Morrison is credited as the first Protestant missionary to China, arriving at Macau on an American ship in 1807. Working in secret in a factory (warehouse) of Yankee traders on Shameen Island, he translated the complete Bible into Chinese by 1823, while illegally learning the language. Only partial portions and a few books had previously been translated into scholarly Chinese. Earlier Jesuits and Franciscans did not make their translations available to their own believers, much less non-Catholics. Morrison consulted only his Hebrew Bible and Matthew Henry's Commentary. A different translation was finished in India by Joshua Marshman and his son John the same year. These works inspired the Swiss-based Basel Evangelical Mission Society to initiate work in China in 1835.

In 1844, Guetzlaff founded the Christian League for the Propagation of the Gospel in the fledgling British colony of Hong Kong. His goal was to promote the Christian faith in China using native evangelists. His plan was to send trusted and enthusiastic new local converts into the hinterlands with quantities of printed material and scant funding. These evangelists were to return after a given time, bringing their converts with them. Guetzlaff's optimistic reports may have exaggerated his success using this method, but the publicity inspired several mission societies in Europe.

China itself had become the major focus of American missions after the opium wars and Tai Ping rebellion that concluded in 1864. Following the American Civil War, the development of the steamship, and the global network of the British Empire, Victorian travelers visited Asia and reported on Chinese charms and curiosities. In addition to Hudson Taylor's China Inland Mission (CIM), founded in 1865, enterprising missionary efforts were carried out by the London Missionary Society, the American Board of Commissioners for Foreign Missions, and a multitude of smaller Christian groups. Colporteurs were itinerant sellers of inexpensive Bible portions and gospel tracts, who traveled the remote roads and trails of eastern China. Unsung Christian heroes in bringing the printed word to a sprawling civilization, they were often the first men to introduce Christianity into remote areas.

Indigenous Bible women, converted by pioneer missionaries, brought the gospel to families in isolated villages. Their grassroots deaconess-like services were essential. By 1905, Lutherans (six European synods and four groups from America) had begun work in central China where the silt-laden Han River empties into the Yangtze at Hankow. Here, China's only north-south rail line met the equivalent of a major east-west water highway—the mighty 3000-mile long Yangtze.

A great fervor had emerged in America and Britain by the late 1800s toward Christianizing China. Industrialists also yearned for China's perceived mineral wealth; bankers and investors saw the potential of developing Chinese markets and infrastructure—especially minerals and railroads—and Christians envisioned the vast open fields of heathens who yearned for the word of God. Several international conferences heightened awareness of China's potential. Within China, missionaries organized large gatherings in 1877 and 1890. In 1907, a major planning and strategy conference at Shanghai embraced the coordination of the

# Missouri Synod Sketches – Part One
## History

    A brief history of Lutheran Church-Missouri Synod should clarify many of the developments in this story.  The Missouri Synod is a conference or union of Lutheran congregations, organized by geographical districts. The one exception is that there are two districts which span the entire nation but are identified by language, namely the Synod-wide English District and the Slovak District, which reflects an earlier time when English- and Slovak-speaking Lutherans were minority groups in a German-speaking synod.

    This group of congregations began with German Lutherans who had migrated to Perry in 1839 and Bavaria in 1842 to several American regions, partly as a result of the German State church wanting to join various Protestant and Lutheran groups together. The group that emigrated Perry County and St. Louis, MO, felt that the Biblical doctrines of Luther's reforms of 1517 had been compromised. They saw their mission to preserve the inerrancy of Holy Scripture and the integrity of the Lutheran confessions (as recorded in the 1580 Book of Concord) against rationalism and unionism.

    Missouri Synod, LCMS, Missouri, and The Synod are all titles used for what was originally known as the German Evangelical Lutheran Synod of Missouri, Ohio, and Other States (shortened to The Lutheran Church-Missouri Synod in 1947.)  More than 20 ethnic Lutheran groups (Norwegians, Swedes, Finnish) also settled in North America throughout the 1800s. From its founding in 1847 with C.F.W. Walther as first president, the Germans did cooperate with several of these other synods. (Arndt was in the last theology classes of the aging Professor Dr.Walther at Concordia Seminary, St. Louis). Altar and pulpit fellowship signified doctrinal harmony. Recognizing the Unaltered Augsburg Confession (UAC), the (Evangelical Lutheran) Synodical Conference was federated in 1872, including Missouri, Ohio, Wisconsin, Norwegian, Minnesota, and Illinois Synods. A controversy over the doctrine of Predestination aborted the potential union of most Lutheran groups in 1884. English did not become Synod's official language until 1917, when, during World War 1, many US citizens looked with suspicion as groups that continued to identify themselves as German.

    Ethnic and doctrinal concerns have made Missouri Synod leaders historically wary of working with other Lutheran church bodies (one major anxiety is "unionism"). Doctrinal purity and historic tradition have been a hallmark and driving force. Latin words in the official seal of the Synod sum it up: *Sola Gratia, Sola Fide, Sola Scriptura* (By grace alone, by Faith alone, by Scripture alone).  Joint projects such as a common hymnal, membership in National and World Federations, and community programs have been problematic.

    Synod operates upon democratic governance, with each congregation independently directing its own property management, staffing, educational and social programs, local outreach, etc. While the pastor is regarded as the ultimate congregational servant and leader, Synodically-trained teachers and other professionally trained church workers are highly respected.  These career church workers regard their positions as a Divine Call, coming from God through congregations and schools.

More about The Missouri Synod on page  34

various mission groups, referring to as comity. The event was held on the centenary of Robert Morrison's arrival to China.

Five thousand Christians gathered in Chicago in May, 1910 to hear addresses by many missionaries in advance of the World Missionary Conference that June in Edinburgh. The Scotland meeting drew 500 delegates and 670 representatives. This watershed Protestant gathering stressed the urgency of "evangelizing the world in this generation." Most conferences presented the image of a wretched humanity—heathen and uneducated—worshipping the wood and stone images of Buddhist, Taoist, and Confucian idols. Missions became the focus of Christian writers including Andrew Murray (*Key to the Missionary Problem*) and Roland Allen (*Missionary Methods: St. Paul's or Ours?*).

The decline of the Ch'ing Empire with the overthrow of the Manchu occupation (1644–1911) was declared on Oct 10, 1911. The Republican Revolution meant political and economic situations in China were ripe for infusions of new thought from Leninism to western culture and Christianity. The new regime cordially allowed the Christian mission enterprise. The defeated Manchus, especially the women, were apparently more open to the good news than were the native Han Chinese. Barriers to the Christian occupation of the Middle Kingdom were inching open. Missionaries were less frequently regarded by the Chinese as demons, possessed of evil spirits come to destroy the Chinese. However, Christianity was still associated with the evils and controls of colonialism and opium.

British miner and businessman Rowland Gibson summarized the optimism about China's future writing in 1914:
"Old clouds of obstruction are slowly rolling away as we stand watching this (Chinese) sunrise. We watch it with pleasure because it is grand. As rosy tints mount upwards to the skies, we recognize it as something more than a new political dawn. We recognize it as one of God's pictures."

A few articles about China had appeared in the Missouri Synod's bi-weekly national newsletter, the Lutheran Witness. Numerous journals and personal accounts had been written by former and current missionaries from other Protestant denominations, but there was scant news about the only overseas LCMS mission in India. Independently, at a Lutheran mission to the Chinese in St. Louis, Teacher Olive Gruen began teaching Sunday school. Eight years later, at age 37, she was called to become part of Arndt's Missouri Synod China enterprise in 1921 (see chapter 4).

Ironically, the status of Chinese laborers in America at the time was a sad one. Chinese men migrated to California between 1849 and 1865 on the slender hope of earning quick riches in the mines and railroads of *Gum Shan* (Gold Mountain) to send back to relatives in South China. Once those projects were completed, America's need for cheap labor was filled by a wave of European immigrants, mostly Irish and German. These sojourners planned to return to their home villages in Kwangtung [Guangdong] and Fukien [Fujian], but only a small percentage actually did come back. Chinese day laborers (coolies) were relegated to life in the shabbier parts of many American towns, especially in the west near the railroads or port cities, and became the object of discrimination, sanctions, and outright derision and murder. Oregon and Washington states were among the more hostile.

The Federal Exclusion Act of 1882 cut off any further Chinese immigration, until its modification in 1915 and repeal in 1943. In many urban areas, local ordinances restricted the Chinese to residence in inner city pockets—Chinatowns—and were forbidden to own land. Typically, they earned low wages in laundries and restaurants, especially after the American craze for chop suey developed circa 1903. Seemingly unintelligible regional languages, undecipherable written characters, and the hybrid sing-song of pidgin English all perpetuated poor communication with Americans. Asian foods, spices, and odors were not fa-

Hankow presented the Arndt family with a wide perspective of China in 1913. They were fascinated by the people, especially the young children clothed in layers of quilted garments. Western buildings lined the waterfront Bund in the areas of the foreign "concessions." More unique was the warren of streets in the "native" city, where several schools would be later established. Shops dedicated to pet birds and their cages lined one street. Another wider street contained mostly linen and cotton merchants.

miliar to westerners. Strange clothing, footwear, and hairstyles (e.g. men with the long Manchu pigtail) all contributed to isolation. There was little opportunity for educational advancement in this minority community. Sojourners were generally not from the educated society of China, although some were merchants, a class wanting to improve the lives of their children through education and marriage.

## The Evangelical Lutheran Mission for China

Aware of these factors, Arndt proposed to the Missouri Synod that missionary work begin in China. Synod was economically strapped by its first overseas mission field in India, initiated in 1895. Arndt was somewhat discredited amongst synodical leaders because of his episode at CSP. Disappointed that his proposals received no action, the professor determined to initiate work in China on his own.

Arndt took matters into his own hands. In 1911, he wrote an English-language collection of his sermons for each week of the church year. *Green Pastures* was printed in English and hardbound in Blair, Nebraska, by the Danish Lutheran Publishing House, and sold to congregations, pastors, and individuals throughout the LCMS. Each sermon is preceded by an outline, and presents insight into Arndt's understanding of the proper distinction between law and gospel, a format pioneered by founding LCMS president C. F. W. Walther, his former seminary professor. There is no mention of the proposed China project within the covers of the book, although its purpose in raising support for a China mission was known. Arndt produced and sold a German language edition of the

book, **Eins ist Not: Predigten uber die Evangelien des Kirchenjahres** (One Thing is Needful: Sermons on the Gospels of the Church Year).

Another tool used by Arndt to promote his concept of a China mission was a monthly newsletter. Initially mailed to about 200 supporters, within a year over 1000 copies were being printed and distributed. Published in German, these **Missionsbriefe fuer China** (Mission letters for China), presented various topics related to China, mission work, and fundraising. The bilingual format of Arndt's writing would continue throughout his career. By the spring of 1912, over 700 pastors, teachers, and congregations had pledged their support for a China mission. These were acting independently from **Der evangelish-Lutherischen Synode von Missouri, Ohio, und andern Staaten** (LCMS).

Arndt organized the Evangelical Lutheran Mission Society for China (**Missionsgesellschaft fuer Heidenmission in China**) at a conference in Gaylord, Minnesota, on May 1, 1912. Another meeting on July 14 formalized the Mission Society, composed primarily of Missouri Synod supporters. The constitution allowed membership to anyone subscribing to Lutheran doctrine, thus crossing synodical boundaries, which left the mission open to the charge of unionism, a tension that festered within the mission for years to come.

Arndt was elected as first president, and commissioned to be its first missionary. The **Gesellschaft** extended calls to five other pastors to become China missionaries but all of them declined the opportunity. Disappointed, frustrated, but undaunted, Arndt determined to pack up his family, leave his three oldest children behind, and start work in China.

## Significant Sources

| | |
|---|---|
| Arndt, Edward L. | *Green Pastures,* |
| Carroll, John | *Edward Arndt,* |
| Gibson, Rowland | *Forces Mining and Undermining China,* |
| Latourette, Kenneth | *History of Christian Missions in China,* |
| Meyer, Richard | *The Missouri Evangelical Lutheran Mission in China,* |
| Suelflow, Roy | *Challenge in China,* |

## China and the U.S.A. Superimposed (same scale and latitude)

Comparing the size and location of China and the continental United States reveals that both countries are on the same latitude, and that Hankow and the area of Hupeh Province served by the LCMS Mainland Mission straddles the 30th parallel, with approximately the same type of climate as the Gulf Coast.  St. Louis, home of the Missouri Synod, rests at the approximate area of the Northern Mission field of Rev Pi in the 1930s, south of Peking [Beijing]

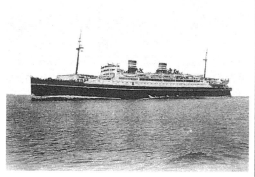

*Even, though I walk through the valley of the shadow of death, I will fear no evil; for Thou art with me.*                                                                Psalm 23:4

## Chapter Two

# China in the Early Twentieth Century

With their steamer trunks of worldly possessions beside them on the Hankow bund that March 3 in 1913, the Arndts were at the beginning of a learning curve of major proportions. The Chinese world they encountered that frigid morning was a milieu of political, cultural, religious, and linguistic factors that would require a lifetime to assimilate. They were little prepared for the experiences ahead, but were equipped with the missionary's determination and a deep faith in their Lord and Savior Jesus Christ. Buoyed with scriptural assurances that God would protect them and that angels had charge over them, they began an adventure which would radically change their family life. And would set the course of Missouri Synod history in Asia.

The Chinese world they experienced merits a chapter of explanations.

### Government

The China Arndt found was a chaotic society without a firm government in control. Over two thousand years of Imperial dynastic rule had been overthrown in 1911 by a grass roots Republican movement. Inspiration for revolt came from overseas Chinese. Medical doctor Sun Yat-sen, influenced by youth in Macau and experiences in Hong Kong and Honolulu, became the first president of the Republic. He retired from politics, turning over the reins of power to Yuan Shih-kai. Yuan had once been part of the Manchu gov

ernment, and had bridged the transition to the Republic. In his attempts to replace the emperor, Yuan was unable to hold together the complex diversity of interests and elements contending for power, which led to a *Second Revolution.* Democracy foundered as regional warlords maintained independence from Yuan's ambitious leadership, squelching his own Imperial ambitions.

The result was a breakdown of governmental structure. The infrastructure of empire was gone. Local warlords, many initially supported by Yuan, exerted their own influence. The populace existed in a lawless matrix at the mercy of vigilantes, bandit gangs, and feudal landowners.

The recently overthrown Ch'ing [Qing] dynasty had been an occupation by the northern Manchu peoples. Han Chinese males had to declare their loyalty to the minority intruders by braiding their uncut hair in a long queue or pigtail. Women continued the practice of foot binding—the painful wrapping of young girls' feet into hoof-like lily buds regarded as both erotic and symbolic of luxury and gentility. The major domestic vice was the smoking of opium (foreign mud). Though recreational use of opium had been in China at least since the early 1500s, it became a major trade commodity by European maritime traders in the late 1700s. China's distaste for the opium trade led to several Opium Wars, which opened major port cities (Canton, Amoy, Foochow, Ningpo and Shanghai) to western

   The vast majority of Chinese people lived on and worked the land. Extensive plains surround Hankow and Hanyang, where the Han and Yangtze merge. Canals, sloughs and marshes dominate the landscape. Traditional fishermen using trained cormorants were commonplace. Drinking water had to be carried from wells, or from the riverside. It had to be boiled before drinking. Water for rice fields needed to be raised over banks, utilizing a variety of traditional human-powered "pumps," before seedlings could be planted with labor-intensive hand field-work.

residence and trade, and led to the ceding of Hong Kong to Great Britain. Attempts in the early 1900s to replace opium agriculture with market gardening and wholesale grain production were only moderately successful. Opium was grown in all 18 provinces.

Internationally, rumblings of a major confrontation among European powers would soon result in "the war to end all wars," with global repercussions affecting nearly every aspect of 20th century life. China broke off its alliance with Germany in 1917, making most German-speaking businessmen and missionaries persona non grata.

Neighboring Japan, riding a tidal wave of recent naval victories over the Russians and Chinese, claimed Shantung province in 1914, when Germans there were distracted by the war in Europe. One year later, Japan presented its Twenty-One Demands to the Nanking government, claiming control and occupation rights in northern China. Yuan Shih-kai was in over his head. He abandoned the presidency in March 1916 and suddenly died that same June.

China splintered with the growth of a strong revolutionary movement in the south, challenging the provisional government at Nanking. Sun Yat-sen inspired a break from the struggling government to form a rival movement around Canton, 90 miles from the European enclaves at Macau and Hong Kong. With help from Russian agent Michael Borodin, Sun established the "restore China society" Kuomintang [Guomindang] based on a Leninist model. This national party united his Alliance Society (*Tung-meng hui*) with several other secret societies.

Sun reluctantly re-assumed the presidency. Then followed the warlord era; disaffected troops, unpaid militias, and disorganized armies roamed a lawless landscape, inflicting uncertainty, depravation, and untold misery and death upon the populace. Anarchy dominated much of China for a decade. For a time, there was also a Christian general, Feng Yu-hsiang, who required his men to carry Bibles. Sun controlled the three southernmost provinces, becoming known as the Southern Forces. But he died in March 1925.

Sun's philosophy laid groundwork for future Chinese governments. Revered as the father of modern China, he modified Abraham Lincoln's "of the people, by the people, and for the people" into the three principles of nationalism, democracy, and social livelihood.

## Language

The pronunciation and the tonal system of Chinese speech, and the complication of many differing dialects complicate Chinese language. From ancient times, it has been difficult or impossible even for some Chinese to communicate with Chinese of a different dialect area. Until recently, it had not been possible to effect a complete and true unification of the Chinese nation. To encourage national unity, the young government mandated that the language of the Peking [Beijing] region would be the national or common language. Outsiders came to refer to it as Mandarin, namely the language of government officials. The spoken language uses various tones in pronunciation, depending on the region; one basic sound can take on a variety of meanings when spoken with different tones. The tonal pronunciation needs to be absolutely and unmistakably correct for clear communication. Unrelated or totally opposite meanings often result from careless attention to the tones.

One early missionary noted, however, that to learn the Chinese language one must have "bodies of brass, lungs of steel, heads of oak, hands of spring-steel, eyes of eagles, hearts of apostles, memories of angels, and lives of Methuselah."

## Chinese Religious Beliefs

Chinese society has traditionally been grounded in at least three concurrent and non-exclusive religious systems. Foreigners

The earth is a major part of traditional Chinese religious belief. Grottos and caves were often designated as sacred spaces, in which altars or shrines were built, and offerings were made. On certain hillsides identified as having good *feng shui*, ancestral bones were buried in clay pots. The removable lids enabled annual cleaning during festivals. Doorways were decorated with images of guardians. Each lunar new year printed paper figures and written characters were pasted afresh.

may be prone to categorize Taoism, Buddhism, and the teachings of Confucius simply as Chinese folk religion. What seems to be common among the first two of these systems is the avoidance of the terrifying aspects of an afterlife. Reverence for the gods is not as powerful as the fear of their displeasure. An extensive use of charms, omens, and paper imitations of religious offerings are thought to appease the gods. Corporate worship, as a function of a congregation is not practiced, but large groups do assemble at temples on festive, religious, and social occasions for theatricals.

Traditionally, it is believed that each departed person has three souls or manes. These may be also referred to as spirits (shen). The first soul remains at the grave site. The second soul resides in a 12in. by 3in. ancestral tablet which bears the name of the deceased, usually placed on the family altar, and eventually in the family or clan temple. The third soul is subject to transmigration. This roaming spirit is of great concern of most Chinese. It is stipulated that after death, humans are re-incarnated into other forms, as men, cattle or other animals, insects, and lowest of all, a woman! Hence, the eating of meat is not universal for fear of devouring one's own relatives. Superstitions surround the presence of spirits and genii or ghosts.

Colors have meaning. Red is lucky. Scarlet is said to create fear among the spirits; yellow is used for charms to protect people and buildings; blue is the color of the emperor; white is the color of death.

Taoism grew from the teachings of Lao Tzu (Latinized as Laocius) 604-520 BCE, enigmatic figure who reputedly shared his wisdom in the form of the Tao Te Ching, sacred book of Taoism, and then wandered off into the mists of history, never to be seen again. The core value of Taoism is creative quietude—the way to do is to be. Matters will come to a proper balance and harmony without intrusive effort, just as muddy water will clarify when at rest. These Taoist observations are reminiscent of parts of the Old Testament Book of Ecclesiastes. Equilibrium is attained by balancing complementary forces of energy, termed yin and yang. Yin is dark, cold, north, earth, square, and female, while Yang is light, warm, south, heaven, round, and male. One form of equilibrium is the practise of feng shui (literally, wind-water), namely determining the auspicious placement and arrangement of buildings to align with the energy flow (chi) [qi] of the earth. This si not unlike the practices in Europe of placing the great cathedrals east and west.

Paradise (Hills of Longevity) is depicted in art as rustic mountain landscapes with lakes and streams, rocky banks, pathways, bridges, pavilions, pine and fruit trees, veiled in mist, where mastery of the mysteries of the cosmos allows one to commune with Taoist immortals.

Confucian thought springs from the fertile mind of K'ung Fu Tzu (Latinized as Confucius) who, like Lao Tzu, lived (551–479 BCE) about the time of the Babylonian captivity of the Jews, and the prophets of the exile. Confucius' discourses or Analects are largely ethical teachings delineated social propriety, filial piety, and political justice or righteousness. They also linked the structure of family, clan, tribe, and emperor in a communal whole. Humans were born without inherent evil, and needed to be disciplined to avoid being tainted by their surroundings and experiences. Leaders were respected for their position, and assumed to be worthy of being followed if they had the "mandate of heaven." Scholars studying classic literature were assumed to be wise and worthy when they passed the Imperial examinations.

For millennia, Confucianism was not only the culture of learned men, but also provided a privileged guild for those who had passed the rigorous tri-annual examinations, as they ascended to positions of power (mandarin) and prestige (literati). The unique pictographic Chinese writing system had been the exclusive domain of the classical scholar

Buddhism influences the landscape in China , Japan, and other Asian regions. The pagoda is the Chinese multi-storied equivelant to the original *stupas* of first century India. ImAges of Buddhist saints (*bodhissatvas*) are found in local temples, where coils of incense smolder to signify prayer. The immense Japenese bronze Buddha at Kamakura was a common destination of missionaries en route to China, including Olive Gruen in 1921.

and religious priest for millennia. This would change in the 1900s. China's second president, Yuan Shih-kai declared Confucianism to be the state religion or moral code.

Buddhism came to China from India in about the first century BCE, contemporary with the Hellenistic and Roman empires to the west. The teachings of Buddha Shakyamuni (Siddhartha Gautama, (563-483BCE) added the element of doctrine to foundational Hindu beliefs, Three gods dominate Hindu beliefs—Bramha the creator; Vishnu, the preserver, and Shiva, the one who reincarnates through *nataraj* (dance of death). Buddha taught meditation and retreat to an otherworldly philosophy would overcome the possessive desires of the earthly condition.

Mahayana Buddhism (the greater path) identifies incarnations of gods, goddesses, and saints who control and can assist every aspect of life and death. A multitude of saints to whom worshippers may address their prayers are bodhisattvas—beings who have become enlightened but have chosen to be reincarnated in order to help others through chants, incense burning, and almsgiving. There are three great bodhisattvas or *p'u sa*—Wen Shu, P'u Hsien, and Kuan Yin, the goddess of mercy. Believers hold that Kuan Yin, in particular, delayed Buddhahood so that she may help mortals. She is the most popular of the bodhisattvas, originally known in India as Avalokitesvara, with many variations of her name among Asian civilizations. Heaven is the western paradise.

Hinayana Buddhism (the lesser path) is not as complex, and identifies no saints. The practice is much more meditative, withdrawn, and ascetic. It took deep root in Indo-China.

Alongside and interwoven with the three major religions is the undercurrent of folk religion. One aspect focusses on Chinese heroes and gods who are honored in temples, which range from large and ornate to small shrines dotting the rice paddies of China. Iconography of gods, spirits, and folk heroes have been carved or formed in all sizes, from wood, stone, clay, plaster, or bronze in both realistic and abstracted images. Gilding, bright paint, and semi-precious gems often cover a statue's surface. Elaborate clothing and headdresses may adorn figures, usually depicted in seated positions. Symbolic positions (*mudras*) of fingers, hands, and arms represent various aspects of Buddhist images, and multiple arms are often used to depict all-powerful and all-knowing deities. The Chinese pantheon includes hundreds of powerful lesser deities—the gods of fire, war, literature, longevity, wealth, and of the hearth or kitchen.

Priests in a local temple may sometimes know chants and liturgies better than intricacies of theology or doctrine, and serve the faithful more in ritual terms than in terms of theological instruction. As intermediaries between the spiritual and the earthly worlds, they know which god (*shen*) controlled which part of the Universe or what phase of life was under whose jurisdiction, and can help the faithful enhance their favor with the gods as well as appease various gods who may be bringing hardship on their lives.

Another point at which a person's life touches the world of the spirits concerns the ancestors. Filial children, no matter their age, have obligation to venerate the spirits of their deceased ancestors. This is most commonly done daily at the family altar and in public at temples or family halls on designated days. This deeply held tradition has presented to children, young or adult, the greatest roadblock to Christian conversion, as this was seen as a form of worship in conflict to the worship of God. Fortune-telling also is related to the spirits, and communication from the spirit world can be interpreted by a medium or by other religious implement (sticks, tiles, papers) to ascertain answers for questions about health, fertility, investment, warfare, and the concerns of individual, community, and empire.

## A Brief Overview of Christian history in China, related to Lutheran Missions

### Phase I - Nestorlan era - T'ang Dynasty

635 - Alopen arrives from Antioch via Persia writes **Sutra of Jesus the Messiah**

781 - Nestorian Monument (Steele) erected at Ch'ang An [Xi'an]

845 – Christians persecuted; banned 907; but continues into Mongol era at Peking

1245 - John of Plano dispatched by Innocent IV; Kahn demands submission

1268 - Niccolo and Matteo Polo visit churches and monasteries in Hangzhou

1284 - Rabban Sauma visits Europe; common front against the Saracens rejected

### Phase II - Franciscan Era - Yuan Dynasty

1294 - Franciscan John of Montecorvino, arrives; trains 40 men by1328;

1299 – Marco Polo returns to Venice; writes Il Milione about his travels

1313 - See of Zaitun founded; Bishopric endowed; many churches built

1339 - Embassy sent to Pope Benedict XII; Pope sends John of Marignolli (1339-53)

1362 - Bishop martyred; Franciscans work with Tartars, not Han Chinese.

1369 - Christians expelled from Klanbaliq (Peking) under Ming restoration

### Phase III - Jesuit Era - late Ming - early Ch'ing

1552 - Francis Xavier uses Portuguese empire to work India, Japan, Borneo

1557 - Portuguese establish Macau - trade thru Canton (Guangzhou)

1579 - Michael Ruggieri resides @ Macau- Matteo Ricci joins in 1583

1601- Ricci in Peking; introduces hydraulics, geography, math & astronomy;

1615 - Paul V allows vernacular mass & compromised practices

1616 - Catholicism attacked as heterodox sect

1671 - Jesuits banished to Canton; Rites Controversy & Term Controversy

1720 - K'ang Hsi decrees "No westerner shall preach in Chung Kuo"

### Phase IV - Protestant era - 1807-1949

1807 - Robert Morrison begins translation of Bible at Macau

1831 - German Lutheran Karl Gutzlaff sends colporters into China;

1842 - Opium War Treaty of Nanking cedes Hong Kong Island to England;

1847 - Rhenish Mission sends Koster to China

1847 - Norwegian Mission Society established

1858 - Treaty of Tientsin ends Taiping Rebellion; Peking Kowloon & Yangtze, interi
      or Treaty Ports, Extraterritoriality (extrality): worship freedoms

1865 - China Inland Mission founded by Hudson Taylor

1890 - Augustana Mission - Daniel Nelson is first USA Lutheran missionary

1900 - Boxer Rebellion put down with foreign help. 57 Treaty Ports

1911 - Ch'ing Dynasty toppled by Republicans in the name of Sun Yat Sen

1912 - Edward Arndt organizes mission society; sails for Shanghai & Hankow

1915 – Evangelical Mission Society "calls" Erhardt Riedel from Missouri Synod

1917 - Arndt offers mission to Missouri Synod

1928 - The "Troubles" - Nanking "Incident"; Term Controversy crests

1937-45 - Japanese occupation; Pacific War

1946-49 - Missouri reopens work at Hankow, Chungking, Wanhsien, and Enshih

1949-52 - Missouri ends Mainland work; opens Hong Kong, Macau, and Taiwan

## Foreign Religious History

As mentioned above, some early scholarship gave credence to thought that Isaiah 49:12 made reference to China, as the farthest distance to the east. The prophet's reference to the Land of Sinim, was thought to reflect both Arabian and Syrian awareness of the land of the Seres, or Sinenses (hence our terms, Sino and silk). Jewish communities are documented in ancient Kaifeng on the Yellow River. Theories exist as to their origins, including the possibility that they could have been the remnants of the ten lost tribes of the Babylonian captivity. They may have been descendants of merchants and traders using the Silk Road.

Better documented is the arrival of Christianity in northwestern China via the Silk Road in the third century with Christian merchants from Syria and Persia. In 635 a monk named Alopen led a Christian mission from Baghdad to Chang'an. Received by Emperor T'ai Tsung, Christianity established roots in China, and soon Christian churches and monasteries were built in major cities, and Christian literature written (Scripture portions, sutras of Jesus the Messiah, worship materials). The clearest testimony to this era is a nine-foot tall memorial stone carving, commissioned by Emperor De Tzung in 781, commemorating and commending this "Illustrious Religion (*jingjiao*) from the West," as Christianity was called. An estimated 200,000 followers flourished in at least 15 cities, until about 845 when the illustrious religion fell into imperial disfavor.

Christianity was banned in 907 when the T'ang dynasty fell. The stone was buried for seven hundred years, but was unearthed by construction workers in 1625, giving irrefutable proof that Christianity had touched China a millennium earlier. The monument is on display in the Forest of Steles Museum in Xi'an. Centuries later Christian documents from this era (Life of Christ, Gloria in Excelsis, Christian teachings and worship materials) were discovered in caves at Tun-huang in the western desert of China.

When Christianity was driven out of Chna, some Christians fled to Mongolia, where it took root in local tribes. In mid-twelfth century there arose one Genghis Khan, feared as the Scourge of God. One of his sons married a Christian princess of one of the northern tribes, and this marriage produced Kublai Khan, the first emperor of the Yuan Dynasty (1271–1368). These were the days when Marco Polo traveled in China, and his journeys have interesting descriptions of Christianity in the court of Kublai Khan. This is the time when the western church sent its first missionaries, Franciscans, to China in 1294. Unfortunaly, when the Ming Dynasty overthrew the Yuan Dynasty in 1368, Christianity was eraicated.

Jesuits from Portugal lead the third arrival of Christianity to China in 1583. Matteo Ricci and others introduced western science and education, and sent the first knowledgeable reports about China back to Europe. Impressed by the high cultural and moral level of life in China, the newly-formed Jesuits sought to introduce Christianity in a way that affirmed what was positive about traditional Chinese culture. Spanish missionaries (Franciscan and Dominican) entered China as well, but with a less positive estimation of Chinese culture and of perceived Jesuit willingness to accommodate elements of Chinese religion too readily. Those debates bounced back and forth between the mission groups and also between the papal court and the imperial court. Eventually, Emperor K'ang Hsi who had officially welcomed Christianity in 1692 forbade the existence of Christianity in 1720—the third such expulsion.

Protestant missions began with the arrival of Robert Morrison in 1807. His greatest contribution was his translation of the Bible and the preparation of a six-volume dictionary of the Chinese language. Such infrastructure allowed production of printed Chinese tracts and publication of the Bible, in portions or in its entirety, which in turn empowered literate Chinese to study Scripture directly. Bible So-

Chinese Christians identified strongly with the parable of the Prodigal Son told in Luke 15:11-32. Often depicted in word and illustration, these particular uncredited prints were found in 2011 amongst mission artifacts in Wuhan. Several Lutheran enterprises illustrated Biblical subjects in black-and-white or color on tracts, in books, with paint, or overglazed on ceramics.

cieties, Mission Alliances, and English and American denominations began evangelistic work after China was opened through the Opium Wars, which led also to the founding of Hong Kong. Soon schools, orphanages, and hospitals were established. When a Chinese accepted Christian beliefs, unfortunately, his peers derisively accused him of "eating the foreign religion" (*ch'i tao*). Beginning in the initial five coastal treaty ports, protestant missionaries, some with wives and children, were among the first foreigners, along with oil, tobacco, and banking representatives to live in China. With later negotiations in 1860 and 1901, over fifty additional cities opened as treaty ports.

Islam was present in the Chinese capital within 100 years of the death of Mohammed bin Abdullah (lived 571-632 AD). Teachings were recorded in the Koran (Qur'an), which had been revealed to Mohammed by the angel Gabriel. Descended from Abraham through his first son Ishmael, Moslems proclaimed that there is only one god (Allah), that complete surrender (Islam—submission) to Allah is the only life acceptable to God, and that Mohammed was the final prophet. Islam co-existed with Nestorians at the T'ang capital Ch'ang An, and continues to be practiced, especially in western regions of contemporary China.

In all cases, scholars learned from literature; the illiterate from pictures and images. Visions of punishment and hellfire were not countered by the promise of a good eternity.

## Trade and Anti-Foreignism

One of the most unsettling aspects to the nineteenth century Chinese was the impact and influence of Europeans. With a few exceptions, China had been a closed society since the first unification of China in 216 BC by Emperor Ch'in Shih Huang Ti (famous for his tomb and ceramic army, unearthed in 1974 at Xi'an). China regarded itself as the Middle Kingdom since it saw itself as the center of its universe, needing no contact with other parts of the world nor requiring anything from outsiders.

Complacency and self-sufficiency meant there was no interest in establishing trade with emerging empire-building and trade-oriented nations of Europe and America. Islamic merchants and traders had carried on most of China's commerce with the outside world, Moslem Admiral Cheng Ho briefly pioneered maritime trade expeditions to Africa in the mid-1400s, but China's largest trade emporium remained Indo-China.

The Portuguese first reached China about 1517, and were granted a limited trading system at Macau about 1557. Merchants were interested in clocks, matches, mirrors, and certain foreign goods, but officials did not want foreigners living on Chinese soil. Trading was limited to exchanges only as far inland as Canton, 90 miles up the Pearl River estuary from Macau. When the British and other nations balked at the limited trading season of six months each year, and at the unwillingness of China to honor a balanced trade partnership, gunboat diplomacy, known as the First Opium War, secured their own trade colony, Hong Kong, in 1841.

Chinese intermediaries of all trading firms (*hongs*) were required to use silver bullion cast into taels, bars, or coin to buy Chinese exports. British traders lacking such bullion began illicitly trading opium from their India colonies to unofficial coastal Chinese traders for silver, which then was officially traded for silk, tea, and porcelains at Canton. Opium usage became endemic at all levels of Chinese society, labeled "foreign mud" by the Chinese. All of the health, moral, and financial woes related to its misuse were associated with Europeans, primarily the British, and anything English was therefore suspect—including Christianity and its agents. Some early missionaries, like Karl Guetzlaff, confused the situation by working for the East India Company as translators. Not only was an inseparable connection

Many men left their families in Southern China to labor abroad in mines, railroad construction, stevedore, laundry and restaurant work, so that they could send their earnings back to impoverished family or clan. In their village temples, a tablet existed for each ancestor. It was the responsibility of the living to honor the dead. Overseas Chinese rebuilt their "Chinatown" in San Francisco after the 1906 fire; workers in Portland carried on their homeland traditions, wearing the required queue until the revolution of 1911.

The chicken selects a message from among the tiny scrolls, which the fortune teller interprets to the superstitious believer.

suspected between dealing in opium and in Christian mission, but Christian mission was financially and militarily supported by the opium trace.

Manchu commissioners were not successful in policing illegal trade. Western merchants were restricted to tiny Shameen Island in Canton, and only for a six-month trading season each year. Western incursions and trade replaced traditional Chinese craftsmen and laborers with the import of manufactured goods. Poverty, the neglect of irrigation systems, and natural disasters further created an atmosphere of despair. Corrupt officials increasingly taxed peasants to satisfy growing financial demands from Peking. The greater the geographic distance from Peking, however, the more ineffective was government control. Hence southern China became the source of several rebellious movements.

One of these was the disastrous Tai Ping Rebellion of 1850-64, when a young newly converted schoolteacher from Kwangtung [Guangdong] province became convinced he was the younger long-lost brother of Jesus. Hong Xiuquan had failed the Imperial examinations, suffered a nervous breakdown, and had seen visions. His charisma and message of reform attracted followers who declared rebellion against the inept Manchu dynasty in 1851, and declared their determination to create a heavenly kingdom on earth. Launching an anti-government campaign, which destroyed villages, towns and cities, along the waterways of Kiangsi Province, the lower Yangtze, and the Grand Canal, the Taipings reached Nanking in 1853. At one point, they controlled two thirds of China, with Nanking as the capital. Under their government, land was evenly divided between all men and women over 16; opium and infanticide were declared illegal; they abolished foot-binding, slavery and polygamy; and women were declared equal with men.

Tai Ping attacks against Peking never materialized, but they did threaten the International Settlement at Shanghai in 1862. Internal corruption and paranoia weakened the movement, but the rebellion was put down only after the Chinese government accepted help from European militias. The British and other western powers got involved, laying a siege on Nanking that ended in 1864 with the deaths of over 7000. It was the worst civil war in world history, causing an estimated 20 million to 30 million deaths and destroying entire cities. In some provinces, the population would not return to pre-1850 numbers for over 100 years. Christianity, however, suffered much guilt by association, due to Hong's claim to be Christian.

During the combination of Opium Wars and Tai Ping Rebellion, more coastal cities were designated as treaty ports. Europeans could headquarter and establish communities where they enjoyed exemption from local law. The privilege was known as extraterritoriality (often shortened to extrality). Through these few toeholds, most areas of China were incrementally commercialized. Chinese officials tolerated European presence, while perpetuating their ancient culture, but impotently managing the drain of local wealth. Hankow became a treaty port in 1858, a prize of the second Opium War.

Infrastructure development over the 30 years was slow and corrupt, leading to the Boxer Rebellion of 1900. The Boxer Protocol allowed foreign powers to garrison troops in twelve cities. When in 1904, once small and powerless Japan defeated the Russian Empire, and by the Treaty of Shimonoseki gained land concessions on the Chinese landmass. More treaty ports were added until, by 1911, there were 53 such coastal and inland cities throughout China, including Hankow 600 miles up the Yangtze. European nations maintained a military presence at these areas to enforce the unequal agreements, extraterritoriality, and guarantee of safety for European residents. This reality created the missionary bind—they could not safely exist in China without those forces, yet their credibility and progress were hindered.

Nearly completed two story faculty houses at the new seminary compound were submerged. Flooding occurred while missionaries were at their annual Conference, 160 miles east at Kuling. Local staff tried to salvage stored furnishings through openings in the tile roofs. One house was totally destroyed, and never replaced

Annual flooding of the Yangtze and Han River was usually controlled by a system of dykes and the upstream overflow areas of Tung Ting and Po Yang lakes. But severe flooding during 1931 saw the worst deluge creating a lake 60 miles wide and 300 miles long. It took six months for the floodwaters to recede.

During early years of Arndt's mission, the real plague in China was the disintegration of a central government. Sun Yat-Sen was re-instated as president of the Republic by 1921. Although unsuccessful at bringing unity to China, he did formulate the San Min Chu I, the three people's principles of self-determination, self-government, and social livelihood.

Rival anti-government warlords would seize great tracts of the countryside, taxing peasant farmers to equip their own armies, causing fear and panic among both urban and rural dwellers. The destruction was wanton. Rape and pillage was the order of the day. Nationalist soldiers appropriated whatever they wanted from the local peasantry, including food, shelter, and comfort. Missionaries hoped the Christian general, Feng Yu Hseng, would prevail. His soldiers were rumored to sing hymns and baptize masses with fire hoses. Some of his men certainly did behave in a more Christian way, but Feng was driven out by Chiang Kai-shek.

Overlaying the situation was China's history of natural calamity—cycles of drought, earthquake, typhoon, flood, and insect invasion that wreaked havoc on crops and the population of nearly 450 million. While China is about ten-percent larger than the continental United States, the vast majority of the population was and is concentrated in the valleys and plains of the northeastern mineral-rich provinces, coastal provinces on the China Sea and interior floodplains on the three major river drainages—Yellow (north), Yangtze (central) and Pearl Delta (southeast).

The latter, composed of the West [Xi], North [Bei], and East [Dong] rivers, does support the lengthy navigation of the Yangtze or Yellow Rivers. Diphtheria, dysentery, malaria, cholera, and tuberculosis were common; sanitary systems were non-existent; hospitals were a rarity; care for orphans, especially girls, was rare; social welfare beyond family or clan was non-evident.

Technology advancements were being introduced that would also change China. Mechanical clocks were among the first items of western modernization to appear. The iron horse had been introduced, but railway tracks only connected a few cities. Transportation and mail to North America required four weeks, six weeks to England via the Suez Canal. Telegraph (lightning letters) to Europe was introduced in Hong Kong in 1871 and Shanghai in 1883. Morse code was used for English messages. About 32,000 Chinese characters were sent by numbers. Local telephonic services were appearing by 1910. Transpacific radio wave telephones would be introduced in 1934 at the cost of $39 USD for the first three minutes (one-third of a month's salary for a missionary). Clipper mail to the u.s. was initiated in 1935 by Pan American airways, an expensive innovation that reduced one-way postal communication time to less than a week.

It was a world in transition.

## Significant Sources

| | |
|---|---|
| Ching, Julia | *Confucianism and Christianity,* |
| Chodron, Thuben | *Buddhism for Beginners,* |
| Crow, Carl | *Four Hundred Million Customers,* |
| | *Foreign Devils in the Flowery Kingdom,* |
| Dunn, George, S.J. | *The Missionary in China – Past, Present, Future,* |
| Kang and Nelson | *The Discovery of Genesis,* |
| Latourette, Kenneth | *A History of Christian Missions in China,* |
| Moseley, George | *China Since 1911* |
| Williams, C.A.S. | *Chinese Symbolism and Art Motifs,* |

| **Chapter Three Arrivals** | | **Origin** | **School** |
|---|---|---|---|
| 1913 - Feb 13 Arndt | Arr via *SS Tamba Maru* from Seattle: Edward & Johanna Marie (nee Solomon), Walter, Christian, Karl, Edward | Pomerania; St. Paul, MN | CSL |
| 1915 - Jan 12 Riedel | Arr via *SS Awa Maru* from San Francisco: Erhardt & Carmelia (nee Beecher) | Lincoln, IL | CSF |

The "Treaty Port" Hankow that Arndt found consisted of a waterfront at the junction of the Han and Yangtze rivers. Passenger ferries vied with junks and ocean-going vessels. A large "native" city of compact buildings and streets centered on the mouth of the Han. The international section housed "concessions" for several European communities.

28

*You are the light of the world. A city set on a hill cannot be hidden, nor do people light a lamp and put it under a basket.*                                        Matthew 5:14–15

## Chapter Three

# Let the Work Begin – 1913–1917

Upon arrival in Hankow, Edward Arndt immediately secured the services of a language teacher and the family became fully immersed in learning Mandarin, day and night. The missionary also met Rev. Charles W. Kastler, formerly of the Basel Mission Society but by then pastor to the German community in Hankow.

Soon after his arrival Arndt visited with several missionaries of the Hsien-I-Wei, the Lutheran Church of China. These were the Augustana Synod (headquartered coincidently in St. Paul, Minnesota) and twelve other European Lutheran groups. Organizing in 1907, they had recently built their Lutheran Theological Seminary at Shekow about ten miles north of Hankow. Arndt preached his first Chinese sermon there in August.

The Bible used by Arndt was the Union Wenli translation, the result of a long process of literary work beginning with British Missionary Robert Morrison in 1807. Several partial translations of the Gospels were the first to be printed, but a complete version was not published until the 1860s. Seventeen years of fitful efforts continued until a standardized version was finished by committee in 1907. When the May 4, 1919 movement precipitated a vernacular language, Mandarin Bai-hua Union Version, Arndt adopted it. In his copy, Shang-ti was the Chinese name used for God, the name most preferred by protestant churches. A Union Version of the four Gospels was also produced in Braille.

The Arndt family moved to upstairs housing on Wha Ching Kai, a busy street in the Chinese quarter. Kastler shared his German chapel near the International Cemetery with Arndt, and they discussed a joint mission to the Chinese. They visited Peking together in 1913, proposing to open a chapel in the area. But Kastler's German congregations offered to increase his salary if he would stay in Hankow. Arndt felt betrayed, even though Kastler proposed to help Arndt without salary. They parted company, and with that went the use of the German chapel. On February 26, 1914, Arndt opened his own street chapel on Hai So Li, near his family quarters in the French Concession area at 12 Rue Novelle. In March, the Wha Pu Kai chapel was opened in the Chinese quarter. Names of chapels were taken from the Chinese street name. As some chapels grew into congregations, they adopted congregational names—Grace, Truth, Trinity, etc.

Arndt tried out several methods to reach the Chinese with the Christian message. Some practices that were first used by Karl Guetzlaff in the 1830s involved learning the native language, spoken and written; becoming familiar with the practices and beliefs of the local Chinese; and dressing and living as the locals. Guetzlaff had helped Robert Morrison revise Bible translations into wenli, the learned language of the classics. Arndt's translations were in the vernacular (baihua) language. The use of tracts, pamphlets, and incomplete translations was

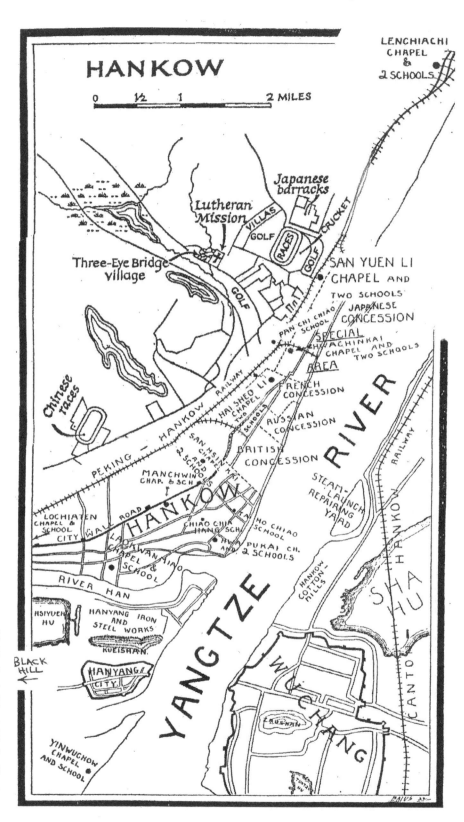

Early Missouri effort was concentrated in the native and International sections of Hankow between the rail line and the Yangtze. Land was purchased north of the railway in 1925 for the future seminary compound, to be built in 1932.

a common practice. These created a curiosity, but required substantial follow through. The key to success lay in explanation and instruction. Arndt's audience was the common man, and his contacts were often with the laboring class, meeting on the street or in a tea house. The concept dates back to Peter and Simon the tanner in Joppa (Acts 10:34–48).

Most beginning missionaries partnered with a local evangelist, a Chinese believer with some education who helped with preaching in Chinese. Often, a new missionary of the Hsin-I-Wei would borrow an evangelist to get started. Together, they would go to the streets and market places. Interested locals were then invited to the mission station for instruction on Sundays. The first major sin to overcome was the common worship of idols and ancestors.

Four adult baptisms took place that September, after the new believers had received instruction. To accept Christ was known to the Chinese as "eating the foreign religion" (chi daoli), and to worship God (tso libai). Christians faced rejection from their families, as they abandoned obligations of ancestor veneration. This was a betrayal of Confucian expectations, since the departed would not receive essential smoke-borne gifts, nourishment, and veneration in the afterlife. Such a decision was not to be lightly considered.

While some other missions sought conversionary experiences as the mark of a new Christian, Arndt's practice seems to have emphasized a thorough and informed commitment to Christ before baptism was allowed. Arndt held fast to this missionary practice, which would characterize future baptism procedures for new believers in the LCMS. This may have been to avoid apostasy, when seemingly converted new Chinese Christians abandoned their new faith for a more profitable opportunity. In poverty and desperation, many Chinese were seen to feign acceptance and church involvement for the sake of food benefits. These were called rice Christians. Bible study and continual reinforcement in worship was called for.

To reach youth Arndt began the operation of primary schools as soon as possible. Few schools of any kind existed for a child of the laboring class. Education was a major part of the Missouri Synod tradition and was a key in Arndt's plan. His first school served 35 pupils, opening at the Wha Pu Kai chapel in May, 1914. The curriculum included reading, arithmetic, good behavior, geography, singing, English, catechism, Bible study and hymns. A small tuition was required, as was the practice with all primary schools in the area. Success was immediate, and four more schools opened in Hankow within a year:

| | |
|---|---|
| Hai So Li | June 1914 |
| Kong Pang Lung | October 1914 |
| T'ieh Lu Wai | October 1914 |
| Chiao Hin Hang | June 1915 |

The mission provided the rented spaces. The small tuition fee was the teacher's only salary. Local teachers were paid about 16 cents each month, or about 500 "cash"— old Chinese brass coins (also called coppers) with a square hole in the center for easy stringing.

The printed word was essential. Translation of the Bible into Chinese had taken several centuries of isolated work by many linguists from Germany and England, beginning with the Gospels and scattered other books. A single book of the New Testament was often first printed as a booklet, called a Bible portion. These were inexpensive, easily distributed, and provided printed Scripture without the bulk or expense of an entire Bible. Utilizing his knowledge of the printer's craft, Arndt had brought to China a small hand press, and his family helped in the set up and printing.

Arndt became dissatisfied with the existing hymnbooks in Chinese, as they contained few of the German chorales he favored, especially for Christmas and Lent. In

Erhardt Riedel, a farm boy from Lincoln, IL, was the first seminarian to accept a call by the Evangelical Lutheran Society for China Mission, after his 1915 graduation from Concordia Seminary in Springfield. With his new bride, they sailed that September, arriving to rent a small apartment near an archway on Rue Novelle in the French Concession. Riedel and Arndt quickly established four schools. In this faculty picture, Riedel and Arndt are in the back row. Within a few years, Carmelia Riedel could pose with her 3 oldest children for a passport photo prior to furlough.

1915 he set about translating these hymns and as he completed a stanza, he would try it out with his evening service. Congregants had no voice training, were not familiar with hymn-singing, and spoke the Hankow dialect. Simple words were best; the challenge was to adjust the Chinese text to fit the melody and metrics of the tune.

Arndt volunteered to work with the Hsin-I-Wei to publish a Chinese Lutheran hymnal even though he was not a member of their conference. On the committee were Germans C. W. Kastler and Karl Reichelt, who years later founded a Lutheran mission to Buddhists in Hong Kong. About 200 hymns were translated, not all of which were of Lutheran origin. Arndt translated ten hymns, and added 65 verses to existing hymns. The first lines of each hymn were printed in German, Swedish, Norwegian, and Finnish. (This activity would one day earn him the accusation of unionism.) The LCMS in America had published a tune edition of its German-English hymnal in 1905. Arndt developed a system of numbered notes in the sequence of pitches and thus enabled the Chinese to sing the hymns or play them on a small portable reed organ. This seemed to help with learning the tunes. Both piano and melodian were new and fascinating sources of music to the Chinese, as was western harmony.

Synod acknowledged Arndt's unauthorized China mission at the 1914 convention, but chose not to support it. References to the mission appeared occasionally in the Lutheran Witness. Without official LCMS recognition, new missionary candidates were reluctant to consider going to China, especially in some sort of untried operation. Six men declined Arndt's offer. The Evangelical Society (Gesellschaft) continued to support Arndt with its adequate treasury from donations. The shortage was in manpower, not money.

## Erhardt Riedel

A second missionary accepted the call to serve in China from the Concordia Theological Seminary, Springfield, Illinois graduating class of 1915. He was to be financed by Arndt's mission society, not the LCMS. Erhardt Riedel spent his summer making travel plans; conferring with Arndt, who was in the U.S. to visit his ailing father; and meeting and marrying a winsome Iowa school teacher named Carmelia Becher.

The Riedels arrived in January of 1916, and began language training. Arndt wanted Riedel to work across the Yangtze in Wuchang, but Riedel preferred serving and living in Hankow; working together with Arndt in the schools and chapels.

In October their first daughter was born. The Chinese consoled the new parents with the hope that the next child would be a boy. Dorothy was the first of 40 girls and 54 boys born to 40 synodical missionary couples while living in China over the next 33 years. Another 30 children were born to these families after they left China. The Klein family raised ten children; the Zieglers bore nine; the Riedels eight. There were no twins.

Frustrated over the difficulty in recruitment, Arndt, Riedel and the Evangelical Society in Minnesota offered their China mission to the Synodical Conference in 1916. This conference included several synods, of which Missouri was one. At the Missouri Synod's 1917 convention, the success of Arndt and Riedel was recognized, and the Synod agreed to take over the mission should the society formally make the offer. This happened in September 1917. Synod's new Foreign Mission Board now included Rev. August Rehwaldt from the society. The China funds were to be separate from those for India, and the China mission field was then declared part of the Synod. And yet, a book of mission stories written by seminary professor Theodore Graebner and published by Concordia Publishing House (CPH) a

# Missouri Synod Sketches – Part Two
## Education

Synod is distinguished for its emphasis upon education. From the time of Martin Luther, education has been seen as the primary avenue of both service and mission. A literate membership supports individual growth. Predating the national Sunday School movement, congregations emphasized the training of young people, primarily using a question-answer format. Luther's Small Catechism, written 1529 by the Reformer, and Americanized in 1896 by Synodical president Rev. H. C. Schwan, is used as an educational mainstay, re-edited in 1943.

As synod grew, the need for trained pastors and teachers became apparent, and regional schools were established. In 1913, there were 11 Synodical preparatory schools, 7 junior colleges, 1 senior college, 2 teacher training colleges, and seminaries at Sprlingfield, IL, and St. Louis, MO. Most of the schools were named Concordia, referring to the Book of Concord (harmony; literally "with heart"). (see appendix for specific locations)*. Professional church workers, usually trained at these institutions, include pastors (including missionaries and chaplains) and men and women  teachers. Later, Deaconesses were first officially trained in 1922, nurses from the 1930s, and Directors of Christian Education beginning in the 1970s.

From its earliest days, the Missouri Synod congregation has supported local elementary schooling, following Luther's stress on a well educated laity. Classrooms are an integral part of any church facility, and many larger congregations support a parochial school. Some focus on early childhood education programs while most include all elementary grades, and some continue through Middle School. A few congregations support a full high school program as well.

The called teacher is regarded as a minister of religion, and traditionally performs multiple service and leadership functions within the congregation - musician, coach, youth and/or  Bible class leader, etc. Alternatively, congregations without a day schools may staff a Director of Christian Education (DCE). The DCE is also a trained and called minister of the gospel, specializing in parish education at all levels. As a teacher of the faith, they work with pastor, staff, and lay teachers in implementing Sunday school and after-hour programs, youth groups, and community outreach.

Today congregations support approximately 1000 pre-schools, 1000 elementary schools, and about 100 community high schools. The Concordia University system in 2010 includes 13 self-financing universities and  seminaries at St. Louis and Ft. Wayne (formerly at Springfield).

More about Missiouri Synod on page 64

year later made no mention of this China connection, making reference only to the Augustana Synod's activities.

The Great World War ended in 1918, a year after America entered the international fray.

In the U.S., German speakers were suspect and worked to keep a low profile. Many German towns and family names were altered. This situation was particularly traumatic for the German heritage of the Missouri Synod. Bibles, hymnals, church publications, and worship had remained primarily in German, except for the non-geographic English District. The China mission continued to use German as its primary language well into the 1930s.

Synod was also in financial straits, but at the 1917 Milwaukee convention, a group of non-clergy delegates organized the Lutheran Laymen's League to help relieve indebtedness and supplement finances. Their support would positively affect the mission field in future years through financial support, volunteerism, witness, and sponsorship of The Lutheran Hour radio program by the 1930s, and much later as International Lutheran Hour Ministries.

The China mission was established!

Arndt's first chapel was the Hai Sheo Li, opened Feb 26, 1914 in the French concession at #3 Rue Novelle, where he held services six nights each week. Erhardt Riedel opened the second chapel at San Hsin Kai (3rd New Street) in 1915, which later became Faith Congregation.

## Significant Sources

Arndt, Edward H.  *A History of the Evangelical Lutheran Mission for China*
Carlberg, Gustav  *Thirty Years on China*
Meyer, Richard  *The Missouri Evangelical Lutheran Mission in China*
Suelflow, Roy  *Challenge in China*

**Chapter Four**
**Arrivals**

| | | | Origin | School |
|---|---|---|---|---|
| 1917- Dec 9 | Arr via *SS Columbia* from San Francisco: | | | |
| Meyer | Lawrence ("Lorrie") & Magdelene (nee Brauer) | | Righton IL | CSL |
| 1918 - Dec 30 | Arr via *SS Nanking* from San Francisco: | | | |
| Gebhardt | Arnold ("Gybs") | | Forrest Green, MO | CSL |
| 1919 - July 24 | Dep via *Empress of Asia* from San Francisco: | | | |
| Arndt | Walter | | St. Paul MN | CSL |
| - Oct 5 | Dep from West Coast: | | | |
| Bentrup | Herman & Martha (nee Hinnefeld) | | Sylvan Grove KS | CSF |
| Gihring | Hugo & Adelle (nee Mathias) | | Freedom, MO | CSF |
| Schwartzkopf | Louis & Emma (nee Gerlach) | | Marysville, OH | CSL |
| 1921 - June 5 | Arr *via SS Tenyo Maru* from San Francisco: | | | |
| Lillegard | George & Bernice (nee Onstad) | | Calmar, IA | Colq. |
| - Oct 11 | Arr via *SS Nanking* from San Francisco: | | | |
| Gruen | Olive | | St. Louis, MO | Valpo |
| Klein | Herman & Edna (nee Schuessler) | | Zanesville, OH | CSL |
| Scholz | Arno & Louise (nee Hartenberger) | | Granton, WI | CSL |
| Theiss | Henry W ("Heinie") & Erna (nee Halboth) | | Oakland, CA | CSL |
| Zschiegner | Max | | Wellsville, NY | CSL |
| 1922 - | | | | |
| Nagel | Christian ("Spike") & Mathilda (nee Maroske) | | New Zealand | CSA |
| Schmidt | Carl & Paula (nee Ehlers) | | Pittburgh, PA | CSL |
| Ziegler | Albert & Laura (nee Strommen) | | Sibley Co, MN | CSL |
| 1923 - Sept 28 | Arr via *SS President Jackson* from Seattle: | | | |
| Fischer | John ("Bud") | | Algoma, WI | CSL |
| Oelschlaeger | Frieda | | West Point, NE | |
| Oelschlaeger | Marie ("Metz"), RN | | West Point, NE | LH-SL |
| 1924 - | | | | |
| Kleid | Peter, MD | | Germany | |
| 1925 - Jan 28 | Arr via *SS President Hayes* from San Francisco: | | | |
| Baden | Martha, RN | | Independence, KS | LH-SL |

**Marriage**

| 1922 | Zschiegner | Max | to Helen Rathert (in Hankow) |
|---|---|---|---|

**Resigned**

| 1919 | Arndt | Walter (continued as friend of the Mission; married Rhoda Bente, 1924) |
|---|---|---|
| 1924 | Kleid | Peter, MD        (continued in Hankow as a friend of the Mission) |

**Departed**

| 1922 | Gihring | Hugo & Adelle | (dysentery) |
|---|---|---|---|
| 1924 | Schwzartzkopf | Louis & Emma + Elmer, Luther, Dorothy | (health) |
| 1925 | Bentrup | Herman & Martha + Herman C, Edmund | (health) |

**Deaths**

| 1920 | Gihring | Leonard | (age 1 - dysentery) |
|---|---|---|---|
| 1925 | Ziegler | Virginia | (infant - stillbirth) |

*And let us not grow weary of doing good, for in due season we will reap, if we do not give up. So then, as we have opportunity, let us do good to everyone, and especially to those who are of the household of faith.*

Galatians 6:9–10

## Chapter Four

# Expansion and Development – 1917-1926

Kindled by the new Missouri Synod connection, staffing of the China mission swelled, as 22 divine calls were issued from 1918 to 1928.

St. Louis and Springfield seminary graduates, most with new brides, swelled the ranks. Four missionary families permanently departed from the field for health reasons.

Seminary graduate Lawrence Meyer and his wife Magdalene (Lenchen) were initially called by the society in 1917. They received a new call from the LCMS that September, arriving in Shanghai on December 9. The couple spent a year at the Peking Language School learning Mandarin in a more systematic program from trained teachers than from individual tutoring, which was comparatively haphazard. They savored discovering Chinese customs and practices, and wrote extensively about unique facets of Chinese culture for LCMS publications. They learned the Peking dialect of Mandarin, which was soon to be advocated as the national language.

The men decided they could establish a second location. In the newer section of the crowded native city west of the City Wall Road, they rented a storefront on Third New Street (San Hsin Chieh). The semi-western two story building was across from a popular tea house on the busy street. Missionary Erhardt Riedel opened the location with daily street evangelism (*wai-tong*) services and preaching on Sundays.

*Fu Yin Tang* read the characters on the sign over the door, meaning Gospel (Joyous Sound) Hall. Backless benches to seat about 80 were set up; a small reed organ was bought; and a speaker's platform was placed in front. In the rear, were a tiny living space and a two foot by four foot cooking area with an oil-can stove. The upstairs space was soon outfitted as a schoolroom, with a small clothes-drying platform on the outside. Riedel gathered evening passersby by singing loudly, issuing an invitation to enter and sit, attracting a reluctant but curious crowd. He would preach to anyone there—the elderly, men smoking cigarettes, screeching children or wanderers from the bustling dark street. He talked into the night, as long as any listeners remained.

A few regular attendees became interested, loyal, and would not allow others to pester or steal from the pastor (muh-si). Interested Chinese were known as enquirers, who wished to know more of the God-man, Yesu. If they renounced their Confucian training and embraced worship of the Christian God, their families would say they "ate the foreign religion." One attendee, a Mr. Sen, had been converted previously, in Shangtung Province by Rhenish missionaries. He became a helper and an inspired story-teller, his favorite tale being the parable of the Prodigal Son. Evangelist Sen eventually returned to Shantung, leaving his equally loquacious son in Hankow to continue the story-telling work.

Peking was selected for language school, where the new missionaries and wives could concentrate on intense instruction in mandarin. The sights of the city included the walls of the Imperial city, famous gateways, bustling markets, and viewing the occasional camel train ending its journey from the Gobi dessert along the Silk Road.

Door-to-door evangelism was not possible during working hours, and cultural standards prohibited foreign men from talking to Chinese women in public. Printed tracts could be distributed, but sitting in a tea house or conducting waitang street preaching encouraged more regular contact with idlers, workers, and enquirers.

The Meyers moved to Hankow after their language study year in Peking, and rapidly involved themselves in the mission. The reverend took charge of another new location, the San Yuen Li, next to the Hankow-Peking rail tracks at the rear of the Japanese Concession. He started a primary school, recruiting local children whose parents wanted their youth educated and were willing to pay the school fees (hsiao fei). In 1921, it became the location of an evangelist's school, headed by Missionary Meyer that would soon become the seminary. Magdalene held regular Bible classes for women, assisted by a Bible woman. These un-named Chinese women were earlier converts, essential to missionary work in they could speak personally with other women, whereas male foreigners should not do so in public. After a woman became an enquirer it was acceptable to talk with a male missionary in public.

Four green seminarians were called within a year. Arnold Gebhardt, a bachelor, arrived at the beginning of 1919, and immediately began language training in Peking. Three married men were also called from the class of 1919, and they and their spouses arrived on the same ship. The Bentrups, Gihrings and Schwartzkopfs lived in semi-European quarters on Milan Terrace in the same terraced apartments as the Riedels. They studied Mandarin from Mr. Fung, a scholarly Christian. Adelle Gihring and Carmelia Riedel were cousins, from Westgate, Iowa.

Arndt's son Walter returned from seminary study in St. Louis, anticipating medical mission work. Daughter Lydia returned at the same time, as a registered nurse. After some initial work using his Chinese, and helping with exploration of new sites, Walter joined the Dollar Steamship Company, an American line often used by the mission for trans-Pacific travel to the American west coast. Walter married and continued living in Hankow, Shanghai, and Hong Kong, supporting and advising the mission until the Japanese War.

Arndt's younger daughter Agnes joined the family, and convinced her frugal father to move their family into a Milan Terrace flat in the French Concession. She bought a blue enamel stove to ease her mother's housework, helped raise the younger boys, and became involved in many aspects of the mission. Within the next decade, she would perform monumental, but largely unrecognized, services for her father, and the mission.

## Shihnan - the Second Station

In 1919, the five missionaries felt ready to begin a second field. They consulted with the non-denominational China Continuation Committee, headquartered in Shanghai, which coordinated Christian efforts. The CCC noted that no work was currently being done upriver from Hankow in vast parts of western Hupeh, which included cities in the formidable Yangtze Gorges.

Riedel and Arnold Gebhardt volunteered to make a survey trip of a five county (hsien) area west of Ichang, a river city of "second importance." They met the Nelsons, a Swedish Covenant mission family there, who helped the LCMS pair get outfitted with supplies. They hired a guide, four chair coolies, and two baggage carriers. The relative urbanity of Hankow had not prepared the men for the rural conditions they found after crossing the Yangtze. Their diaries record a 19-day expedition, covering 317 miles on narrow trails, rutted cart paths, muddy slopes, and the rare stone path. Not until 1936 would there be a paved road.

Walking through 101 named towns and hamlets, they found mostly poor and

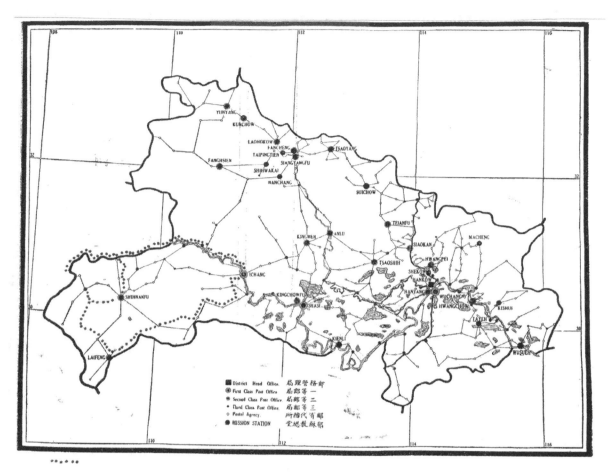

Hupeh Province Postal Map, indicating towns with mail service and routes used by mail carriers. There were no roads. Distances were measured in li. One mile equals 3 li, so that a walk of 60 li would equal 20 miles. The dotted route westward from Ichang to Shihnan circling back along the Yangtze marks the 1919 route of missionaries Riedel and Gebhardt, on a month-long journey seek a suitable new mission field.

isolated villages, much disease, and desolate living conditions among the peoples farming in the picturesque rugged mountains. Fording many rivers in southwest Hupeh, they ascended mountain passes as high as 6500 feet, and descended into river valleys averaging 1500 feet above sea level.

Overnights were spent in farmhouses, sheds, local temples, the occasional inn, and in open fields, sleeping on their own bedding to prevent lice infestations. Food was locally cooked rice with occasional vegetables or hardtack and tinned meat carried from Ichang. As always, drinking water had to be filtered and boiled.

Exploring the third importance towns of Laifeng, Shihnan, and Li Ch'uan brought them into contact with a few outposts of Episcopalians, Finnish Lutherans, Roman Catholics, Scottish missions, and the Pittsburgh Bible Society. They did find several Chinese Christians. The area was politically unsettled, a stronghold of southern Nationalist rebels (Jin Kuo Juin) claiming allegiance to Sun Yat-sen. One of the generals, Lee Si Jui, was known to use his spare time reading the Catholic catechism!

The return trip downriver took just three days on a *Pa Er* "creeper" junk, loaded with a shipment of "idol paper" (used to burn spiritual gifts and messages to dead ancestors). They headed to Ichang [Yichang] via Wanhsien [Wanxian] and Kweifu [Fengjie] All three would become new mission stations by 1923. Oarsmen were required to negotiate rapids and whirlpools on the swollen river. From the mouth of the Gorge, the two men walked the last day to Ichang, then boarded an east-bound steamer. Their return to Hankow coincided with their Missionary Conference, held at Kikungshan, the mountain retreat and school of the Hsin-I-Wei Lutheran.

Shihnan was selected to be the second station of the LCMS China mission. It was the largest city in southwest Hupeh, once an imperial administrative center (fu)

over five counties (hsien), with an official headquarters building (yamun). The hinterland included ten counties, roughly the combined area of Massachusetts, Connecticut, and Rhode Island. Located on the Clear River (Ching Kiang), the ancient walled city was set in a picturesque valley of terraced paddies that produced abundant crops of rice, vegetables, and fruit. It would be re-named Enshih [Enshi] in 1927.

Shihnan was seen as a fresh, almost virgin, field—a populous center far distant from the distractions and "evils" of the Wuhan conurbation. It was destined to be the most remote of the mission stations, and not always the first choice of married missionaries. Depending on where the traveler left the Yangtze, three narrow trails led to isolated Shihnan. The shortest, from Kweifu and Tai Chi, required crossing three mountain ranges in five days of walking, or being carried. A trek from Badong to the east required seven days, and it took eleven days from Wanhsien to the west. Travelers brought their own bedding, food supplies, and several porters.

Erhardt Riedel and Hugo Gihring returned to Shihnan and established a connection with a Reverend Chang, who ran an Episcopalian chapel. A large recently built two-story traditional courtyard house near the city's eastern gate was rented. Owned by the Hu family, the house had been occupied by marauding troops and rebel bandits who called themselves "home guards." Its two shop fronts faced the East Gate Road with a wide gated entrance between, contiguous with a stone-paved courtyard. About 20 rooms with latticed paper windows faced the open space. There would be plenty of space for housing missionary families upstairs, and areas for a chapel, school rooms, and clinic were on the main level. The men returned to Hankow, enthusiastic and excited to begin work.

In March, 1919, all was ready. Gebhardt joined the two families, along with Dr. Elizabeth Shapleigh, a Methodist and grad-

Just west of Ichang [Yichang[, the mighty Yangtze emerges from its treacherous course through 120 miles of mountain ranges. Upriver travel remained hazardous for millenia until the completion of the Three Gorges dam in 2006. Passage by wind-powered traditional craft had to be assisted with human labor, using teams of trackers hauling boats upriver through narrow gorges.

uate of Johns Hopkins Medical School, and a nurse, Ms. Tang. Freight included bedding, clothing, foodstuffs, tinned milk, kerosene stoves and heaters, kitchenware, an Estey organ, and Gihring's wedding present—an upright piano! Remingtons (typewriters) were considered essential. The party boarded a steamer to Ichang, where a 60-foot freight junk was hired to run the group and its supplies 60 miles up the Gorge to Tai Chi. This was easier said than done.

A week of rowing, tacking by sail, and trekking to negotiate reefs, brought the 13 passengers (three missionaries, two wives, four children, the two medical women, plus a cook and houseboy) up to Wind Box [Qutang] Gorge. The eight oarsmen and a "boss" (lao ban) at the rudder navigated the quiet reaches, but negotiating the narrow rapids required about 50 local men, women, and children harnessed to the boat as "trackers" by a long woven bamboo rope to pull the craft up the turbid watercourse. Passengers disembarked for safety whenever rapids were to be breeched. More than once they witnessed a loaded junk break loose, and bob uncontrolled downstream, at the whim of swollen currents. ."

Life aboard a Yangtze junk had few equivalents. Younger children were tethered with a rope to prevent a fall overboard. There were no guard rails. Women and children slept under an arched canopy of matting in the center of the barge, with woolen blankets hung as crude partitions. Men and crew rested on the open deck. All freight and supplies were stowed under the deck in compartments. The cook prepared rice and fried bean curd settlings over a clay stand (chattie) and charcoal fire, with occasional turnip greens plucked from the riverbank.

There was no privy or restroom. On the river, men relieved themselves over the gunwale, and women modestly used a chamber pot under the matted canopy.

Once Tai Chi was reached, passengers and freight were off-loaded onto the bank.

Gebhardt negotiated with coolies to carry baggage, boxes, crates, plus the piano and melodian for the five-day overland trek to Shihnan. Crossing mountain ranges and numerous rivers, creeks, and freshets, the party spent most nights at small wayside inns. Women and children rode in sedans and the men gladly walked. They arrived during a downpour, and found the Hu house rooms dry, but in need of a thorough cleaning and clearing of detritus and opium paraphernalia, left from the soldiers and rebel occupants. They were delighted to set up their beds—boards over sawhorses, and enjoy the flickering light of their simple kerosene mei foo lamps.

The first order of business was to have a sign painted in traditional characters reading *Chi Doh Chiao Fu Yin Tang*—"Christian Good News Hall." This was hung over one of the shop fronts. Backless benches and a pulpit were built, and the men began wai-tang preaching on the busy street, attracting curious passersby fascinated by the foreigners.

Dr. Shapleigh and Ms. Tang were expected to set up a clinic with their medical supplies. However, this did not materialize. It seems the nurse had friends in the army nearby and the women were drawn to work with soldiers, rather than townspeople and attendees at the *Fu Yin Tang*. They even procured a donation of $10,000 in national currency for their work, until it became clear they did not intend to work with the mission. Apparently there was also unclear communication between the women and missionaries over practices. The two medical workers resigned to work with the rebel army and the money never materialized. Disappointed at this development, the medical goals were shelved. Missionary Gihring, with no training but a humanitarian penchant, took care of minor medical situations, using a Red Cross guide book to learn basic procedures and use of the medicines and ointments which had been brought from Hankow. A year later, the mission was able to obtain a

Shihnan was the largest city in western Hupeh, but isolated many day's journey from the Yangtze. Trails from the Yangtze ports of Wanhsien, Kweifu (Tai Chi), Badong, and Ichang required as long as an 11-day trek, utilizing porters to carry bedding, food, and mission materials. Within the walled city, the LCMS mission acquired a traditional 2-story courtyard house near the East Gate, with a loggia facing the narrow main street

West of Kienshih

mortgage on the Hu house at about $1,500 USD for five years, after which the house ownership could be transferred.

By January, 1923, a group of seventeen Chinese were baptized. Each had a western sponsor; seven belonged to one family; two were sons of a man being baptized, four were foundlings supported by famine relief funds. The newly baptized took Christian names.

The missionaries became familiar with the poor living conditions, disease, and poverty in the Shihnan area. Their letters to relatives, the Board of Foreign Missions, and articles for church publications informed the home Synod of the urgent situation. In the winter of 1920–21 severe famine, resulting from drought and poor land management drove local Chinese to desperation, often grinding up dry leaves, chaff, and weeds for meager sustenance. Infants were sold or abandoned.

Synod's German language 𝕷𝖚𝖙𝖍𝖊𝖗𝖆𝖓𝖊𝖗, the 𝕳𝖔𝖒𝖊𝖑𝖊𝖙𝖎𝖐𝖘 𝕸𝖆𝖌𝖆𝖟𝖎𝖓, and the 𝖂𝖆𝖑𝖙𝖍𝖊𝖗 𝕷𝖊𝖆𝖌𝖚𝖊 𝕸𝖊𝖘𝖘𝖊𝖓𝖌𝖊𝖗 carried a series of dire reports as more missionaries sent accounts and requests. Missionaries suggested that groups of congregations could combine forces to finance the mission and relief efforts. Famine ravaged parts of Hupeh province again in 1922. Local famine relief associations were formed and the weak government tried to help by sending 500,000 "strings" of copper coins, but the funds never reached the people. In the words of Luther, "I give food to a hungry person, or drink to one who is thirsty, or clothe him that is naked, not only that he may eat or drink, but that I might get in touch with him and bring him to Christ, to His kingdom." Monies were collected in stateside LCMS organizations, raising $18,833 USD for famine relief, and sent to Shihnan.

That same spring, Synod merged the China and Indian mission funds. In response to the growth of the China mission as well as the continuing work in India, Synod's first vice president Frederick Brand was elected to also serve as General Secretary of Foreign missions, visiting both mission fields several times. More significantly, he set a conservative tone and tried to manage every aspect of the China mission for 28 years, maintaining his influence until after WW II.

## The 1921 Missionary Conference

The mission secretary's first trip to China began in May 1921. Brand visited all schools and chapels, examined ten potential Chinese evangelists, and conducted the first China General Conference of the Evangelical Lutheran Mission in China. That July, all the called missionaries assembled at Kuling [Guling] in the LuShan mountains. Also present was George Lillegard, the only experienced missionary ever to join the mission. He had spent 1912–15 in Kwangchou, Honan, serving with the Norwegian Synod. Returning to Chicago for divinity school and then serving a parish, he applied to the LCMS and received a call to China. With his bride Bernice, he arrived in June 1921 and was stationed to help open the new station at Ichang.

Many patterns and policies were established by the first conference with Dr. Brand. Present were Arndt and Riedel, the two veterans from the original China Mission Society, the Meyers, Gebhardt, and three new couples finishing language training.

At Kuling, Brand directed the course for the future of Missouri's China mission. Historically, Christian missionaries had been divided into two philosophies. A "hard gospel" missionary goal would implant the teachings and rituals of the home church and denomination. These were authentic, conservative, and focused. Synod taught that biblical discipline, continuing instruction, and adherence to doctrinal purity required an organized church. Avoiding possible heresy meant that leadership must be in the hands of seminary trained, credentialed, and ordained men.

A soft approach would proselytize and bring salvation as soon as possible and at all costs to the "heathen." That involved the

Schools were the first and most effective entree into Chinese culture, as every parent desired an education for their children. A small tuition charge was paid monthly. Storefronts were rented, mostly Christian teachers were engaged, and Olive Gruen's residential Girls school was eventually located in the former home of a German family.

Olive Green's classroom and school

possibility of syncretism, namely incorporating and adapting certain local pre-Christian practices (most notably ancestor veneration) into Christian spirituality. The Jesuits in the 1600s had been accused of this by later Dominican and Franciscan missionaries. The feuding Roman Catholic orders appealed to the pope for a decision. When the Ch'ing [Qing] emperor Kang-hsi [Kang Xi] learned of a foreign leader interfering in China's internal affairs, he simply banned all foreign religions.

The LCMS mission must avoid unionism—cooperation and fellowship with any church body not in complete accord with synodical teachings. A major point of disagreement was predestation, or the doctrine of election—who will go to heaven, and is that known from eternity? Any unresolved disagreement could dictate separation from errant Lutherans in fellowship, prayer, worship, and sharing the Eucharist. Seven other Lutheran missions in central China and three German missions had first organized in Shanghai at the 1907 all-China Centennial Mission Conference. These proudly were united into the Lutheran Church in China, called *Hsin-I-Wei* ("Justified-by-Faith Church"), operating their seminary at Shekow, a large residential school for missionary children at KiKungShan, and the Lutheran Home and Service Agency in Hankow.

LCMS policy on separation was to be China conference policy. A conviction that most Lutheran churches taught some kind of error there would be little sanctioned cooperative work in the China field. From St. Louis, this was absolute. More than once, charges of "unionism" would be laid upon well-intentioned long-term experienced missionaries in the field for decisions they made in China, lacking St. Louis' approval.

## Schools

It was the policy of Synod to establish Christian schools for missionary purposes in all fields. By 1920, the mission operated eight schools for boys and three for girls with a total of 427 pupils. Teachers were to be Lutheran Christians whenever possible. Primary education was available to Christian and non-Christian students, all paying a small tuition. Middle schools (equivalent to U.S. high schools) were designed for the education of potential teachers and theological students. From the middle school in Hankow would grow an evangelist's school and seminary. Ambitiously far-sighted, the conference set a goal to graduate teachers capable of superintending a system of Chinese Lutheran schools for boys and girls.

## Women's Work

Already in 1919, missionary wife Magdelene Meyer began conducting classes for local women at her husband's San Yuan Lee chapel, with the help of an elderly Chinese Christian woman. The San Yuan Lee became the largest Hankow chapel, with a boys' school for 200 students, and a girls' school accommodating 45 students. A dispensary with a Chinese doctor served 60 to 70 patients each day, and above the clinic were two rooms used to start an evangelist's school. The 1921 conference did recognize that no mission in China could expect any great success without women workers. It was assumed that missionary wives would do all they could in working with and training women and girls. Experience showed that Chinese women were best evangelized by other Chinese "Bible women." Then the children would be sent to Lutheran schools, and it was hoped that fathers would eventually accept the gospel as well.

Bible women were essential in other protestant missions, but references to them are scant in LCMS literature. Some were paid, but most seem to have been volunteers. Segregation of the sexes in Chinese culture necessitated that only women talk to women in public. Yet, Chinese men would never be Christianized unless the women were also converted. Unmarried Bible women could intinerate, visiting in homes, villages, and out-stations.

They would teach Bible classes and distribute tracts and Bible portions. Scant in-

Women formed the bedrock of Chinese and European living. Chinese women trained initially as "Bible Women" who could witness and serve other women. The women of the Mission were gifted musicians, teachers, medical assistants in addition to their family roles. They greatly enjoyed the annual retreats at Kuling, and the rare opportunity to be with other western homemakers.

formation is available on their training, evangelism methods, or literacy levels. A few also did basic medical work, and often witnessed and distributed literature to women waiting at clinics.

In the primary schools, youngsters received religious instruction every day from an evangelist or student pastor. Another teacher taught the secular subjects. Rote recitation facilitated memorization. Classrooms were most often on the second floor above a chapel. Most were on or near noisy market streets. Only natural daylight from a verandah supplied illumination. Walls were generally bare, except for large etched or lithographed Bible story pictures. Simple wood benches or stools had no backs and each table served as desk for two pupils. On cold or rainy days, students usually brought a heated rock or brick set in a covered bamboo basket as a foot-warmer.

The 1921 conference resolved to open a girl's boarding school (junior high) in Hankow, with a division for evangelistic workers as well. Considering the low estate of girls in Chinese society, the girl's school was directed towards the education and preparation of the LCMS-equivalent of Bible women. Chinese females were shy to be in public places where there were men. Many Bible classes and catechumen work took place in private homes. Chinese families of the better classes preferred to send their upper grade girls to boarding schools, rather than have them out on the public street going to and from school each day.

Miss Olive Gruen arrived in late 1921 with five other new missionaries. With 17 years background in education, she was the first woman and fulltime teacher of the mission.

At 39, Olive was a veteran, having also taught eight years of Sunday school with a Chinese mission in *Hop Alley* eight blocks from Old Trinity Church in St. Louis. The St Louis Sunday School Association paid part of her salary in China. Olive was re-assigned from her work in Shihnan to Hankow, to open the girl's board-

ing school in February 1924. Classrooms and dormitory were housed in the two-story brick home originally used by Charles Kastler, the German pastor who had first befriended Arndt.

Educating potential Bible women presented challenges in that most were semi-literate and required much help with reading. All the girls were from the mission primary schools. Memorization of large portions of scripture and the Small Catechism was expected. Student training included an apprenticeship with a more experienced Bible woman.

In 1922, the major non-denominational all-China Missionary Conference was held in Shanghai, organized by the China Continuation Committee of Protestant Missions. Intentionally, the LCMS mission was neither officially nor unofficially represented, although its existence was recognized in the 468-page report, and the new Shihnan field was mentioned. "God grant that our mission ever zealously guard against this great evil and remain separate!" wrote Missionary Arno Scholz.

Lack of mission board confidence in the ability of the Chinese to maintain an indigenous church, relegated workers to a long trial period as evangelists. The General Missionary Conference was to be an assembly of ordained missionaries only, subject to the Board of Foreign Missions. Conference minutes outlined requirements for native workers including academic instruction, probationary work, and rigorous internship to satisfy the LCMS that a candidate could actually become ordained.

Whether this was fatherly, conservative, colonial, imperious, cautious, doctrinal, or micro-management, in retrospect it is apparent that the missionaries rarely saw their Chinese converts as equals. Arndt expected his new members would organize much like American congregations, with officers, elders, etc. Most seminary students and candidates spent long years as evangelists until they passed and could be ordained. The mission conference maintained the stated goal of an indigenous clergy,

## Women's and Girls' Work in China –

The work of the Missouri Synod in China is still in its infancy, but that for the women and girls especially is in its very beginnings, as heretofore there have been no women workers.

In Hankow, where Rev. Arndt started to preach almost ten years ago, Mrs. Arndt always attended the services when it was possible to act as a chaperon for the Chinese women who might be encouraged to come into the chapels. About two or three years ago a regular women's meeting was arranged once a week at two o'clock in the afternoon. An elderly Chinese woman, a Christian for a number of years, assists Mrs. Meyer who so far has had charge of the meetings. As practically none of the women attending can read, progress is very slow. They memorize mostly. They learn Bible stories, some hymns and prayers. A Scripture reading and Catechism lesson is given by one of the missionaries or evangelists at each meeting.

At Shihnanfu the plan is the same as at Hankow, the meetings being held twice a week at five o'clock in the evening, which is a more convenient time for the women to come out. Here, where very few of the girls go to any school at all, we always have a larger number of girls attending than women, the average attendance of both being twenty  Much individual work must be done in assisting the women to learn to read, so that some time they may be able to read the Bible and Catechism themselves as well as hear the Word preached. Mrs. Lillegard, Mrs. Klein and myself do as much of this as is possible. There is always a Chinese woman, the guest-room attendant, who talks to the women and helps them at any time they happen to come in.

You understand that in China it is almost impossible to get the women to come to public places where there are men. It is contrary to their custom and in the interior, where there has been no foreign influence it is more noticeable than in port cities. So there must be a great deal of personal visiting done, and later we hope to have catechumen classes in the homes of some of these women until Christian knowledge and love will discard not only heathen practices, but also customs that hinder their growth as Christians.

At Hankow there are about four hundred girls in our schools where they receive religious instruction every day from the evangelists. The teacher teaches only the secular branches. But these schools at present are only lower primary schools, that is, their work covers the first four grades. There are no upper grades or high schools for our girls for two reasons: first, because we have no Chinese teachers, and, second, because the Chinese prefer to have their older girls attend boarding school than have them out on the street going to and from school every day. Do not imagine these schools are well equipped and warmed buildings such as you are used to seeing in America. They are good schools for China, but at best, even in the large cities, where mission and government schools have been established for many years, we find mostly bare walls, benches and stools without backs, and desks that look like tables with shelves below where the books not in use may be placed. In Hankow our eight girls' schools are mostly a room or two on the second floor of the houses where the chapel services are held, no windows, but like all Chinese houses open to the street in the front. If you had any idea how noisy a Chinese street is you could imagine that these would not be very quiet places to study, but that does not disturb Chinese – they are accustomed to noise. Also on dark, rainy days they are most gloomy and cold. Sometimes the children bring footwarmers to school in the shape of brass charcoal burners or earthen pots set in a covered bamboo basket. However, the boys and girls are at school early and late, so that special study hours are arranged for them before school time in the morning, and in the evening.

Our plans for future work with the women and girls is that there may be many women workers among the wives of the missionaries, as well as women sent out specially, that they may visit them in their homes and help in the individual instruction so that the Chinese women may be sooner brought to a deeper and fuller knowledge of the Truth by a personal reading of the Word of God, necessary to make true Christian homes  We shall have to find and train teachers from those who become Christians that there may be Christian schools for our girls as well as for boys.

**1922 letter from Olive Gruen**

but they were extremely cautious; concerned about the teaching of false doctrine, misrepresenting Lutheranism, apostasy, and *rice Christians,* an unfortunate but common term among Protestants that referred to Chinese people who may have professed Christianity only for its material benefits.

Communion was celebrated. Five converts of communicant age were baptized on the first Sunday after Epiphany, and missionaries and confirmands celebrated the Eucharist the next Sunday, signifying that all are one in Christ as stated in 1 Corinthians 10:17.

Many in the mission truly loved and enjoyed the Chinese converts, but the times and condition of China in the 1920s and 1930s usually perpetuated the historic wall erected by both cultures. With the conviction that they knew a better way, neophyte missionaries had not learned much about the Chinese way of life, history, or culture in depth, except as it may touch on religious territory. Several missionaries, looking back on their careers, have noted that what was needed was a deeper understanding of aspects of the Chinese world view that had an effect on local church work.

Although Frederick Brandt was to return to St. Louis, he was elected president of the Missionary Conference.

## Ichang, the Third Station

Ichang, the treaty port since 1877 at the foot of the Yangtze Gorges, was chosen as the third mission station. It was the largest city between Hankow and Shihnan. At 47 feet above sea level and 950 miles upriver from Shanghai, Ichang sits where the Yangtze transitions from narrow up-river rapids and treacherous torrents into its broad mild arterial reaches. Until the 2006 construction of the Three Gorges Dam, lower Yangtze passenger steamers and junks had to transfer their payloads to traditional wind- and human-powered native junks and barges for the 30–35 day trip upriver. (Smaller boats with high-powered steam engines made for a faster, but more expensive five-day trip.) Teams of over 50 trackers were needed at low water to assist vessels through certain narrows and rapids westward towards Patong [Badong], Kweifu [Fengjie], Wanhsien [Wanxian] and Chungking [Chongqing]. On average, one in ten craft foundered or was lost.

Ichang sits in a beautiful basin on the Yangtze's north bank, facing red clay conical hills across the river. It is the Upper Yangtze transshipment point for anything destined for Western China. Steamers and gunboats were ever present. Several distinct regional river craft were also common. Besides cargo junks and reed rafts, there were floating dwellings and tea houses, tenders and sampans, dragon boats, and special isolated barges for the quarantine of cholera sufferers. Industrial installations from the oil companies made Ichang an early petrochemical hub, and its airstrip a strategic military location in wartimes.

Setting up each mission station followed a similar pattern, but with unique quirks. George Lillegard, with three years of previous China experience, and Louis Schwartzkopf, just completing first-year language study and their wives were assigned the task at Ichang, in September 1921. On an exploratory trip, the men rented a newer foreign-style building (meaning it was a two-story structure). On a busy street near the South Gate, there was space for a 150-seat chapel, and rooms for a school, with small quarters for a resident gatekeeper and evangelist. In 1923, land nearer the river and an airstrip would be purchased for a western-style residence. Land was also bought in Hankow and Shihnan about the same time. New WuHan chapels were also opened in Hanyang, and its suburb of Ying-wu-chow.

## Wars and Rumors of Wars

At the 1921 conference, bachelor missionary Arnold Gebhardt was assigned to Shihnan, after his year of language training, to replace the Riedels (on furlough), the Gihrings (who had left due to health reasons), and the Schwartzkopfs (reassigned to Ichang). He arrived to find the city caught in the chaotic martial atmosphere dominating central

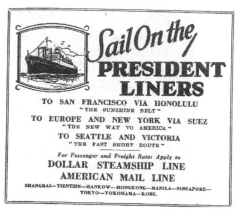

Two Indiana sisters arrived seperately, Ella with her missionary husband Lorenz Buuck in 1930, and Clara Rodenbeck as a deaconess-nurse in 1931.

In many respects, the Missouri Lutherans were a transplanted family, enjoying the Christian fellowship of co-workers who had come from the same Synod, and trained at the same seminaries. In 1923, Marie and Frieda Oelschlaeger arrived together from Nebraska (front row, right). The arrival of each new group of missionary recruits was a great occasion, as the group surrounding Rev and Mrs.Arndt in their Hankow home on Milan Terrace in 1923

China. The official Republican government capital at Nanking was not in full control of Hupeh. Regular Chinese postal service was sporadic. Gunboats patrolled the Yangtze near the larger treaty ports.

Contesting with the government were troops from neighboring Szechwan province. Mercenaries of renegade warlords and factions from the south also ravaged the province. Soldiers held the most power. During six days in November, Shihnan changed hands four times. As the neutral foreigner, Gebhardt became involved in negotiations. Much like the biblical spies at Jericho, he was clandestinely lowered from the city walls in order to hold negotiations with the warring factions until a truce was determined. Even so, the Roman Catholic and Episcopalian missions were ravaged, businesses looted, and many injured Chinese were brought to the Hu house, where an army doctor provided treatment. Mission work was briefly abandoned, as families retreated to the newly-opened station at Ichang. A clinic and school eventually opened, and an out-station was established three miles away at Ch'i Li P'in.

## Reinforcements

Four fresh seminarians arrived in Hankow late in 1921, including bachelor Max Zschiegner, three newly-wed couples, and Olive Gruen, the mission's first called woman, mentioned above.

Two of the new men, Henry W. Theiss and Max Zschiegner, were fully financed by the Walther League, whose support came entirely from the small Pennsylvania District. Half of Olive's support was provided by the St. Louis Sunday School Association. She would spend 40 years in the China field. All missionaries anticipated a full career in China. Herman Klein's career spanned 21 years. Zschiegner died in his nineteenth year of China service. But Arno Scholz left because of war in 1927, and Theiss left for the same reason in 1928.

Three more married young missionaries arrived in 1922—Carl and Paula Schmidt, and Albert and Laura Ziegler came from the St. Louis seminary; Christian & Mathilda Nagel arrived from Concordia Seminary, Adelaide, Australia. Official LCMS workers then totaled fifteen. Those who arrived in 1921 and 1922 took their language instruction in Hankow at a school set up by the mission. Many wives participated in teaching, wartime welfare, and health care activity as they learned basic Mandarin as spoken in Hankow.

Statistics for 1922 show 14 missionaries and one woman teacher; nine native evangelists, 42 native teachers and other helpers; 11 chapels; 12 schools, as well as the seminary and middle school. The mission included 230 communicants, 381 baptized, 132 catechumens, and 1,073 pupils.

Olive took language training in Peking, before her assignment to open the junior high school for girls in Hankow by 1924. In 1923, the National Walther League had proposed opening a stateside Training School for Lutheran Women Missionaries, but that did not happen, at least not in the format anticipated. A widowed pastor in West Point, Nebraska, was inspired at a 1923 conference in St. Louis, to suggest that two of his daughters Frieda and Marie Oelschlaeger become workers in China. They agreed and sailed that same fall. (As the years passed, other women were sent to China after completing a Deaconess program at Lutheran hospitals in St. Louis or Ft. Wayne.) The sisters worked at Shihnan, Frieda teaching in the mission school and Marie operating a dispensary. Martha Baden arrived in 1925 to help with nursing at Shihnan. The fifth single woman would arrive in 1927—Nurse Gertrude Simon. Frieda, Olive, and Gertrude would each give nearly 40 years to China mission work. Marie, Frieda, and Martha married career missionaries.

## Kuling and the Walther League

Missionary Arndt's second daughter, Agnes, came to Hankow in the early 1920s to help her family, and also procured employment with a local German firm. After several years of helping her family and the mission, she

### Missouri Synod Sketches - Part Three

### Auxiliary Organizations

Three nation-wide auxiliary organizations developed over time to further fellowship, evangelism and social work of Missouri Synod congregations. Composed of energetic and dedicated congregational members, each League originated from a grass-roots movement, before gaining Synodical recognition

Named for the founder of the LCMS, the **Walther League** (WL) had its beginnings in 1893 as a youth organization for members under 35 years of age. Leaguers participated in wholesome co-ed activity, spiritual growth, and service through community and national projects as well as fund-raising for international projects.

The largest initial project was the founding and support of the Tuberculosis Sanatorium at Wheat Ridge, Colorado. Walther League was a social mainstay for LCMS young adults, a model democratic corps within the church, raising huge monetary sums for many worldwide projects. Zone, District, and National gatherings encouraged service projects, fortified leadership roles, and promoted careers in church work. Walther League supported the acquisition of Valparaiso University in the 1920s.

Several missionaries were totally funded by Walther League connections. The League financed four retreat houses built at Kuling in 1923, organized "China Nights, and fostered individual projects.

The League lost Synodical support in 1976, undone by issues around the Vietnam war and internal tensions within the Synod. Wheat Ridge Ministries has provided continuity in ensuing years, especially in its work with faith-based health and human care ministries. LCMS ministry among young people has continued to develop, both with congregational activities ane national gatherings.

The **Lutheran Laymen's League** (LLL) organized in 1917, uniting non-clergy into a support organization, especially to fund special outreach projects. It's major endeavor since 1930 is The Lutheran Hour. This world-wide radio and media ministry is more commonly known as "Bringing Christ to the Nations."

Urban and rural audiences participate in various correspondence Bible courses, and uncounted thousands have come to faith in Christ through these efforts. Listeners are encouraged to affiliate with active local congregations where possible, so as to benefit from fellowship and corporate worship. Asian broadcasts have originated from Hankow, Shanghai, Hong Kong, Taiwan, and the Philippines.

The **Lutheran Women's Missionary League** (LWML), formalized in 1942, provides the opportunity for women to fund local, national, and international projects that support missions, provide human care, foster Bible studies, and promote fellowship. LWML has financed entire buildings, schools, and self-help programs around the world.

On the local and congregational level, the LWML is a powerful networking system, channeling the enthusiasm, energy, and effort of church women into a wide variety of social services and programs. LWML projects support orphanages, medical work, and schooling in Hong Kong and Taiwan.

More about the Missiouri Synod on page 64

toured the USA in the summer of 1922 as a guest speaker at District Walther League conventions. The Walther League (WL), named for LCMS founder C.F.W. Walther, was the young people's organization of the LCMS. The League was founded in 1893 in Buffalo as the "𝕲eneral-𝖁erband der evangelisch-lutherischen 𝕵ugend- and 𝕵ung-𝕸aenner-𝖁ereine der 𝖲ynodal-𝕶onferenz. At the time of Miss Arndt's speaking tour, there were 1122 senior chapters and 249 junior chapters meeting at individual congregations The 𝖁ereinsbote (later Walther League Messenger) publicized and supported Agnes's campaign, alongside similar efforts supporting the Wheatridge tuberculosis sanitarium in Colorado, and the growth of hospice boarding houses in 12 larger cities. The league also supported the LCMS's acquisition of Valparaiso University in the late 1920s.

The Walther League already supported two fulltime China missionaries, Max Zschiegner and Henry Theiss. Agnes seized upon the enthusiasm within the league for ambitious projects. She spoke to over 100 groups nationwide and led the Walther League in raising $7,000 USD for the construction of four stone retreat houses at Kuling on mountain property in Kiangsi [Jiangxi] already purchased by the mission. Collections were also taken for a "Chinese Students Fund" in 1925. Ground was broken for the houses at the 1923 Kuling conference, and workmen were supervised by Missionary Nagel. Workers tended to expropriate surplus nails, bricks, and other materials as part of their unpaid benefits, so Nagel counted out the spikes, screws, lime, and various materials meticulously. Ironically, the Australian reverend's last name means *nail* in German, and his nickname was Spike.

Construction of three houses was completed in time for the 1924 conference. The houses were to become the venue of annual conferences and summer holidays, with healthy, cooler air and welcome relief from the humid furnace of Hankow summers. A larger house was constructed a few years later, making the four contiguous properties into a very inviting and practical retreat. A Kuling escape made life in China tolerable for many western church workers and business families, including the family of Pearl Buck, and later, Chiang Kai-shek and Mao Tse-tung. The role of Kuling in the psyche of the mission cannot be overstated.

## Literature

Chinese interest in reading escalated greatly after the language reforms of the May 4 movement of 1919. Classical writing was gradually replaced by a simpler system of characters and vast numbers of Chinese wanted to use this skill once reserved for elite scholars. Mission flyers were printed inexpensively and distributed at chapels, tea houses, public assemblies, and on the streets. Bible stories, individual books of the Bible, and tracts were translated and printed.

By 1921, a regular church newsletter with a distribution of over 1000 copies was started by Gebhardt and Meyer. By 1924 this became the Chinese Lutheran Witness, which included doctrinal materials, Bible stories, and Lutheran news stories.

The Gihrings had to leave for health reasons in 1923 and the Meyers took a furlough. The Meyers would briefly return, but soon quit China for health reasons in 1925. Back in the States, Lawrence went on to become a leader in the Synod. Magdelene was one of the six women who founded the Lutheran Women's Missionary League, in 1942.

## 1923 General Missionary Conference

Like the other Lutheran China missions, the Arndt mission was originally named "Faith-Righteousness Church" or Hsin I Hui (Hsin Yi Huei). At the 1923 conference, the mission re-titled itself as "Gospel Doctrine Lutheran Church" (Foo-Yin Tao Lu deh Huei) to distinguish doctrinal purity and stress the church's evangelical nature. Arndt was not in attendance at this conference, and questioned the name change.

The cool climate at 4,000 ft elevation provided welcome relief from the sweltering summers of the Yangtze Plain. Kuling was a four-hour hike from the river port of Kiukang, up the "Thousand steps" into a valley in the Lushan mountains. Here, europeans from eastern China sought refuge and regeneration, mixing business, political, and religious worker and families

Doctrinally sound Lutheran literature was desperately needed for use in the schools and in proselytization. Early on, Arndt wrote and translated the most essential works—Luther's Small Catechism, hymns, tracts and Bible portions. Copies were produced both by mimeograph and letterpress. The founder became intense in providing more Chinese Christian literature, choosing to not waste his time going to Kuling for the 1923 or 1924 conferences, when he could remain engaged in literary work.

Arndt had been asked to present a paper on "The Chinese name for God" at the 1924 conference. This was a question and topic which had vexed Christians in China at least as far back in Chinese history as Marco Polo. Arndt sent a different paper, on the "Chinese name for Hell." Missionary Lillegard then suggested a discussion on the term for God. That presentation was to have far reaching effects (chapter 6).

In addition to work in the schools and chapels, Meyer and Gebhardt began writing and editing the Chinese Lutheran Witness (*Lu-teh-chiao chien-cheng*). The newsletter contained devotions, sermon suggestions, feature articles, news of various congregations, plus tidbits of various subjects. It was published until 1937. Copies were sent to all stations and distributed in some market places.

Conversions and baptisms grew from chapels, schools, medical work, street preaching, native evangelists, and evangelism waiting sessions in the open marketplace. Bible women brought the good news of the "one thing needful" to Chinese women, bridging the gap with local women. Baptisms totaled 68 in 1924; 182 in 1925. While these new Christians gained roles in their local congregations, missionary recommendations for a Chinese advisory board were denied by the St. Louis board as pre-mature. Local Chinese were not given decision-making responsibilities in 1924.

## Three New Yangtze Stations -Shasi, Kweifu, and Wanhsien

With several new missionaries now arriving annually, the conference decided that new stations or fields should be opened. Studying maps and surveys the board encouraged investigation of an area westward up the Han River from Hankow. Missionaries Bentrup, Scholz, and their cook traversed a dozen larger towns in the Han valley somewhat parallel to the Yangtze. They discovered hostility, hospitality, extortion, and brigades of government and warlord soldiers. A few evangelists were found along the way, which proved helpful. In each seven- to twelve-hour day they covered about 90 li (three li equals one mile). About 150 miles upriver, they turned south overland to Shasi on the Yangtze. Their research did not lead to any work in the Han valley until the extensive flooding of 1931.

The 1923 conference proposed three additional mission stations to be on the Yangtze, rather than the Han, bringing to six the total number of mission locations:

**Shasi** [Shasi], a mill town 100 miles downriver from Ichang, commands a vast plain, where the Yangtze breaks into several braided distributaries. The ancient walled city of Kingchow (Chiangling) [Jingzhou] lies three miles north. On the river between Shasi and Ichang is Itu, where the Clear River (Ch'ing Kiang) flowing east from Szechwan past Shihnan empties into the Yangtze. No significant hillock is in sight for 50 miles south toward the Dong Ding Lake [Tungtinghu], nor 100 miles eastward toward Hankow. Consequently, seasonal flooding is frequent whenever the Yangtze's dikes are breached. About 30 miles northeast of Shasi, flows the Han River, connected by the overland route explored by Bentrup and Scholz in 1921.

**Kweifu** (Kueifu) [Fengie], just beyond the border of Szechwan [Sichuan] was chosen because of the potential of its large hinterland. It was not a treaty port, but a rare anchorage for steamers, junks, and foreign gunboats within the Yangtze gorges. Ten river miles south was the village of T'ai chi on the right bank, the start of the shortest (five-day) trail to Shihnan.

Re-named Fengchieh in 1927, Kweifu lies west of the scenic, majestic, and treacher-

Expansion westward from Hankow added five locations by 1923. Shashi, Ichang, Kweifu, and Wanhsien were all accessible from the Yangtze. Shihnan was three mountain ranges south of Kweifu, accessed at the village of Tai Chi.

Kweifu, near the Wind Box gorge, was a traditional walled city where the river level seasonally varied by over 100 ft. Salt was mined under the river at low tide. Several shacks were built onto the crenelated walls, including the home of evangelist Tai.

ous Wind Box Gorge. The ancient walled county seat, also called K'wei chou fu, is nestled on the steeply-terraced north bank, surrounded by pockets of coal mines. More unique are the salt-brine wells, submerged under the Yangtze during high water. When the shingle stone reefs are exposed, wicker huts are built over wells dug about 12 feet deep. In the huts, seeping brine is collected and boiled off nearby. The fuel for this process is local anthracite, burnt in an iron pan over primitive mud burners. Smoke and steam mingle into a mystic pre-industrial atmosphere. Salt is scarce in inland China, and therefore a commodity highly prized, controlled, and heavily taxed.

Nagel and Klein were assigned to open the Kweifu station. Gebhardt helped Klein negotiate the rental of half of a dilapidated courtyard house, a process that took two months. The Chinese were in no hurry to rent to foreigners, and were concerned that they would lose "face" in their community by renting out part of a family home. The anti-foreign atmosphere was especially strong in Kweifu. Property in China is traditionally owned or controlled by every member of the family, and all had to agree on its usage. A rental figure was finally reached that allowed the owners to make "face" by boasting that the foreigners were paying a price higher than the local rates.

Preparing their half of the Hsin Kung-kuan property for living quarters meant rousting resident pigs, chickens, and other domestic animals, building chimneys, filling in *spirit holes* with glass, stretching netting under the ceiling to keep out falling bits of the roof, building wooden floors, and applying several layers of whitewash. Scarce metal hardware items from Hankow were delayed and subject to disproportionate customs charges. The superstitious landlord restricted where and when gates, doors, and partitions could be made, and it was winter before the chapel was dedicated.

Suddenly taken ill, Klein asked Nagel to preach at the opening on February 24, 1924. With only a year of language training, the new missionary led a small but successful service.

After less than six months at Kweifu, the Kleins were called back to Shihnan, leaving the Australians to evangelize, manage a chapel, and start two schools in the next four years. The most successful school was uphill from the city wall. Nagel's first baptismal class consisted of four adults and four children. Christian and Mathilda spent their entire China service in Kweifu, leaving in 1927. They had laid a foundation of the faithful that lasted over 20 years.

**Wanhsien**, 70 miles upriver from Kweifu, is the third largest city in Szechwan province, the ricebowl of China. A walled city perched at a major Yangtze bend; it is halfway between Ichang and the head of major navigation at Chungking, 1487 river miles from Shanghai. Cypress lumber (*pai-mu*) from surrounding forests supplied the second largest junk-building docks on the Yangtze. Outside the city walls, local warlords forced farmers to grow high value opium poppies, more lucrative than rice or vegetables. A nine-story white pagoda on a 1000 foot hill set Wanhsien apart from surrounding hills. Stone steps rising to a 1200 foot elevation behind the city lead to a verdant 30 acre plateau, and a smaller walled city of refuge whose name translates as *Celestial City*.

Lillegard, having the experience of opening Ichang and working at Shihnan, was selected to open what was to become a very active and diverse station.

## Concordia Seminary

The drive to train its own educated and doctrinally sound workers led the mission to found a school for evangelists in 1922. In Hankow, a training school for native teachers and a seminary for evangelists was begun in the upper rooms above the dispensary at the San Yuan Li. Fourteen Chinese men, all graduates from the primary schools, began the training to become teachers. Twenty-one men initially enrolled in Arndt's rudimentary seminary.

As the forerunner of Concordia Seminary, Hankow, it set a course of separatism from the Hsien-I-wei or other Lutheran institutions, such as the Union seminary at Shekow, or the Ki-

WANHSIEN, 173 miles above Ichang.

Three new stations were established by the 1923 Conference. Shasi and nearby Jingzhou became a favored mission spot since it was a commercial hub between Ichang and Hankow.  The walled city of Kweifu (also called Kweifuchow) overlooked the Yantze above an area of intense rapids. Salt was mined from under the river, and boiled-off using fires buil from local coal.  Beyond the Gorges was Wanhsien, a tung oil center on a loop of the Yangtze. Mission operations would be established both in the city and at a compound two miles uphill from the river.

kungshan American School, 40 miles north of Hankow.

Gebhardt reinforced the importance of the evangelists' school at the 1923 conference when he stressed the goal of a self-supporting, self-governing, and self-propagating Chinese Evangelical Lutheran church. Such a church would require a well-educated Chinese clergy, quality Christian teachers, and intense thoroughgoing evangelism.

A native clergy was being nurtured in Hankow with a seminary curriculum, without classic language study. Class time was reduced the second year so that the men could work and gain experience at the various Hankow chapels. The seminary was moved in 1924 to the Wa Chin Kai chapel in a relatively quiet section of Hankow, where student housing was better. The first class of four men graduated in 1926. From the class

of nine men started in 1922, three had not passed the examinations, one was not ready for exams, one had died, and two others had suffered chronic lung trouble. But it was a start.

Graduate Pi P'ei-ying would go on to evangelize and develop congregations to the north in Hopeh [Hebei] province on the route to Peking. This he accomplished without the permanent presence of any missionaries. Pi's classmate, Ch'en Huai-jen, was to become pastor of the largest and most isolated congregation - Shihnan/Enshih.

Reports from the Missionary Conferences of 1924 and 1925 tell of progress at all stations as start-up efforts matured into functioning schools, chapels, clinics and orphanages. These many and various programs would soon become stymied by a "perfect storm" of developments from 1926 to 1928.

## Significant Sources

| Arndt, Edward L. | *Our Task in China* |
| Baepler, Walter | *A Century of Grace* |
| Blumer, Deborah | *Called According to His Purpose (Lillegard)* |
| Fuerbringer, Ludwig | *Our China Mission* |
| Meyer, Richard | *The Missouri Evangelical China Mission* |
| Polack, W. G. | *Into All the World* |

## The Yangtze and Mississippi River Sytem compared at the same scale.

Central in the history of the Missouri Synod mission to Mainland China are two remarkably similar river systems. In America, the Missouri Synod's core is within the drainage of the Mississippi (Ohio and Missouri rivers included) centered at St. Louis, 1100 miles upriver from its mouth at New Orleans.

In China, the Missouri Mission centered at Hankow (Han and Chia Ching rivers, and linkage with the Yellow River via the Grand Canal)), 600 miles upriver from it mouth at Shanghai. Both rivers are silty, prone to seasonal flooding, and function as interstate water highways enabling distant inland commerce and settlement long before the advent of highways, railroads or airports.

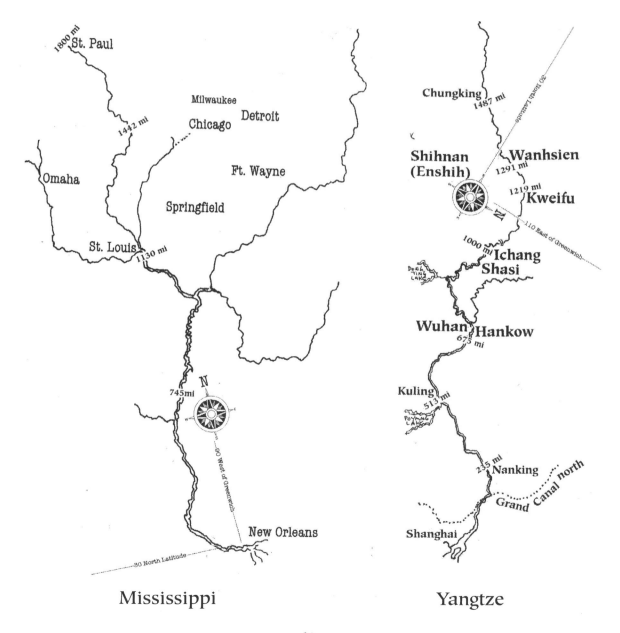

Mississippi                                    Yangtze

*Because you have made the Lord your dwelling place—the Most High, who is my refuge—no evil shall be allowed to befall you, no plague come near your tent. For he will command his angels concerning you, to guard you in all your ways.*

Psalm 91:9–10

## Chapter Five

# Missionary Home Life and Activity

Who were these men and women willing to leave their families, automobiles, telephones, and other modern conveniences to spend years in war-torn and disease-laden China? Where did they come from and what drove them? What were their living and working conditions? How did they raise families? How did they cope with separation from family and friends back home?

### The Divine Call

Above all else, these men and their families believed unconditionally in Jesus Christ as Lord and Savior—that the historical Jesus Christ died for the redemption of the soul of every person on the globe; that each individual needs to know of and accept the love of Christ; that the Creator of the universe is also its Redeemer; and that they could rely on what the future holds because they knew who holds the future.

Christianity is not a spectator sport. Mission workers inherited the enthusiasm of the New Testament apostles in commitment to share this eternal good news. These 20-somethings had chosen careers as pastors in a conservative and doctrinally-driven denomination—the church in which they were raised. Years in a Missouri Synod prep school, junior college, and at seminary had confirmed and reinforced their knowledge and intent to spread the word, and their conviction to do so. *For the son of man is come to save that which was lost.* (Matthew 18:11).

The Missouri Synod issues "Divine calls" to pastors, teachers and deaconesses to a specific ministry (or mission), believing that they have a spiritual directive and destiny to serve God wherever the LCMS Call Board determines each person is best suited and most needed. It is an appointment from God extended through the church. Just how this is decided is a mixture of requests from congregations, schools, and LCMS districts submitted to an annual conclave of representatives from the colleges and the two seminaries, together with synodical and district leaders. The Board and the candidate prayerfully consider the options, but a seminarian would rarely turn down his first call.

Missionary writings, letters, and reports exhibit an unfaltering faith as they relate personal successes or struggles; medical well-being or devastating onslaughts of tropical diseases, even death; cooperation with local government or conflicts with authorities; constant financial concerns; and matters of doctrine. A scripture passage was always at hand to reinforce their belief in God's presence and blessings; their second source was the writings of Martin Luther.

Music, especially the heritage of Lutheran hymns, played a significant role in their morale, and in their pedagogy. After acceptance of and baptism into Jesus Christ and education in the one true faith, the third leg of the mission schools and chapels was singing. Hours were spent with students and new believers practicing and performing Lutheran chorales. Many missionary wives took on the task of musical instruction, some taught piano or reed organ playing. Singing

# Missouri Synod Sketches - Part Four
# Men, Women, and Family

Historically, men of a Missouri Synod congregation were expected to serve as head-of-household, leader of the moral development of the children, and a responsible voting member of the congregation. Luther's expectations were that the father educate the children, using the Catechism to explain the doctrines of the Christian church, divided into six parts: The Ten Commandments, The Apostles Creed, The Lord's Prayer, The Sacraments of Holy Baptism and the Altar, The office of the Keys, followed by an expose on behavioral expectations, the Table of Duties.

The role of women in the Synod has slowly evolved from that of domestic helpmate and mother, to active service and leadership in the congregation, with involvement at local and national levels. The majority of Lutheran elementary parochial school teachers are women.  Since 1922, over 80 women have completed deaconess training and serve a variety of ministries in some congregations.  Regional Lutheran Hospitals also have had schools of nursing, notably St. Louis and Ft. Wayne.  In addition, women have served many forms of ministry in administrative, medical, social, and office roles.  Ordination has not, however, been open to women, given the church's understanding of biblical teaching.

Congregations are to support the Synod financially with a recommended 15% of their budget. In exchange, Synod provides a national and world mission program, welfare services, health and retirement plans for church workers, and several commissions charged with the study of theological issues, educational policies, fundraising, and making recommendations to congregations through the 5 synodical districts and at  triennial conventions.

At the time of the origin of the China mission (1913), there were about one million members, 2,100 congregations, 700 preaching stations, nearly 1,500 parish parochial schools, over 3,000 pastors, numerous parochial school teachers, and 20 overseas missionaries in India. These numbers have grown and fluctuated with national events such as World War 1, the Great Depression, World War 2, the ecumenical movement, and post-denominationalism.  Membership of the LCMS today is 2.3 million baptized souls, about 1% of the national population and 3% of acknowledged Christians in the US and Canada.

More about Missiouri Synod  on page 184

was always part of the program at the school for missionary kids, and a major part of worship. Most missionaries were also instrumentalists playing violin, horns, piano, harmonica . . . and the phonograph.

All spoke German and English, and had studied biblical Hebrew, Greek, and Latin. This may have helped them learn the challenging spoken and written Chinese language. They were prepared to accept the directive "divine call" of the Synod to serve where needed. But most had no inkling that their destiny would be far-off China when they first enrolled at seminaries nor even after vicarage, as they neared graduation. Until the 1940s, not a single graduating candidate indicated a vague interest in China in their pre-call applications. In other mission societies, like the China Inland Mission (CIM) and London Missionary Society, individuals applied and prepared specifically for Chinese work, often waiting for years before they were finally allowed to go. And missionaries were a motley crew—not unlike Jesus's first disciples.

Twenty of these missionaries were sons of ministers in the Missouri Synod. Several were the progeny of LCMS parochial school teachers. The third largest group was sons of midwestern farmers. Several were inspired to become church workers through activity in the Walther League, the youth organization of the church. All but four were called to China directly from the seminaries, with just a year of vicarage experience in a parish. Most were about 26 years old when they left, and almost all were newly married. Many of their wives were recently graduated from Lutheran nursing schools or teachers colleges. Three bachelors sent for brides within a year of arrival.

Roy Suelflow, briefly a China missionary himself in 1948, identified another type of "China hand" in his 1971 doctoral thesis. He and seminary professor Dr. William Arndt noticed a tendency in a few men who could become "somewhat cracked" as missionaries. Charitably, this referred to individuals who were over-enthusiastic, perhaps too eager to go into foreign fields without a realistic or informed knowledge of the complex stresses of overseas work. Altruism is not a guarantee of success. Nor is faith alone.

What does this mean? Some individuals could be attracted more to the image of being in charge of neophyte evangelists and a staff and servants responsible only to him. Men of several denominations had reputations for creating a local bureaucracy as a top dog foreigner. Some, duped by flattery or self-importance as a foreigner, often collected a following of self interested rice Christians. Another temptation could be extreme individualism in some missionaries, exceeding the discipline and scrutiny of a local church council or responsibility to their denominational leadership in America. There were also "loners" who had difficulty maintaining concord with fellow missionaries over doctrinal disagreements, housing policies, positioning, daily fellowship with Chinese people, or cooperation with non-LCMS people. A missionary thought to be stepping out of line, despite the best of intentions, could attract the concern of any mission board, to the point of being recalled.

By and large the LCMS China Mission was a congenial group who liked each other and respected and supported one another. Only in Hankow were there ever more than four mission staff at a station. Missionaries unable to return after furlough were deeply disappointed.

First and foremost, to be a successful missionary, one has to love the Chinese people. Secondly, one must be sent by a united church body. A church divided against itself cannot be in mission.

## Raising Families - Home Life

Annual allowance for a missionary couple was $1100 USD in the 1930s, with a stipend of $35 for each child up to a maximum of $150. Housing was provided by the mission. A griffin (bachelor intern) for Standard Oil Company in China earned $2500. In America an assembly line worker averaged $1400 (Henry Ford paid $5 per day). During this post-revolution period in China, at least three currencies were in circulation. America was on the gold standard until 1935. U.S. gold dollars were worth about two

All missionary couples, except the Arndts, were newly married just prior to their terms of service in China. Over 100 children were born from 1916 to 1937 in the Mission. Herman Klein is shown with 8 of his 10 children. At annual Kuling retreats, there were often 15 children under the age of five.

and a half Mexican silver dollars. Each Mexican coin was worth about 800 old Chinese cash, known as coppers. With a hole in their center, the low value coins were threaded onto a string or wire for ease in carrying. And there was government paper money, called Yuan, which fluctuated unpredictably. Mexican silver was the standard of exchange. During the Japanese occupation after 1937, Japanese military Yen were ubiquitous.

Missionaries were paid out of a monthly bank transfer to the entire mission, which often did not arrive on time. Assignment as mission treasurer was a time-consuming position. Some families frequently borrowed advances from the mission treasurer. Many families drew from stateside savings accounts.

By American standards, local living conditions in China were below primitive. The centuries-old lifestyle of the working and rural class Chinese resembled frontier American living with an occasional touch of elegance, but sometimes with a foundation of the medieval. Human waste was deposited in commodes and night soil was collected daily for use in agriculture. A stench was ever present during the hot languid summers on the Yangtze Plain. Flies were ubiquitous.

Water was hauled in buckets from the Yangtze, Himalayan snowmelt containing runoff from a third of China. In a few instances, a well or nearby stream of dubious purity provided water. Using alum to flocculate and settle sediment, all drinking water had to be filtered and thoroughly boiled. Twenty minutes was standard. Fresh vegetables had to be rinsed in a disinfectant solution of potassium permanganate (permanganate of potash) or *Condy's Crystals* to kill bacteria, or had to be thoroughly cooked. Fresh fruit was doused with boiling water before being peeled.

Without refrigeration, food needed to be purchased daily, usually in the open markets or stalls, or from Chinese farmers who brought their produce to town, or the mission, in huge baskets. Pigs and chickens arrived in wicker cages. The shopping was done by servants or amahs. They spoke the market language, knew local varieties, and haggled for best price in the time-tested Chinese fashion. It would be rare to see an unaccompanied western woman in the market stalls.

Larger cities like Hankow or Shanghai had provision stores in the concession areas, selling some European foods—dried, powdered, or tinned. Most of these foodstuffs were British, part of the colonial empire network (the raj) stretching from South Africa, Egypt, and India thru the Malay States, Straits Settlements, Hong Kong and Shanghai. British brand names became familiar (*Lyle's Syrup, Bird's Custard,* etc). Some products were familiar, yet different—corn flour (cornstarch), salad cream (mayonnaise), treacle (molasses), and tinned bully (corned beef). European stores after 1930 might also have cold storage—refrigerated or frozen meats, dairy, and best of all, ice cream.

Cooking was done over wood, coal, or charcoal fires. Unvented indoor cooking generated a dingy and acrid smoke. Chinese cooks often prepared meals in an outside or open cooking area, with a *wok* (iron curved-bottom pan with two handles) mounted over a hole in a brick *kang*, which was a large vented masonry platform that retained heat. The more basic *chatty* (a perforated low clay stand) was also used. Paraffin (kerosene) was refined and marketed by the Standard Oil Company and used for light and some cooking. The SOCONY Man delivered kerosene to most urban dwellings, Several missionaries used enameled kerosene cookers or stoves, some with ovens. Electricity was still a novelty, unreliable and not available at all hours. There was no home refrigeration, but block ice could be delivered for ice boxes, which kept the day's dissolved KLIM (powdered milk—spelled in reverse) adequately cool. Some foods were dried, others bought fresh in the open markets. Chinese style cooking pots, crockery, and tools, were available in local shops, but expensive foreign pots and pans could be purchased from the Wing On department store in Shanghai or by mail thru Ward's catalogues from America.

Furniture was most often locally made by native craftsmen, in wood, bamboo, or wick-

## Missionary Cookery

Missionary wives were determined to create a family diet that duplicated their home cooking in America with familiar foods for their families. Most were "comfort foods"; many for children.   Carmelia Riedel's sailed to China as a new bride in 1915. Her ring-bound cookbook contains a 20-year accumulation of recipes for "down home" German-American favorites, with some substitutions for ingredients not available in China. Most are hand-written recipes, and credit  the source. Most women would also teach these recipes to their cook amahs.    So for the fun of it, let's call these *"Sino-Teutonic"* cookery. A few samples:

**Sausages and Fried Apples**                              Carmelia Riedel
Prick the sausages well with a fork. Place in a deep frying pan. Pour in enough boiling water to cover the bottom. Cover and cook over a moderate fire. When the water evaporates, remove the cover and turn several times, that they may be nicelty browned. Turn onto a platter.
Core a number of large tart apples (sub: Chinese pears), cut them in rings an inch thick, and fry in the sausage fat.  Garnish the sausage with the apples and serve.

**Apple Fritters**                                        Mother Beecher
1 1/3 cup flour                    2 tsp baking powder
1 egg                              1/4 tsp salt
2/3 cup milk or KLIM               3 medium sized sour apples
Pare, core and slice apples, stir into batter and drop by spoons-full into hot grease. Serve hot with syrup.

**Bran Bread** (for health and constipation) (no directions given)
2 cups of bran or whole wheat flour        2 cups white flour
4 tbs of treacle (sub: molasses)           A pinch of salt
1 cup of sour milk (sub: milk + 1 tsp vinegar) 2 tsp of soda

**Butter Scotch Pie**                                     Irmgard Koehler
1 1/2 cup milk                     2 eggs
1 cup brown sugar                  2 tbs butter
3 tbs cornstarch                   2 tbs powdered sugar
Heat 1 cup of milk and the sugar until the sugar is free from lumps. Mix the cornstarch, 1/2 cup milk and egg yolks and add to hot mixture slowly. Cook in double boiler until thick, stir, Cool 10 minutes. Add butter.

**Marshmallows**                                          Laura Ziegler
Boil 2 Cups sugar and about 3/4 cup water until it ropes. Soak 1 pkg Knox Gelatine in 3/4 cup cold water. Add to syrup when it has boiled enough and beat all together until it is quite thick and white. Add vanilla or fruit coloring.
Line a pie tin with browned coconut on which to pour the candy. Let stand until set firmly. Then cut in squares and roll in coconut or powdered sugar

**Sugar Cookies**                                         Mathilda Nagel
Beat thoroughly 8 eggs, add 4 cups sugar, 2 cups shortening. Beat well with 1 cup milk. Add sufficient flour with 4 tsp cream of tartar and 2 tsp soda.

**Butter Scotch Cookies**                      Martha (Baden) Fischer
4 cups brown sugar                 1 cup butter
4 eggs                             1 tbs vanilla
1 tsp cream of tartar              1 tbs baking soda
6 1/2 cups flour                   pinch of salt
Mix & shape into loaf the evening before. Chill. Next day, slice & bake in moderate oven.

er. Chinese or European styles were crafted from drawings and photographs provided by the client, but made using traditional Chinese techniques and joinery. An elegant room might have a Chinese wool carpet, made in Tientsin [Tianjin], or an imported carpet of congoleum (linoleum). Very few large items were brought from America, although the Gihrings did ship their piano. Western hardware items were rare, and subject to taxes.

To survive, families needed the services of a Chinese cook, houseboy, or amah, who knew how to select and bargain for foodstuffs, manage laundry, and tend the children. Trying to maintain an American domestic lifestyle in China would have driven most women to apoplexy. The mission gatekeeper also arranged handyman services, worked with other locals for everything from repairs to furniture construction, and often dickered to hire rickshaw pullers and other laborers. This practice dated back to the earliest European households in China, providing work for the locals and ease of lifestyle for the Europeans. Freedom from having to deal with mundane tasks like housework, cooking, and laundry allowed the missionary and his wife to do more of the work for which they had been sent to China.

Westerners needed little reminding to be cautious of consuming unboiled water, unpeeled fruit, and uncooked foods. Those who did not often paid a price.

A case of malaria or dysentery would confine them for weeks, some even in hospital. Several individuals had to return to the States because of illness. Two-year-old Enno Buuck died from intestinal disease.

Several missionary wives, once they learned about food shopping in the local stalls and markets, would dismiss their helpers to save money. Some were not comfortable being waited on. More often the *amah* (household woman) and other domestic help became essential members of the household, and surrogate mothers to the children. They were paid a pittance, but in this arrangement, foreigners helped locals earn their rice bowl. Many of the earliest Lutheran converts and their children were such servants, workers, or rickshaw pullers.

In the case of the Arndt family, supporting papa was a joint effort. Johanna raised their youngest sons—Walter, Christian, Karl, and Edward—amid crowded and spartan housing. Daughter Agnes moved to China in her early twenties, not long after the family's arrival. Good at finances, she obtained employment with the Hong Kong Shanghai Bank in Hankow. She prevailed on her parents to move to better living quarters with the other missionaries at Milan Terrace. She helped manage the household, equipped her mother's kitchen with a modern blue enamel stove, and participated in evangelistic, medical, and educational work. She took care of her father, but was also creative in finding ways to work around his reluctance to spend money. She traveled back to the U.S. on behalf of the mission to raise funds, especially toward the construction of the retreat houses at Kuling.

Two basic housing choices were available to the early missionaries. They could live and conduct mission work in part of a modified Chinese courtyard house. In Shihnan, they did so at the Hu house, a large two-story wood structure with all rooms facing onto a central open courtyard. The other choice was to rent one or more rooms in western-style buildings. Such buildings were common in the concession areas—the sectors in treaty port cities designated for foreigners. Several families rented adjacent flats in Hankow's French Concession, the largest being a complex on Milan Terrace. It was there that Arndt did all of his work; that pastors Pi P'ei-ying and Ch'en Huai-jen were graduated from the first seminary; and that missionaries home-schooled their youngsters. While outwardly resembling European architecture, the interiors were often rudimentary. The urban Chinese shophouse was narrow and deep, with the street-level containing the business or shop front, and the living quarters upstairs.

All cities were crowded. Kweifu and Wanhsien were still contained within medieval walls. Narrow irregular lanes separated windowless walled compounds. Rooms inside the walls faced open-air dirt or paved courtyards,

As families grew, the need for schooling was initially satisfied at home, but students were soon sent to attend the Kaiser Wilhelm schule or the British school in Hankow. Norille Nero started the full-time missionary school in 1931, until his untimely death from ulcer surgery in 1934. Gilbert Wenger took over until Theobald Breihad arrived that same fall.. He would arrange for his Concordia Choir to sing Christmas songs over local Hankow radio XHJA in 1936.

where everything from old furniture to spare potted plants were stored. Open *nullahs* (Indian: deep gutters) carried away grey water and some waste. The air was pungent with the odors of humanity, more so in the summertime heat and humidity. Hankow was renowned as one of the three furnaces of China, yet snow occasionally fell in winter. Homes had no heat, save a rare brazier or small kerosene stove. In the cold of winter, it was common to wear several layers of quilted and padded garments, outdoors and indoors. One noted how cold it was by how many layers one needed. Some well-wrapped up youngsters were nearly as wide as they were tall!

Starched white shirts, ties and jackets of white duck were standard dress for the men, usually with braces (suspenders). Casual clothing was for children. Women tried to dress fashionably. No foreigner would wear Chinese clothing. Many of the pastors' wives were also accomplished seamstresses. Much correspondence with mothers and sisters was dedicated to patterns, sewing notions, and the redesign and re-sizing of men's and women's clothing. More than one letter home included a snippet of silk taffeta or crepe with a request for mom or sis to find and send trim, rickrack, buttons, and thread. Chinese tailors in the larger cities were masters at duplicating just about any garment for which they had a picture or drawing. Tailoring was a trade with very low payment, which was per day, not per garment. In rare cases, ready-made clothing from the Ward's or Sears catalogue was ordered. For the large families of several missionaries, a Singer (sewing machine) was an essential luxury, equal in importance to a Remington (typewriter), and a Hoover (vacuum cleaner).

## Education

Missionary children were and are a unique lot. Their youthful minds absorb information without discrimination or filtration. So the learning of the Chinese language from amahs and other domestic help was natural. Living in or near the foreign concessions, they developed street friendships with peers speaking French, German, Japanese, or Italian. They may have been taken into the Chinese city by servants to shop for food and household goods. They played Chinese and western games, rode wagons and bicycles, scraped their knees on cinder-covered pathways, and even broke their arms falling from trees.

Europeans and Americans tended to live in isolation, socializing within their small circles. One particular Hankow German business family, Frederick and Eva Titus, befriended the missionaries over decades. Mr. Titus even assumed responsibility during the Japanese war for mission finances. In Hankow were social clubs for each nationality.

Fourth grader Dorothy Zimmermann raised silkworms. Joe Riedel and several others collected postage stamps. They listened to grammophone recordings of classical music (but no any secular or dance tunes!). Board games were popular, especially a new game called Monopoly. Since the adults so frequently used the mission's only game board, the children made up their own version of Monopoly, drawn on scrap cardboard with currency cut from colored paper scraps.

School was basically home schooling, taught in German. First grader Dorothy Riedel, on furlough with her family, had to learn English when she attended a Lutheran parochial school in Illinois, in 1922. When the number of missionary children reached critical mass, mothers shared group learning of the three "R's" and dads guided religious instruction.

By 1931, a full time teacher was needed, and Norville Nero was called from Concordia Teachers College (River Forest, IL) to teach, coach, and direct music programs. With the completion of the seminary building in 1932, two rooms on the main level were set aside for a proper school. Textbooks, illustrated flip charts, maps, and grade cards came from Concordia Publishing House in St. Louis. Nero's untimely death, due to complications from abdominal surgery, greatly dispirited the Hankow missionary families. McLaughlin and others assumed teaching responsibilities until Theobald Breihan arrived in late 1934. As a dramatic reader and

Transportation was often an adventure for the mission staff.  Children could use their Radio Flyer wagons, and adults could ride the streetcars of Shanghai, but more unique was crossing the river on a small junk. or riding in a rickshaw across Hankow. Children often were hauled by carriers riding one or two in a basket at the end of a *kang* shoulder pole

musician, he arranged choral performances by Concordia School children on the local radio station. More on that in chapter 8.

## Getting Around

Transportation in China could be a tricky business. Travel within a city was accomplished primarily by walking. A sedan chair carried by two or four carriers or coolies (depending on the occupant's weight) could be hired. Charges had to be agreed upon beforehand. This *k'u kung* (bitter labor) method of carrying passengers, freight, coffins, or furniture on shoulder poles was one way laborers or porters eked out a subsistence livelihood—their rice bowl.

More humane and prevalent with foreigners was the ever present rickshaw, a two-wheeled device first developed by a missionary in Japan, but rapidly adapted to all sorts of hauling in China. These were pulled by one man. In later years, a bicycle would be welded onto the front of the rickshaw, making a trishaw or pedicab. Citizens of moderate means often had their own rickshaw "boy," but most were for hire, similar to a cab or taxi today. Again, the fare had to be negotiated prior to the ride. The mission did have a few regular, but not full-time, rickshaw boys.

Dodge, Chevrolet, and Ford motorcars and trucks became more common in China after WWI. When the new seminary compound opened in 1932, it was a two-mile walk into the city. Herb Meyer used $700 from his wife's insurance settlement to buy a 1934 Dodge Chassis, which was then outfitted by a local cabinet maker as a bus/station wagon. Meyer took good care of the vehicle, gassed it up, stored it in a make-shift garage, and was the primary driver. He was never fully reimbursed by the Board for his investment.

Getting around the countryside was not an easy affair, and nearly impossible if one did not live near a major waterway. Although most rivers were navigable with shallow craft, the Yangtze was the great artery of transportation in central China. Steamers and wind-driven craft of every class were available for long distance travel to other river ports, east and west. These were operated by both Chinese and British companies. Several classes of travel were available. The two most commonly used classes by the missionaries were third-class European or first-class Chinese. When Arndt was alone, he would go steerage, bunking with the crew. Meals were not included in the lower-class fares, and missionaries often packed enough food for the duration of their journey.

Roads, as defined in the west, did not exist beyond a few miles from larger cities. There were few paved roads, rather dirt ruts just wide enough for one-wheel barrows. Winding trails snaked around slopes as they crossed mountains and valleys. Bridges could be anything from stone to rope and wood. Overland travel was mostly by foot, or by sedan, on switchback routes. While a sedan chair was a luxury device, complete with an awning or shade, it was far from comfortable. The rider was at the mercy of sure-footed carriers and their sing-song rhythmic chanting which coordinated their carrying motions. The passenger was somewhat tossed about, and could rarely relax. The concept of a guard rail was unknown.

The Chinese one-wheel barrow could be pushed or pulled by a porter. Passengers and baggage had to be balanced on either side of the large central wheel. Another short-distance vehicle, usually for use only in town, was the Peking cart, a two-wheeled affair with no springs or suspension.

Long-distance travelers carried their own bedding and sought shelter in inns, temples, or in the dwellings of rural peasants and farmers. Missionaries on such trips usually brought an entourage of several carriers, bringing clothing, bedding, food, and the necessary materials for their work - Bibles, printed tracts, and Bible portions. It was customary for their coolies to do the cooking and set up the bedding.

Rail transportation in China at the time was confined to a few developed lines, and only 6000 miles of track were operational when the Ch'ing government fell in 1911. These were primarily in the north, connecting Peking with the

Long distance overland transportation meant walking or riding narrow trails over mountain passes. Many missionaries preferred to walk alongside. Wives and children usually were carried, but were not comfortable. A trip of more than an hour usually required carriers to haul drinking water food, bedding, and clothing.

Yellow Sea at Tientsin, and with the East China Sea at Shanghai. Major Japanese-built lines linked Peking with Manchuria (Japanese-occupied Manchukuo after 1931), Mongolia, Russia, and Korea. There was only one railway into Hankow, the 800-mile Peking-Hankow line, built after 1897 by a Belgian syndicate with French and Russian funding. Coal-fired American-built locomotives made the trip in just 36 hours.

That line also had stations in Honan near Kikungshan and Sinyang, where there were Augustana mission operations.

There was no rail bridge over the mighty Yangtze. A southern 700-mile rail connection from Wuchang to Canton through Hunan via Changsha had been laid out in 1899, but was not completed until 1936. From Guangzhou, the Kowloon-Canton route connected to the British Crown Colony on the South China Sea. One other line that would become important to the mission later in wartime was far to the south, from Haiphong and Hanoi in French Indo-China connecting with Kunming in Yunnan province.

Telephone service first linked Hankow with Shasi in mid-1935, a year after the first Pan Am Clippers began air mail services abroad—a convenience and expense that missionaries and the Mission Board used sparingly. Imagine a letter to home arriving in less than two weeks!

## Wellness and Disease

China's eastern plains and lowlands were breeding grounds for many diseases. Queasy readers may wish to by-pass this section, but these situations were a reality in China. Flies and mosquitoes found breeding grounds everywhere, from animal and human excrement to standing water in canals, sloughs, and paddies. Maggots infested open wounds, which actually kept wounds clean and prevented gangrene. Lepers, with deteriorating bodies and flaking skin, walked the streets warning passersby of their ailment by shouting.

Most Asian diseases were unfamiliar and rare to North Americans. The threat of tuberculosis, diphtheria, dysentery, typhus, cholera, dengue and malaria was constant in unsanitary and crowded environments. Such ailments killed many Chinese, who contracted and died of ailments endemic to the tropical climate. The use of antibiotic medicines was years in the future, home nursing, retreats to mountainous Kuling, or medical services and hospitals in Hankow, Shanghai, Hong Kong, and America were the refuge of last resort.

Several missionaries suffered with consumption or tuberculosis, which was rampant in several forms. Exposure to saliva or airborne droplets from sneezing spreads the bacteria, especially in crowded or unsanitary situations. Symptoms include coughing up mucus or blood, fever, fatigue and weight loss. For some, treatment meant returning to the States and healthier air. Several men spent six months to three years at Wheat Ridge, Colorado, where the Walther League had opened a TB Sanitorium. Some missionaries returned after recovery, only to have the disease reoccur.

Diphtheria infects respiratory systems with lesions and blockage of air passages. Toxins produced damage the heart and other organs. Newly-arrived bride Cornelia Meyer contracted diphtheria, dying within months of her arrival in 1932.

Ever-present amoebic dysentery was especially common in the summer, and several missionaries noted their experiences with the disease in their letters home. Spread by consuming contaminated food and water, it is common in tropical areas where human waste is used as fertilizer. Hence, fresh food is peeled or thoroughly cooked, and all drinking water has to be boiled, leading to the universal drinking of tea. Often fatal, inflamed intestinal tracts produce mucus and bloody stools accompanied by fever and abdominal cramps. Children developing dysentery could be cured with an emetine injection, but infant Leonard Gihring succumbed in 1920 nonetheless.

In winter, typhus spread easily by lice or fleas, and often decimated entire families. The bacteria can cause diarrhea, rash, high fever,

The care of the foot took on significance in the warm tropical climate, Many ailments and injuries were treated by the mission clinics.

Foot-binding, the traditional deformation of women's feet into "lilly buds," meant years of pain in their adolescence and difficulty in walking for adult women. Embroidered and elegant shoes were a sign of class.

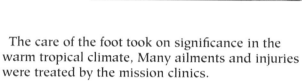

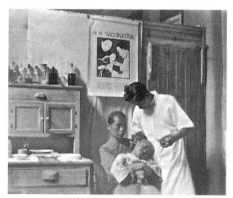

nausea, delirium, and death. Before the advent of antibiotics, treatment included oral and intravenous fluids. Cholera is a bacteria spread through contaminated water or foods. Symptoms are high fevers and dehydration, which can be fatal. .

Malaria is a warm climate parasitic disease spread by the bite of infected mosquitoes. The parasites enter the bloodstream after maturing in the liver. Red blood cells are attacked and destroyed. High fever, shaking chills, anemia, and body aches are the result. Methods of prevention including wearing full-body clothing and sleeping under fine protective netting. Mosquitoes are repelled by the burning of mosquito coils— incense-like spirals of compressed pyrethrum powder that smolder to deter the insects. Dengue is similar, but more common among the indigenous peoples.

Smallpox, measles, polio, and other diseases infected many in some missions. Leprosy was also present, with an estimated one million lepers throughout the country living alongside healthy people.

Teacher Norville Nero passed away (at age 25) after three years in China from complications of ulcer surgery in 1934. Edward Arndt (at age 64) and Max Zschiegner (at age 43) died of natural causes. Several children died—Leonard Gihring of amoebic dysentery at age one; Dickie Thiess of polio at age four; Enno Buuck of dysentary at age two; Dorcas Ziegler at age two; and three infants who died at birth. Yet over 90 missionary babies were born in China without losing any mothers in childbirth. Two German doctors, Kleid and Schneider, worked occasionally with the mission. Marie Oelschlaeger and several other women performed midwifery services.

Maintaining a positive mental health was a challenge in these circumstances. A few individuals lost their enthusiasm and yearned to return to the familiarity and comfort of American life and family. The constant threat of disease, political unrest, isolation, and unfamiliar foods took a toll. Separation of families during recovery from various diseases was emotionally draining on families, especially on wives who had to assume head of household duties and positive attitudes for the sake of children while the ailing one recovered. Five missionaries who did retire to the States for medical reasons went only as a last resort, yearning to return to China. Three did.

Weddings, Baptisms, Confirmations,and Funerals, several weddings meant special celebrations. Four marriages among mission staff resulted from co-worker romances. The first was Martha Baden, a nurse, who wed John Fisher in 1926. Teacher Frieda Oelschlaeger married Elmer Thode in 1930; her sister Nurse Marie Oelschlaeger married Arnold Gebhardt in 1931; in 1933 Nurse Clara Rhodenbeck married Eugene Seltz. Five bachelor missionaries sent for their brides and were married in China — Max Zschiegner, Herb Meyer, Herb Kretzman, John Wilenius, and Paul Kreyling.

Missionaries became extended family to each other, standing in for distant loved ones at times of joy and sorrow, and especially during holidays. Each child born to missionaries inherited a gaggle of instant uncles and aunts (tanta), and baptisms were celebrated in Kuling and all of the mission stations. Several missionary babies were named for other missionary children, Dorothy being especially popular.

Sadness tested the closeness of the community. Four funerals and the burial of two children were especially wrenching; events some of the other children would never forget. Edward Arndt's funeral was a major event when he passed away unexpectedly at age 64 in 1929. Funerals for young workers like Cornelia Meyer and Norbert Nero were times to reinforce each other. Many wrote condolences to families of the deceased. The mission established a cemetery for Chinese Christians in 1925, but foreigners were interred in the Hankow International Cemetery near the German church once used by Kastler.

## Communications

America was at least five weeks away by Pacific steamship. Letters written at Christmas received an answer by Easter. Airmail was not even an option until 1935. Most missionaries wrote regular newsy letters to someone back

Social events around weddings, baptisms, and confirmations celebrated the family nature of the mission staff. Max Zschiegner hired a car for their Hanow wedding with Helen Rathert. Kreylings were married in 1948.

But four funerals also took place at tne old German Chapel during the 36 years of the mission - 4-year old Dickie Theiss, founder Edward Arndt, recent bride Cornelia Meyer, and teacher Norville Nero (photo), Pioneer Max Zschiegner was laid to rest in Wanhsien, and toddler Enno Buuck lays in Shasi.

home, who would then send the letters on to other relatives. In Hankow, most Americans knew the dates and hours of ship movements and planned letter-writing accordingly. Using only two sheets of thin paper for the least expensive postage, most wrote to the very edge of the page. Any merchandise sent from America was subject to duty or import taxes. (The western powers were operating the post office and still collecting damages from the Boxer Rebellion, via taxation.)

Missionaries also sent letters and reports to church publications. Several long dispatches and exposes appeared in the Lutheran Witness, the Walther League Messenger, and the church's German periodical, Der Lutheraner. Keeping the accomplishments and goals of the mission in front of parishioners was essential in eliciting prayer and financial support for budgeted and specific projects.

Photography was popular with westerners living in China. Firms in Shanghai and Hankow processed black and white film, printing on American or German papers. With limited missionary finances, most prints were small contact prints. Pictures were passed around and shared with the other missionaries, and many duplicate snaps were ordered. Most were mailed to family back home, put into photo albums and labeled, or sent to the Mission Board for inclusion in various LCMS publications.

One avid photographer was Carmelia Riedel, mother of her own eight children and tanta to most of the mission families in the 1930s. Her Kodak went with her everywhere, especially to family and mission events. The kids dreaded posing for another of mom's pictures, but obligingly posed in line-ups and step formations, especially during general conference times at Kuling. Her fold-out "brownie" captured everything from close ups, landscapes, vignettes of Chinese life, large groups of missionaries, school children, and members of the various Chinese chapels. The bulk of pre-war photos you see in this book are from Carmelia's shutter. Other copious photo collections came from the Buuck, Gruen, Klein, Koehler, Theiss, Ziegler, Zimmer-

mann, and Zschiegner family albums.

Radio was in its infancy when the mission started. Several of the young seminarians-cum-missionaries were avid science hobbyists. Henry O. Theiss and Adolph Koehler both applied for ham radio licenses and worked to pick up signals from Shihnan to Hankow. As reception and broadcast power increased, commercial radio stations appeared in Shanghai, Hankow, and other cities. A few missionaries had their own wireless sets by 1940, when shortwave broadcasts from Manila and Quito were regularly picked up. Hankow had two commercial AM stations; from Shanghai, there were thirty-six.

Phonographs were high-tech entertainment for missionaries, families, and friends. Hand-cranked gramophones played symphonic records brought by Wallace McLaughlin in 1928, but when Paul Frillmann arrived in 1936 with Bing Crosby's *Temptation*, it was censored as being too explicit! Two movie houses in the concessions, showed motion pictures like "Alice in Wonderland" and "Babes in Toyland" directly from the U.S. Attending one was, indeed, a special treat. At least once, U.S. sailors hosted a shipboard matinee.

### Furlough, Deputation, and Re-Entry

Missionaries were entitled to a year-long furlough after seven years in the field, based on the biblical practice of sabbatical rest. Everyone looked forward to these trips back home, which meant reunions with family, opportunities to do advanced study, and restore health. Leave also meant "deputation" work - speaking at conventions and congregations, especially those whose prayers and generosity supported the mission program or specific missionary.

Deputation work could also include filling vacant pulpits, raising financial support, and doing other work as requested by the Mission Board. Several weeks of travel time on land and sea were involved.

Churches from Sylvan Grove, Kansas to Frankenmuth, Michigan, held annual mission festivals. These late summer weekend events,

Nestled in the Lushan Mountains of Kiangsi Province, Kuling was the ultimate rest and relaxation spot for families. High altitude air, views of mountain crags and picturesque trees, and time around the fireplace were so welcome. Adults could take advantage of quiet time to write articles for various publications back home, or catch up on correspondence using their Corona or Remmington typewriters

often in the church grove started around 1909. Typically, Mission Sunday involved morning worship featuring sermons from a visiting missionary, a huge potluck meal, followed by more preaching in the afternoon. Missionary wives often met separately with women of the congregation to explain the many other aspects of mission work. Herman Klein dressed his nine children in Chinese clothing for presentations. Young children played games in the afternoons, buying tickets to use for shooting games or bowling. Proceeds were sent to the LCMS mission program.

Festivals were also conducted at several Walther League camps, the first being at Arcadia on Lake Michigan in 1923. Several young individuals were inspired to enter professional church work at these sessions. At such events, many young people from different churches or districts also first met their eventual spouses.

As difficult as it was for missionary families to learn the Chinese language and culture when they first arrived, it was often equally awkward for them to re-adjust to American civilization after having come to understand and appreciate the Chinese and their foods, language, etiquette, customs, and nuanced culture. Many lunged back into life in a midwestern congregation, never bringing closure to their love of China. Children born and educated for years overseas sometimes had great difficulty fitting into a "normal" school setting or making friends who did not speak Chinese. They have since been identified as "Third Culture Kids"—not belonging to either their foreign or home country society. Their lives overseas were both blessing and curse.

## Kuling

The highlight of each year, without exception, was summertime spent in the heights of the LuShan Mountains at Kuling in Kiangsi Province. With dry air and temperatures 15 degrees cooler than the Yangtze Plain, Kuling's lofty waterfalls, scenic trails, rock formations, and glorious sunsets were a welcome change.

Kuling was 190 miles east of, and 4000 feet higher than, Hankow and other cities on the Yangtze plain. The German-speakers called Kuling their **Bergheim** (mountain home). Missionaries would come for about a month, mostly to hold their annual General Conference in the refreshing climate. Families often stayed longer sharing the four retreat houses.

The mission's annual conference determined staffing and programs for the coming season, heard presentations on aspects of mission work, debated doctrine, and provided time to hike, picnic, and play Monopoly and other games. New personnel tried to arrive in China by the mid-summer meeting. Needs and situations of each mission station were analyzed, and new initiatives were considered, always pending ratification from the Board of Foreign Missions. Families could be re-assigned, and relocated to different stations with short notice. Devotions, Bible study, worship, and the reading of reports and papers were also a major part of the two-week sessions.

Missionary Arnold Gebhardt wrote these undated impressions in his diary:

"I wish my camera would take a picture of these beautiful mountains, as they really are showing especially the wonderful color effect that my eye can see and my soul can enjoy. I should like to have the folks back home see these masterpieces of beauty.

Off in the distance I see a beautiful peak. It is at the top of a steep blank wall; but this mountainside is rich in color. There is a natural clay color with streaks of black running down from the top. Then there is a pale sandy red, a mossy black- green, the reddish brown of a dry oak leaf, the brownish black color as you see in fields over which a fire has passed. Further this way, nearer me, there is more maroon red, and then the shades of green, according to the usage of the land and composition of the soil. On the mountain tops you have a glowing moss-colored green. About halfway up and extending up the terraces there is the green of wheat and rye and peas and other early vegetables.

Eighteen missionary kids at Kuling about 1926, rear left clockwise: Dorothy Riedel (glasses); Robert Klein; Keith Nagel; Gerhardt, Paul, and Marie Reidel; Paul Kleid (sailor); Elmer Schwartzkopf, Herman Bentrup; Dorotho Schwartzkopf (crying), Edmond Bentrup, Luther Schwartzkopf; Verna Scholz, Max Zschiegner; Howard Ziegler: John Riedel; Bette Lillegard and Ruth Theiss.

Summer visitors never tired of nature walks and picnics at Kuling, One major highlight was the swimming pool, not far from the Walther League retreat houses.
On the far left is Paul Frillmann, later to become chaplain with the FlyingTigers.

The coloring indeed is beautiful, too beautiful to be reproduced by any painter. These wonderful colors that a painter could not produce, these wonderful mountains several times as large as Egypt's pyramids, and a thousand times as many of them!"

Traveling to Kuling was no small matter. The closest river port was Kiukiang [Jiujiang], 150 miles downriver from Hankow, a full day's trip. Kiukang marks the boundary between the lower and middle Yangtze. Families from Shasi were 500 miles west. Those from Ichang came 600 miles, from Kweifu, 700, and from Wanhsien about 770 miles. From Shihnan, there was first the five-day walk to Kweifu or Ichang. Everyone enjoyed the rare opportunity to be a tourist, especially for those sailing through the famous Yangtze Gorges. Kids reported being very happy to get other kinds of meals than "home-cooking" on the boats. Western-style breakfast from the galley was an especially welcome treat.

Kiukang was just the river port. Kuling's 4000-foot high plateau could only be reached by foot from its base, ten miles south of the Yangtze. Men and children walked, most women rode in sedan chairs borne by two or four carriers, some youngsters were hoisted in baskets on shoulder poles by sure-footed chair-coolies. Approaching the final ascent was a large stone stairway known as the 1000 steps. At the top was the Gap, the welcome little cluster of shops, post office, and church. Kuling had been an ancient sacred temple grounds. It was developed about 1905 by British Missionary Edward Littled, who wrote: "The torrid heat of the Kiukiang summer, which in the opinion of many old and well-traveled residents, exceeds in malignant intensity that of almost any other place in China, necessitated some place of refuge to which the exhausted sufferer might repair. Nature seems to provide an antidote to its own poisons, and in this case has set down lofty and cooling mountains beside the scorching plains."

Only one trail ascended the mountain, hacked into rock around many ledges overlooking shear drop-offs. Hence no motorized transportation was available. Yet about one-third of the mission babies were born at Kuling.

Missionaries and business families from as far away as Shanghai owned European-style stone houses where they brought their household staff and families for summer "cooling." Two boarding schools operated there, one was the Kuling American School for children of Episcopalians and Presbyterians; the other was Miss Tilly's Redcroft School, a British institution, which would later temporarily house the Lutheran American School of Kikungshan.

Locales atop Kuling were named Russian Valley, Lotus Valley, and Missionary Valley. Roads were named Pennsylvania, Verdun, Oxford, Princeton, and Yale. There was Barrie's Hospital and the Kuling Hotel. At the Gap were several Chinese shop-houses, a post office, two chapels, and the China Travel Service kiosk where arrangements could be made for carriers. The mountain was a true respite and refuge, an isolated expatriate asylum. Time spent at Kuling also produced the fondest memories of China for authors Pearl Buck, John Hersey, John Espey, among many others. Missionary living in pre-war China was indeed a unique and never-to-be-duplicated experience.

## Significant Sources

| | |
|---|---|
| Buck, Pearl | *The Exile; Fighting Angel* |
| Buuck, Lorenz | *I am with you always* |
| Crow, Carl | *Foreign Devils in the Flowery Kingdom* |
| Espey, John | *Minor Heresies; Tales Out of School* |
| Hersey, John | *A Single Pebble* |
| Parsons, David | *Wait and See* |
| Pollock, David | *Third Culture Kids* |

**Chapter Six**
**Arrivals**                                                                   Origin        School

1926 - Jan 4    Arr via *SS President Monroe* from Vancouver, BC:
        Simon            Gertrude                                    Zachow, WI   LH-SL

     - Sept 25   Dep on *SS President Monroe* from San Francisco:
        Cloeter          Arnold ("Rusty") & Lola (nee Nollmann)           Adair, IA    CSL
        Meyer            Arnold                                    Fergus Falls, MN   CSL
        Simon            Martin & Ruth (nee Tolzman)                   Bonduell, WI   CSL
        Theiss           Henry O ("Deke") & Frieda (nee Loewe)           Oakland, CA   CSL
        Thode            Elmer ("Deth")                              LaPorte, IN   CSL

**Marriage**
1926  Fischer,          John              to Deaconess nurse Martha Baden

**Departures**
1926   Meyer            Lawrence & Magdelene                              (health)

1927   Lillegard        George & Bernice + Betty Ann, Marjorie, Laura     (evacuated)
       Meyer            Arnold                                       (tuberculosis)
       Nagel            Christian & Mathilda + Keith, Norman             (evacuated)
       Scholz           Arno & Louise + Verna, Lois                     (evacuated)

1928   Cloeter          Arnold & Lola + Rhonda                          (recalled)
       Schmidt          Carl & Paula + Muriel                          (evacuated)
       Simon            Martin & Ruth                                (recalled)
       Theiss           Henry W & Erna + Ruth, Evelyn                   (resigned)

Pastor Max Zschiegner, author of the accompanying article, sends the above pictorial representation of the Reformation Festival gathered at Hsi Tsu Kai Chapel, together with the thought that it symbolizes. Under the figure is our pioneer missionary, Pastor Arndt, in the lower left hand corner.

*Always be prepared to make a defense to anyone who asks you for a reason for the hope that is in you; yet do it with gentleness and respect, having a good conscience, so that, when you are slandered, those who revile your good behavior in Christ may be put to shame.* 1 Peter 3:15

# Chapter Six

# Troubles 1926-1928

Two concurrent issues plagued the mission from 1926 to 1928. Unrelated forces were about to collide and rain havoc on the enthusiastic band of pioneer missionaries. Internally, disagreements over the proper Chinese term to be used as equivalent to the God revealed in the Holy Bible festered and divided the missionaries and their stateside supporters. It is difficult to overstate the passion, angst, division, and paralysis resulting from the Term Question. The tumultuous issue marked the era euphemistically known within the mission as the "troubles."

Externally, warring Chinese factions increasingly disrupted central China and all of the mission stations, causing a near total evacuation of personnel. Many retreated to Shanghai. Some returned to their homeland.

The skirmishes between warlords, the clash of northern and southern forces, incidents in Shanghai 1926 and Nanking1927, and eventual domination by the Nationalist red Communists was summarized, in true British understatement, as the Disturbances or the Evacuation.

The year 1926 had dawned with promising mission programs in six distinct locations, all with out-stations, spread over 700 river miles from Hankow west to Wanhsien. However, external and internal events challenged the very core and survival of the Good News Way Lutheran Society (*Fu Yin Dao Loh Da Wei*).

Synod had sent 22 seminary graduates and five women to China, since 1917.

Three families had returned because of medical problems, leaving four bachelors, 13 married men, and four deaconesses (two nurses and two teachers). The ten remaining families had 23 children, most of pre-school age.

All missionary families assembled in July 1926 at Kuling for a few weeks of cool highland temperatures. For this fifth annual China General Missionary Conference, stations had been left in the care of the Chinese evangelists. Concerned about political unrest, Gebhardt stayed in Shihnan, while the other families steamed down the Yangtze among gunboats from England, Japan, and the U.S. About to devastate the morale and fiber of the mission, several internally divisive undercurrents were flowing.

## The Term Controversy

Reverend Arndt had unwittingly opened a can of worms when he offered the financially stable Evangelical Lutheran Missionary Society for China to the Missouri Synod in 1917. The China mission became a more-publicized Synodical enterprise, calling young dynamic men, wives, and deaconesses to the field. In exchange, independence was relinquished over financial and philosophical control to the Mission Board, 8000 miles away.

Conference recommendations now had to be approved by the Board of Foreign Missions. Communication consumed valuable time and energy, sometimes the recommendations and decisions of the experienced workers in China were challenged. Finances were tightly controlled from St. Louis, requiring reams of

Cartoons from Walther league Messenger, 1927, drawn by missionary Max Zschiegner

The Cause of China's Chaos — If She Only Knew It

1926 Missionary Conference, at Kuling, Seated are Edward Arndt, mission founder, and Frederick Brand, Director of the Board for Foreign Missions. Behind Rev. Arndt is George Lillegard, leader of the group of missionaries opposed to the use of Shang-Ti as the Chinese name for God. Frederick Brand was present to represent the opinion of the St. Louis Seminary Faculty committee that Shang-Ti was an acceptable term.

paperwork, hours of minutely detailed accounting, and long delays. Approval was required before any new field could be opened. Micro-management of expenses required detailed monthly accounting. Furloughs, travel within China, and medical expenses were negotiable. Many instances of inconsistency arose in implementing Board policies.

Most significantly, all but two of the cadre of energetic new missionaries were young, with less experience, and high-minded in their approach to mission. Only George Lillegard had previously been a missionary—for three years in Honan with the Norwegian Synod. Wallace McLaughlin had served three years as an assistant pastor in the United Lutheran Church. The fresh graduates, with just one year of vicarage experience, had anticipated work in a stateside parish. A call to China, of all remote places, was unanticipated. Understandably, no one had adequate language or cultural preparation for overseas work. The men were grounded in LCMS theology, fresh from St. Louis, and Springfield, In their mid-20s, they represented a new generation of Germanic-American values in the aftermath of The Great War. Seminarians had not been permitted to marry while in school, so most were also newly married, some to women they had quickly courted between graduation and embarkation. Nearly all started families soon after arrival in China.

While the new men respected Arndt and his founding work, cutting their missionary teeth under his supervision, a generation gap began to erode harmony between some co-workers, and to distance several from Arndt. Some significant differences of process and practice had emerged by the mission's tenth anniversary. While missionaries became like family with their co-workers and shared many rich blessings of community, they were also mostly strong-willed Germans, fully able to stand their ground over theory and procedure when challenged, agitated, or inspired. Good energy resulted in major accomplishments and baptisms of the Chinese. The same commitment precipitated

stalemate, discord-even chicanery-when applied to contested internal issues.

Living and working in close proximity in alien surroundings at isolated small stations with just one or two co-workers could sometimes fray nerves. There were few Europeans residing inland with which to interact socially. Scant references to discord appear in print, except in a few private letters. Annual conference decisions over stationing were usually cooperative. The needs of each location were factored in with individual language experience, administrative and leadership strengths, and the overall program of the mission. Issues were amicably resolved before re-assignment, although sometimes only after much discussion. Family size, schooling, and health issues seem to have also been significant. The challenge of isolation and difficulty of travel, particularly at Shihnan, complicated the situation.

Arndt did not attend the Kuling conferences in 1923 or 1924, since he was doing more important literary work in Hankow. In advance of each annual conference, various men were selected to prepare papers for discussion. Arndt had been asked to present a treatise on the Chinese name for God but in 1924 sent a different paper on the Chinese name for hell. This was a very significant difference. His choice to substitute, by intention or innocence, re-opened a Pandora's Box of semantics and doctrine.

When Arndt didn't produce the assigned conference paper at the 1924 conference, Chairman Lillegard took the opportunity to lead a discussion by presenting his own conviction concerning the contentious issue of the proper Chinese name, or term, for God.

An intense battle had been fought by the Roman Catholics in the seventeenth century concerning this issue. By eventual papal decree the name *T'ien Chu* (Lord of Heaven) was prescribed as the proper adopted name. Indeed, that name became the name still used for the Roman Catholic Church, namely T'ien Chu Chiao, literally, the Church of the Lord of Heaven. The internal acrimony generated by this and other issues was so severe,

In St. Louis, a new campus for Concordia Seminary was completed in Clayton in 1926. Amidst the various stained glass windows in Wartburg Hall are panes commemorating the India and China Missions. China is represented by a large traditional Asian dragon, shown under the radiance of bright heavenly light. That brilliance eminates from the ideograph for God, equivelent in style to illustrations using the Hebrew word for Yahweh. The two Chinese characters used here are Shang-ti, the term consistently favored by the Seminary faculty (and Edward Arndt) throughout the Term Controversey. Representing the India mission on an adjacent rondel, is an elephant depicted beneath the Star of India.

however, that in 1704 the emperor banned missionaries and Christianity.

A century later, Protestant missionaries were again torn by this issue, although attitudes toward the Roman Catholic Church removed Lord of Heaven as an option. Two other words surfaced (*shen* and *Shang-ti*). The discussion and debate were long-running and divisive.

In a nutshell, the core of the discussion was which of these words, both used in Chinese religious terminology for god/deity/spiritual being, was the more salvageable word and which was freighted to the point of being unusable.

One side opted for shen, as the more generic word, comparable to the Hebrew elohim and the Greek theos. Though it could refer to a variety of spirit beings in addition to god/s, this side felt that with proper education, the term could be refined, and with the addition of true to the term, the term could become a Christian concept, just as in English Christians have become comfortable with true God. In English we can also capitalize a word, which reinforces a sense of a specific God, and not merely some generic god, not so in Chinese.

Shen advocates felt that the use of Shang-ti was fatally flawed. In the Chinese religious world, there was a deity known as Shang-ti, *supreme ruler* or literally *one above (shang) the emperor (ti)*. To use a name that identified a god worshipped in the Chinese pantheon, however, would be comparable to using names like Jupiter or Zeus for the biblical God. A personal name is used in place of a generic designation. What is at stake is sowing confusion in the minds and hearts of Chinese converts about the identity of the Christian God. To the extent that there is conflation of Chinese and Christian ideas of God, that can lead to syncretism which may leave a person content in his or her idolatrous ways.

Those who preferred Shang-ti admitted that Shang-ti was known in the Chinese pantheon. However, they felt that the concept of supreme ruler itself has a generic sense which connotes a much clearer and higher identity than shen, which can bring to mind a wide range of spirit beings, including various forms of spirits that inhabit the human body, and remain (and can haunt) after death. As with shen, instruction would be needed to fill Shang-ti with distinctive Christian content.

Though the debate had all but run its course in the wider Protestant world, it took on new passion in the LCMS mission. Lillegard and many of the more recently arrived missionaries felt strongly that shen was the only legitimate choice and that Shang-ti was an intolerable compromise. Arndt and most seasoned missionaries preferred the Shang-ti Bible and used the name Shang-ti in the mission's various literature productions. Though the 1924 Conference tabled the furtive discussion, when Arndt used Shang-ti in his course materials for the fall of 1924, the younger missionaries felt he was flouting the conference resolution to not use Shang-ti in any printed materials, pending a final decision.

This debate raged for many decades without real resolution, and finally cooled down to a defacto agreement to disagree. There is one interesting relic of that debate, namely when a person wants to buy a Chinese Bible, he has a choice of a shen Bible or a Shang-ti Bible. Printing both is easy, since the only difference is the choice of a two-character word or a one-character word; the Shang-ti Bible is printed normally, and the shen Bible leaves an empty space behind for the character for shen.

Yet another division within the Missionary Conference concerned the location of a permanent Chinese Concordia Seminary with classrooms, library, and living quarters. Upriver men believed a central location, somewhere between Wanhsien and Wuhan, was a logical choice. It woud be away from the congestion, climate, and temptations of worldly Hankow. The Wuhan area was also a political hotbed; site of the original 1911 re-

Missionary George Lille-
gard, shen proponent,

Walter A Maier, St. Louis
Seminary professor.

William Arndt, Seminary
professor not related to Edward Arndt, but a strong sup-
porter of the China Mission

The Lord's Prayer hand-written in cursive Chinese characters. Read Chinese from right to left, top to bottom.

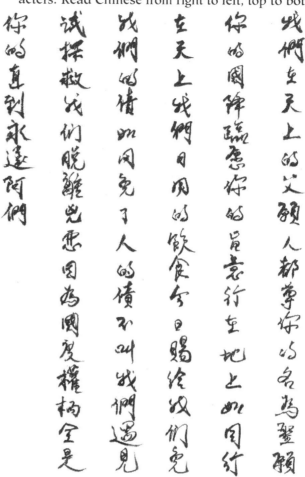

## Addenda to Synodical Reports.

### CHINESE TERM QUESTION.

The following report was adopted: —

WHEREAS, The controversial question in our China Missions
regarding the term to be used for God is a highly complicated one,
which cannot be decided within the space of a few days; and

WHEREAS, Your Committee has spent many convention hours
listening to the arguments of both sides, linguistic, theological, and
philosophical, without being able to arrive at a satisfactory solution; and

WHEREAS, We consider the whole matter worthy of longer consecrated efforts toward ultimate solution; and

WHEREAS, Several of the protests include claims the correct-
ness or incorrectness of which could be proved only by referring to
minutes, reports, and correspondence, which are not available to
your Committee here at Synod; therefore be it

Resolved: —

1. That Synod elect at this session a standing committee of five
impartial men, who have as yet not dealt with the question, and
that this committee work toward an ultimate blessed settlement of
all points at issue;

2. That during the interim in which this committee now functions all further agitation of this matter be dropped.

The following were elected members of above committee: Prof.
W. Kruse, Fort Wayne, Ind.; Prof. E. Koehler, River Forest, Ill.;
Rev. W. Moll, Fort Wayne, Ind.; Prof. W. Moenkemoeller, St. Paul,
Minn.; Rev. L. Schmidtke, Chicago, Ill.

volt and still controlled by warring factions in the mid-1920s. On the other hand the tri-cities were the transportation hub of central China. As a treaty port with more conveniences, Hankow was favored by the missionaries living there. Without full approval, some Hankow men arranged for the purchase in 1925 of a low-lying seven-acre site at Jardine's Estate, in the floodplain two miles behind the French Concession. It was surrounded by frequently flooded rice paddies, a drainage canal, and adjacent to a small hamlet, the Three-Eye village.

With this swirling morass of issues, the conference appealed to St. Louis for a judgment on the Term Question, rather than trusting themselves to reach a conclusion with the help of local Chinese Christians or scholars. The Board of Foreign Missions and the St. Louis seminary faculty both supported Arndt's viewpoint, stating that terms needed proper instruction. Though not academically grounded in Chinese history, linguistics, or culture, their judgment was thoroughly researched, but was conciliatory at best. Coincidentally, a stained glass window in the new St. Louis campus represented the China mission with a dragon and the characters for Shang-ti.

The topic drained so much synodical energy that the issue was barred as a topic of official discussion at the triennial delegate convention, and relegated to a sub-committee for further study. From St. Louis, Fredrick Brand, director of LCMS missions, became a referee in the debate. Trying to soothe ruffled feathers, the director probably did more damage than good by sending opinionated notes to individual parties. He definitely supported the St. Louis seminary faculty decision. The Missionary Conference was in such disarray that it determined again to invite an outside mediator from Synod to the 1926 Kuling conference. That delegate was to be Brand himself, who could visit the China field economically as part of his triennial inspection schedule. He was not neutral. Such distrust existed that several missionaries would not take communion together at the conference. Brand pre-

sented the St. Louis seminary's opinion that the use of Shang-ti should not be prohibited, allowing the use of either term.

Synod's decree was unacceptable to the shen party, who still felt that they were misrepresenting the true God and confounding the Chinese. The topic of predestination became embroiled in the issue. Perhaps some native knowledge of God in Chinese culture could detract from the miracle of conversion. Since Gebhardt was scheduled for furlough, the Missionary Conference delegated him to represent the shen arguments at a hearing in St. Louis in October; Arndt would make the trip to defend Shang-ti.

## Chaos in the Life of China

When the Missionary Conference adjourned August 24, the families hiked down the mountain to a military impasse along the Yangtze, arriving in Hankow three hours before the withdrawal of northern government troops from Wuhan. Missionary focus quickly turned to family safety and survival amid the factions and forces creating New China. While the mission was immersed in its squabbling, civil government in China was being reduced to shambles.

Several popular social movements had emerged in the New China which were to culminate with tumultuous frenzy in 1926.

Social and political stability was tenuous since the 1911 downfall of the Ch'ing dynasty. Replacing two millennia of imperial rule with an ill-defined democratic government gave rise to the growth of contending philosophical and political movements within China, which had direct consequences on foreign interests and on the Lutheran mission.

One factor was the anti-classic movement, revolutionizing the style and form of written Chinese. The formal, classical style *wen-li* of the scholars was gradually simplified *easy wen-li* to a colloquial form that approximated conversational Chinese *bai-hua*. Though the literati disdained this process, it allowed the ordinary person access to newspapers, magazines, books, poetry, and intellectual

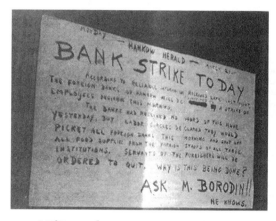

Military elements were omni-present in eastern China during the 1920s. Several leaders be-friended the Mission, in whose clinics many injuries were treated.

treatises. In turn, this allowed introduction of new ideas and exchange of opinions, as in the influential magazine *New Youth*, as well as in local notices and comments written on public bulletin boards.

The ability of the average Chinese to learn and read *bai-wah* was a society-changing development. Other language systems were also devised, including a national phonetic script, which duplicated the sounds of the spoken Mandarin dialect, using 39 non-Roman symbols. There were high hopes for the new system. A phonetic Bible was transliterated. Romanization of the spoken language by westerners generally followed the nineteenth-century Wade-Giles (traditional) system. The current *pin-yin* system used in China was introduced into the People's Republic in 1957.

An anti-military movement advocated a cessation of the on-going struggles of the forces vying for control of the new nation. There was no government with authority. The scramble for power involved the northern republican forces, a parliament in Peking, emerging Communist elements among the southern nationalists, provincial armies, local militias, rogue mercenary troops serving unaffiliated warlords, and gangs of disaffected soldiers called bandits (*min tuan*) or the people's army. Factions contended for control of hearts, minds, food, weaponry, and territory. Intermittent domestic militarism would plague China until the 1931 Japanese Occupation, again during the Pacific War until 1945, and culminating in the civil war and formation of the People's Republic of China (PRC) in 1949.

Anti-capitalism sentiments were a reaction to the expansion of the foreign concessions, an integral part of the colonial treaty port system. Large European residential and commercial buildings dominated cityscapes, especially in Shanghai, Hankow, Tientsin, and Nanking. The abuses of the industrial system with its tedious labor and de-humanizing landscapes of manufacturing and mining had become irritants to student leaders and intellectuals alike.

Not all popular movements were negative. Patriotic nationalism emerged as a new and popular force. Hopes for a strong independent nation of Han Chinese had tantalized Chinese society for several generations. Strong anti-foreign sentiments and movements grew from the long history of colonial aggression and territorial accumulation. Discriminatory and favorable taxation of foreigners, abusive customs control, and privileges of extraterritoriality antagonized the Chinese. Post-war assurances by the Allies to return self-determination disintegrated. Colonial systems failed to satisfy or dissuade anti-foreign energies. Especially targeted were Japanese and British interests, as the Chinese strove for a strong identity and a new nationalism.

Anti-imperialism reinforced the avoidance of western financial and industrial opportunism. Communism appeared in 1919, imported by Russians Mikael Borodin and G. N. Voitinsky and studied by Mao Tse-tung [Mao Zedong]. It was a strategic time to fuel agitation and unrest. Leninist, Trotskyite and Bolshevist elements contended for influence. In 1921 Chou En-lai [Zhou Enlai] established the Young Communist Party in Paris and imported it to China.

An anti-religious movement promoted a nationalistic loyalty to time-honored belief systems. Piecemeal acceptance of western culture brought about a challenge to the long-established religious practices of China. New philosophies threatened long established societal understandings. Religious traditions were rejected as mere superstition, and were not only wasteful of both human and financial resources, but also weakened the nationalistic fervor of the nation. Over and above these issues, to "eat the foreign religion" was to abandon clan loyalty and familial practices, including required and all-important ancestor worship.

Christianity was seen as a paramount threat. The 1850-64 Tai Ping Rebellion was the result of a Christian convert who believed himself to be the latter-day brother of Jesus.

Several missionaries sought refuge in Shanghai during the Disturbances, under the protection of British and American warships. Taking advantage of the situation they continued their language instruction in preparation for return, but only Gertrude Simon (in glasses) was to fill out her career in China.

The carnage and death caused by his followers soured Chinese authorities and the populace on this imported religion. The 1900 Boxer Rebellion further degraded Christianity, weakened the Ch'ing dynasty, and gave further momentum to nationalistic aspirations.

Missionaries were regarded as foreign agents, even invaders, bent on destroying Chinese tradition. Yet, in 1880 the government's Chinese Educational Commission had selected 100 promising young Chinese to study in America. Yung Wing, once a mission school student in Macau, and the first Chinese graduate of an American college, was instrumental in the commission. But it was too little and too late. Recalled by the Empress Dowager before most had graduated, these men later formed the intellectual core of China's eventual adaptation of western science, technology, and engineering. The western ideals adopted by some of these men were later blamed for weakening Chinese society.

## International Sentiments

With the signing of the Treaty of Versailles, the Chinese people expected to regain territories then occupied by Germany, primarily in Shantung [Shandong] province. However, because Japan had entered the war on the side of the victors, the German areas of influence in China were re-assigned to Japan on May 4, 1919, by the diplomats in Paris.

When this news reached China, the outcry was immediate. There were riots. Students assumed a major role in changing popular attitudes. Several social movements would grow from the unrest, including the Chinese Renaissance (also called the New Thought Movement, and the New Tide), and the May Fourth Movement. These developments charted China's twentieth-century history, its relations with world powers, and the status of foreigners and missionaries.

On May 4th, soon after terms of the treaty were published in China, rioting began.

Students initiated street protests with an energy and agenda very different from the unrest of peasant farmer and laboring classes. Student arrests totaled 32. Energized with newly realized powers and awareness, middle school and college students took advantage of lax government control. The vernacular press spread news and ideas with sensational large-type headlines and articles. Japanese goods were boycotted and anti-Japanese sentiments escalated. Chinese business interests, merchants, and railway and industrial workers allied with the students, bringing the government to the brink of collapse. The May 4th patriotic movement following the Great War drew into focus the importance of traditional values, customs, arts, artifacts, and archaeology of historic China that would continue despite the Cultural Revolution into the present.

## The Disturbances –
## Caught in the Middle – 1927

Political and military confusion increased steadily since the 1911 Manchu overthrow, Yuan Shi-kai's tumultuous presidency, the May 4th Movement, and President Sun Yat-sen's restoration to national leadership in 1917.

Sun's philosophic Three Principles laid groundwork for future Chinese governments. He modified Abraham Lincoln's "of the people, by the people, and for the people" into nationalism, democracy, and effective livelihood. With his leadership, the three southernmost provinces evolved into the Southern Forces. President Sun died suddenly in 1925, instantly transforming him into a popular hero honored by all. Chiang Kai-Shek became president.

Warlordism (there were 25 warlords around Tientsin alone) prevented a stable government. Sun's brother-in-law Chiang Kai-shek eventually assumed leadership of the party. To expand their power base, expeditions were launched against the Peking government. Moving north in mid-1926, red southern troops targeted Shanghai and Wuhan, attacking just after the Lutheran missionaries returned from their summer conference at Kuling. Hankow

Shihnan, the mission station most remote, supported a large orphanage and school. In the early days, it was housed within the ancient city walls at the Hu House, where young residents often had their lunch in the open courtyard of the traditional house. Beyond the city at Yang Wan, far more space was available for fresh air activity.

was captured by insiders propagandizing for the southerners, and organizing peasants, laborers, and some northern soldiers before the southerners ever fired a shot. Hankow became the capital. The Wuhan regime thus implanted itself. And so began the disturbances.

Radical and Communistic indoctrination in Hankow led to the rapid formation of unions and the appearance of anti-foreign, anti-imperialist, and anti-Christian posters, slogans, and cartoons. By December, direct agitation against churches appeared, first with professional agitators touting slogans like "running dogs of the imperialists," and worse, "sons of foreign devils." Several confrontations took place at various mission schools and chapels, some involving extortion, occasional vandalism, and unexpected chicanery on the part of local workers. Student Evangelist Mr. Lo, at the Hua Chin Kai chapel, adopted Communism himself, and then permitted meetings of the Kuomintang on mission property.

The 1926 Christmas celebrations were disturbed, but none were cancelled entirely. Max Zschiegner reported that several Hankow chapels had been the subject of anti-Christian propaganda. Christians at the Lo Chia Teng chapel outside the city were denounced as "dogs of the imperialists." Rowdies broke up chairs at the Hsi Tzu Kai in Hankow's Chinese quarter on December 23. Posters slandering Christianity were pasted on several chapels, ripped down by the Chinese Lutherans, and re-pasted quickly by agitators. Christmas Eve worship at the San Yuan Li was interrupted; services at Hua Chin Kai and Hsi Tzu Kai were held behind locked and boarded doors; a rabble of students dispersed families at the Lao Kuan Miao, which was completely looted on Christmas day. At Hua Chin Kai, 200 school children from four mission schools made it home safely when the police arrived and scattered trouble-makers who had scaled the iron bars of the church's windows. The commissioner of foreign affairs offered no help.

## School Registration

In February, relations between the mission and the education bureau of the new Wuhan regime were in crisis. Educational reforms on the national level had been officially implemented in November 1925. Among other regulations, foreign-financed schools were to make application for registration. Foreign schools needed to be designated as privately established. The president, vice-president, or principal of such institutions was to be Chinese. If a board of managers ran such a school, the board was to be 50 percent Chinese. Primary and middle schools were not to propagate religion in their program. The curriculum of such schools was to follow standards set by the ministry of education and was not to include religious courses among the required subjects. Religion was not compulsory; in fact, it was prohibited. The Lutherans were in a bind, but a few schools operated as long as possible, skirting closure on technicalities.

The Wuhan government now insisted on the registration of all schools. No school was to teach or promote religion in any form. Missionary Schmidt attempted a "Lutheran Young Men's Bible Class" after regular school classes. Schools had been the heart of the mission. What to do?

Primary schools were shuttered in March, and the Chinese teachers were advanced three month's salary. Banks had been closed, but a merchant friendly to the mission offered to exchange currency. Riedel conducted workshops with faculties for two weeks to improve their religious knowledge, teaching methods, and classroom control. Still, the teachers joined their middle school students in calling the missionaries imperialists.

The American consulate recommended evacuation of expatriates from inland China in March 1927. That same month, southern red forces seized nearby Nanking, looted much of the city, and killed several foreigners. This soon became known as the Nanking Incident. A treaty port, Hankow had been considered safe for Europeans, and so the upriver missionaries

New arrivals November 1926

Lao Kuan Miao public reading room.
Evangelist Tso in Glasses

The first two ordained pastors of the China Evangelical lutheran Church were Chen Huan Jen and Pi P'ei-ying, also known as "Pastor Bee." Here they are surrounded by their professors (left) Wallace McLaughlin, Adolph Koehler, Max Zschiegner, and Erhardt Riedel. While graduating in 1926, neither was approved and ordained until 1934. Pi had recruited Chen into the ministry, and both faithfully served until their deaths.

from Shihnan, Shasi, and Wanhsien took refuge there. Several upriver missionaries of other denominations had escaped only with the aid of British gunboats. Most foreigners called these times the evacuation.

On Sunday, March 27, policemen entered the San Yuan Li chapel during worship and arrested Evangelist Pi P'ei-ying and Mr. Li Chi-chang, a teacher at the middle school. Being northerners, they were accused of making anti-revolutionist statements against the occupying Bolshevists and jailed at the main police station beyond the concession area. Appeal to the American consulate was beyond extrality protections. Rather, it was suggested that the Americans pack up and leave town. A disgruntled ex-evangelist, Mr. Chow stirred the pot in retaliation for his earlier dismissal by Riedel. Mission image and credibility were besmirched in the local press as imperialistic. Blackmail was threatened daily.

The Wuhan government threatened to take over the Hsi Tzu Kai chapel. Labor unions had already occupied the Yin Wu Chow in Hanyang. The Christians gave up their larger chapels, and rented unmarked spaces but also met in the home of Evangelist Ma Ch'ing-hue. Missionaries arranged for seminary students-in-training to step in.

Pi and Li remained incarcerated. The unregistered schools were illegal. To open them would be defiant and risk forcible closure. The situation was explained to the boarding students. Several of these baptized boys at the middle school, were being subsidized by the mission, or were once orphans from Shihnan. The students held a meeting in the Bolshevist fashion; were agitated by a disgruntled former teacher; and switched loyalties to Communist elements and the Hankow Students Union. Demands were made for changes in the religious curriculum, for co-education with girls from Miss Gruen's girls' school, and for money to cover other schooling and travel.

Missionary Carl Schmidt was accused of "doing away" with a student, the result of a scuffle between assistant principal Mr. Wang and a student ringleader. Even after reconciling with the remorseful student and housing him overnight in their own compound in the French Concession, the boy ran away, perpetuating a murder hoax.

In the interim, more upriver missionaries were urged to evacuate to Hankow. Christian Nagel and family had to leave Kweifu, and China, because they were Australian (hence British). Ichang and Shasi were abandoned, with local evangelists left in charge.

Shihnan's situation was the most desperate and dramatic. Twenty-three days after the invasion of Hankow's British Concession, word reached the Shihnan missions by currier that they were to evacuate. Easier said than done! Bandits and brigands infested the shorter five-day route to Tai Chi. As it was winter, ice and snow made the way treacherous along the longer route to Patong. Along the route, only rudimentary mud huts and mat sheds were available for overnight shelter. Carriers doubled their rates under the circumstances.

Add to this the fact that there were six children included, all less than five years of age. Rev. and Mrs. Ziegler were both abed with dysentery, requiring over a week to regain minimal strength. Klein gathered supplies and supervised the packing of bedding, quilted clothing, foodstuffs, and the construction of enclosed sedans in which the children were to be carried. Nurse Oelschlaeger and Edna Klein looked after the six children. When the evacuees finally assembled in February they left under cover of darkness. It was a weary and relieved party that arrived seven days later at Patong on the Yangtze. Another day was spent awaiting a lone downriver steamer, which they hailed with an American flag and boarded from a sampan mid-stream. Upon reaching Ichang, it was another six-day wait for a steamer and four days on the Yangtze to Hankow.

The native Christians of Shihnan knew they were not abandoned because of Christianity, but because of the anti-foreignism so rampant during the *troubles*. Chinese Christians were viewed skeptically by other Chinese

The orphanage in Shihnan was established at the Hu House, near the eastern gate of the city. School was conducted and instruction in sewing and other domestic arts was given. Expansion of the orphanage to Yang wan provided more space in the country setting

as slaves of the foreigners. Christians would fare better, if invaded, were they not associated with foreigners. The missionaries and the local Christians both realized it was best to leave, hopefully only temporarily.

In Hankow, now firmly in the hands of Bolsheviks, it was also realized that the local Christians would pay a painful price for their association with suspect Americans. About 200 mission personnel from many missions were holed-up at the *Hsin-I-Wei* Lutheran Home Agency Building. Jardine, the British shipping firm, arranged for the steamship Suiwo to transport women and children downriver. Most of the men remaining sailed on March 25 aboard the Loongwo. The last missionaries reluctantly boarded a skow, the *Gungwe*, one day before a riot in the Japanese concession. They anchored for several days off the Hankow bund for safety before transfer to the *Kungwo*. On April 6, they set sail for Shanghai.

Edward Arndt and his daughter Agnes refused to leave Hankow. Arndt had not been involved in school issues while cloistered at Milan Terrace doing literary work. He resolved to tend the remaining mission properties, and felt it his duty to relentlessly intercede for the release of Rev. Pi and Mr. Li. Agnes would not abandon her father, instead cooking and cleaning for him, and taking daily bread to the imprisoned Pi and Li.

## Tested and Not Found Wanting

So it was that crowded Shanghai became a confused place of refuge and regrouping for Europeans and Chinese. Olive, Gertrude, Frieda and Marie were urged to retreat there in early 1927 after the forced abandonment of Shihnan. The Oelschlaegers took care of the three Ziegler children during their parents' lengthy hospitalization in Shanghai. In September the sisters were granted early furlough.

## The Exodus

Five families requested and were granted early furloughs and sailed for the U.S. in late March. Some wives took their children to America while the husbands remained in China. With conditions uncertain, three other men were released on emergency leave and accepted LCMS pastorates in U.S. congregations. Twelve missionaries stayed in the relative safety of the French and international Shanghai concessions for the duration, five of whom had only arrived the previous fall and were still in language study. There was no general conference at Kuling in 1927. These were not the best of times.

The prospects for Protestant missions were worse than ever. There was little hope of ever resuming productive work under an orderly government. Never again would Chinese Christians be under a "yoke of bondage" to a foreign church; conversely they would not have full theological and financial benefits from overseas.

Despair, famine, and chaos dominated large areas of China for a year. Internal dissension weakened the Kuomintang during the summer of 1927. Chiang Kai-shek suddenly ousted his Communist allies, consolidated his financial support in Shanghai, and recaptured Hankow from the Bolshevik elements of the Wuhan regime. Martial law was proclaimed on July 18; about 4000 people were put to death; and westerners were able to return to Hankow by the end of November, after an eight-month absence. Routed forces scattered, to roam as bandits. Communist or red elements would re-assemble in many locations, especially in Kiangsi, south of Kuling.

The military and political strife seemed to have passed. A government was established at Nanking under Chiang Kai-shek. Cautious at first, then enthusiastic, the Lutherans were eager to plunge in again, gradually returning to all of their former locations.

## Picking up the Pieces

Among the group of missionaries who returned to the U.S. in March 1927 were several of the Term Controversy men who had firmly stood by their convictions to only use shen. The theological battle and the secular domestic crisis resulted in the elimination of

Activities continued at the Shihnan Orphange during
the Troubles of 1927-1928.

Winter scenes at Kuling

most of these men from the China field.

Three of the dissidents declined to further serve in China against their convictions. The Board of Foreign Missions did not permit two other men to continue in the China field. Arnold Cloeter and Martin Simon were recalled by the board in the fall of 1928 over their dispute with the optional usage of Shang-ti. Both had spent eleven months learning the language in Hankow and Shanghai during the "troubles," preparing to serve upriver. Once back in the U.S., Cloeter went on to serve several pastorates in Minnesota.

Simon took a congregational call in Oregon, and later distinguished himself in publishing *The Children's Hour* and *My Chum* youth magazines. He wrote the popular family devotional book *Little Visits with God*. These were all distributed and used Synod-wide. His elder son, Paul, became a distinguished long-term U.S. senator from Illinois. Son Arthur founded Bread for the World, the Christian hunger relief organization, in 1974. His sister Gertrude remained a missionary in China and Hong Kong until her death in 1966. Her nephew is a LCMS pastor.

The Term Controversy remained a topic of synodical conversations, conventions, and committees until at least 1947, with no satisfactory resolution. Disagreement over the Chinese name for God would haunt the mission and the Synod for decades, cause individual grief, institutional anxiety, even embitterment and stalemate for workers in China. It remained important only to the individuals and families ensnared by their convictions. Disappointment, resentment, and wasted potentials were the unintended but inevitable results of an unresolvable issue. The debate was never satisfactorily settled and both names are accepted. Time has defused the passions.

Ironically, while of great importance to the contestants, the issue has not been significant to the Chinese church. The question has been adiaphora, a non-essential issue to Chinese Christians, then and now.

A church divided against itself cannot be in mission.

**Significant Sources**

| Arndt, Edward L, | *Is Shang-ti Wrong?* |
| Chow, Tse-Tsung, | *The May 4th Movement* |
| Clark, Elmer, | *What's the Matter in China?* |
| Fairbank, John K, | *The Great Chinese Revolution* |
| Gebhardt, Marie, | *The May 4th Movement* |
| Lillegard, George, | *A History of the Term Controversy in Our China Mission* |
| Moseley, George, | *China Since 1911* |

**Chapter Seven**
**Arrivals**                                                    **Origin          School**

1928 - Oct 29    Arr via *SS President Adams* from San Francisco:
   McLaughlin          Wallace ("Uncle Mac")                    Philadelphia, PA    CSL
   Zimmermann          Elmer ("ECZ") & Anna (nee Backs)         Edwardsville, IL    CSF

1929 - Nov 16    Arr via *Empress of Russia* from Vancouver, BC:
   Mueller             Reinhold ("Mike") & Dorothy (nee Fischer)    Altenberg, MO    CSL
   Seltz               Eugene ("Bull")                         Truman, MN          CSL

1930 - Oct 6     Arr via *SS Shinyo Maru* from San Francisco:
   Buuck               Lorenz & Ella (nee Rhodenbeck)          Van Wert Co, OH     CSF
   Werling             Wilbert & Clara (nee Ripke)             New Haven, IN       CSL

1931 - Sept 19   Arr via *SS Madison* from Seattle:
   Diers               Alvin & Lilly (nee Hollenberg)          LaGrange, TX        CSL
   Koehler             Adolph ("Adie") & Irmgard (nee Elsel)   Nicollet, MN        CSL
   Meyer               Herbert & Cornelia (nee Rau)            St. Louis, MO       CSL
   Muehl               Richard & Ella (nee Schnitker)          Cleveland, OH       CSF
   Nero                Norville & Ruth (nee Kuehnert)          Milwaukee, WI       CTC-RF
   Rhodenbeck          Clara                                   Allen Co, IN        LH-FW

1932 - Oct 4     Arr visa *SS President Taft* from San Francisco:
   Wenger              Gilbert ("Doc")                         Fair Haven, MN      CSL

1934 - Oct 19    Arr via *SS President Lincoln* from San Francisco:
   Breihan             Theobald                                St. Joseph, MI      CTC-RF

1936 - April 1   Arr via *SS President Grant* from Seattle:
   Frillmann           Paul                                    Melrose Park, IL    CSL

**Departures**
1930  Fischer    John & Martha + John, William, Marian        (called to US parish)
1932  Theiss     Henry O ("Deke") & Frieda + David            (health; resigned)
1936  Werling    Wilbert & Clara + Miriam, Wilbert W., David   (health)
1937  Breihan    Theobald & Caroline                          (health)

**Marriages**
1930  Thode      Elmer       to (Deaconess teacher) Frieda Oelschlaeger
1931  Gebhardt   Arnold      to (Deaconess nurse) Marie Oelschlaeger
1933  Seltz      Eugene      to (Deaconess nurse) Clara Rhodenbeck
1936  Breihan    Theobald    to Caroline Sievers (arrived from USA)
1937  Meyer      Herb        to Bernice Hollrah (while on furlough in USA)

**Deaths**
1929  Arndt      Edward              age 64 - (heart)
1931  Theiss     Richard "Dickie"    age 3 - (polio)
1932  Meyer      Cornelia            age 30 - (diptheria / heart)
1934  Nero       Norville            age 26 - (surgery complications)
1936  Buuck      Enno                age 2 - (dysentery)

Chapter Seven

# The Best of Times – 1928–1937

All of the missionaries who had remained in China were back in Hankow by November 1927. No mission properties were damaged by the disturbances. Seven small congregations were holding worship. Under relaxed restrictions from the central government, evangelists organized nine Christian day-schools, in expectation of subsidy by the mission. Arndt had spent the eight months living at home in the French Concession, which was surrounded with barbed wire.

Against the advice of British and American authorities, perhaps all the missionaries could have remained in Hankow. Half of the forty-seven mission personnel had left China.

## Picking up the Pieces

In Hankow, Olive and Gertrude resumed their work with women. Within a year the enrollment at the girls' school stood at nine. Most Chinese still regarded a daughter as a liability, whereas a son was an asset. Very few parents defied traditional regard for their daughters as chattel, arranging marriage for a dowry, and a life of ignorance as a son-producing daughter-in-law. A life of service as a Bible woman or doing zenana work with house-bound women had much more appeal than life as a virtual slave.

The newer missionaries continued language instruction. Arndt, Fischer, Theiss, Thode, and Zschiegner resumed supervision of chapels and schools. Several congregations were now identified by a biblical concept name, rather than the street location:

San Hsin Kai  became Faith
Wha Ching Kai became Faith
San Yuan Li became Zion
Hsi Tai Kai became Renewed Light
Gnen Huei T'ang  became Grace

Committed to the congregations and the new Lutherans upriver, Gebhardt and Cloeter steamed west in June to evaluate the status of stations at Wanhsien, Kweifu, Ichang, and Shasi. They were unable to reach their two locations in Szechwan, Wanhsien Kw and Kweifu. Closed to foreigners and occupied by holy soldiers or joss coolies—troops motivated by a supposed spiritual benefit—western steamers would not anchor at Kweifu for fear of being commandeered. The rented mission house was rumored to have been severely looted and the gate-keeper robbed. No more missionaries were stationed in Kweifu, renamed Fengkieh {Fengjie}, but missionary concern, connection, and conversions continued for years. See chapter 9.

At Shasi, the two missionaries found that most native evangelists and members had remained loyal during the civil strife. Believers had taken care of properties for the most part, managed finances, and had even prepared several candidates for baptism. The mission house, between the town and the river, had sustained minimal damage since the Chinese Chief of Customs there had occupied

Hankow was a city of timelessness, with a native quarter of narrow streets, food vendors, and pedestrian traffic. In contrast stood large modern western buildings. One building well known to missionaries was the Lutheran Home Agency, containing a hostel, library, and offices of the Lutheran Church in China (LCC). Mish kids liked to socialize here. The building was designed by Herr Sachse, the same German architect who would design the Concordia Seminary in 1931.

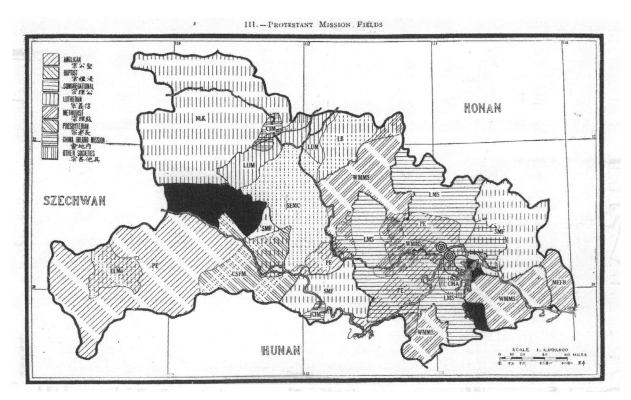

the building. In the rented chapel, benches and the pulpit had been burned. The school had been closed all year, an isolated band of Christians, mostly women, continued meeting on Sundays, and holding a Bible class on Monday afternoons. Thode was able to move back in September 1928, but the Board did not allow the return of Theiss (initially in the U.S. on a medical furlough), to continue in China because of his stance on the Term Question. He went on to serve congregations in northern California, and also was an army chaplain during World War II.

Ichang was not yet peaceful enough for a resident missionary. A recently trained convert there, Ts'ai Paulo, had used mimeographed copies of Riedel's sermons to preach and prepare eighteen women for baptism. A Bible woman also resided in the former rented chapel, although it was concurrently occupied by troops.

The Joyous Sound Lutheran Society was intact, at least in Hankow, Shasi, and Ichang!

Energizing the spirits of American supporters, Board of Foreign Missions Director Fredrick Brand encouraged U.S. congregations to hold their traditional fall mission festivals. He wrote a Lutheran Witness article in February, 1928, identifying four rhetorically positive outcomes from the troubles for Christianity in China:

1. In his judgment, the social gospel had proven inadequate to hold the faith of Chinese Christians not firmly rooted in the vicarious atonement of Christ. He felt the virus of modernism and its doctrinal imbecilities had not survived the crucible of social disintegration. Christianity aimed at fixing social ills and building reliance on the good life were inadequate applications of the true gospel message of the sin-atoning sacrifice of the Son of God.

2. Most native Lutherans had remained loyal and faithful. They had protected missionaries and their properties against the godless troops, risen to stand against persecution for their faith, and had even continued evangelization. Many new Christians were awaiting baptism at the end of civil war.

3. The winds of persecution had sifted out the chaff of rice Christians—those Chinese of the church more interested in material benefits than the promise of salvation. Those remaining were true believers and faithful witnesses for Christ, which were bound to grow. Thus grew a core of dedicated workers for the kingdom.

4. Increased evangelism opportunities were now manifest. The Chinese perhaps now could see the futility of heathen civilization (people who do not acknowledge the God of the Bible). Ancestor worship, praise of political heroes, and a fusion of religions had no efficacy. The Chinese would be ready to hear and accept of Christ crucified. The fields were ripe and harvest waiting.

At 1928 Easter services, missionaries preached, baptized, and gave communion at all seven chapels in Hankow. Schools were still closed, but the mission was reviving.

The Oelschlaeger sisters returned from America in late October 1928, on board the USS President Adams accompanied by recruits Elmer and Anna Zimmermann plus Wallace McLaughlin. The Kleins returned a month later.

None of the other missionaries who had been permitted to travel to the United States in 1927 came back to China in 1928.

New missionaries were needed in the China field. Other denominations were also seizing the opportunity. The China Inland Mission set and accomplished the goal of sending 200 new missionaries by 1931. The LCMS sent twelve new people between 1928 and 1931, including Nurse Gertrude Simon and Norville Nero, a teacher for the one-room school for the missionaries' children. He taught in German and English.

Director Brand summarized his ide-

Frederick Brand's criteria for a successful missionary candidate.

1. Must be a convinced Lutheran;
2. Equipped to meet objections and doubts of non-Christians;
3. Should be acquainted with history, customs, and beliefs of the heathen;
4. Lead a consecrated and Christlike life;
5. Free from class pride to live and labor among the lowly and despised;
6. Not be strongly opinionated and able to do cooperative team-work;
7. Gladly forego western conveniences to put up with primitive lifestyle;
8. Be an able teacher of the Word in the vernacular, and supervise others;
9. Be a Christian statesman and polished Christian gentleman;
10. Be exemplary in physical fitness, language study, and executive skill.

A large house was rented to provide classrooms and faculty residences for the second incarnation of Concordia Seminary. Theiss and Zschiegner lived on the premesis. The student body in 1930 consisted of boys and men in preparatory and seminary programs. Missionaries from left are Erhardt Riedel, Henry O. Theiss, Max Zschiegner, and Wallace Macloughlin.

al missionary in 1930 as a person with the unique qualifications. See page 108

For the fall term of 1928, the Hankow chapels opened six primary schools and one in Hanyang. Registration of the schools was still questionable under the government regulation on religious instruction. Hoping that the local Hankow authority might be otherwise distracted, Missionary Fischer did not register the Christian day-schools. Approximately 500 students were enrolled.

## Edward Arndt (1864-1929)

Rev. Edward Arndt passed away unexpectedly in his sleep at his Milan Terrace home on April 17, 1929 at age 64. He probably died of a heart attack. None of his family was in Hankow at the time of this death. Mrs. Arndt was in the U.S. for major surgery, accompanied by family members. Sisters Frieda and Marie Oelschlaeger had been keeping house and cooking for Arndt. Yet in his ever-frugal ways, he saved money by eating foods from the Hankow street vendors and would not heat his room, confining himself there to do literary work (translation).

The funeral rites were conducted on a rainy April 21, at the courtyard in front of the four residences on Milan Terrace. Many school children and adult Christians paid respects. Burial was in the International Cemetery, near the German chapel which the missionaries used for their worship. Hymns were sung in English, German, Latin, and Chinese. Evangelists Pi, Chen, Wei, and Feng participated. Theiss, Klein, and Fischer spoke at the graveside. His daughter Agnes later had a large stone monument erected in his memory. Four other mission personnel were destined to soon lie in the same cemetery. That burial ground today is reportedly beneath modern buildings.

Accolades were written by many and various churchmen on both sides of the Pacific. They recounted his single-minded dedication, his command of three modern languages and knowledge of biblical linguistics, the poetic quality of his Chinese translations, and his commitment to God and the Chinese people. Former critics were silenced in the posthumous acknowledgement of his multiple contributions—publishing two books of his own sermons; editing and printing the Missionsbriefe; founding the Geschellshaft (Ev. Luth. Mission Society for China); initiating the work, recruiting, converting; organizing Chinese congregations; coordinating the Missouri Synod affiliation; establishing day-schools, middle schools, and the seminary; translating the Small Catechism, sermons by C. F. W. Walther, and other theological works and hymns; authoring many Chinese hymns; as well as penning countless articles for the 𝕸𝖎𝖘𝖘𝖎𝖔𝖓𝖘𝖙𝖆𝖚𝖇𝖊, 𝕯𝖊𝖗 𝕷𝖚𝖙𝖍𝖊𝖗𝖆-𝖓𝖊𝖗, 𝕯𝖎𝖊 𝕬𝖇𝖊𝖓𝖉𝖘𝖈𝖍𝖚𝖑𝖊, 𝖙𝖍𝖊 𝕳𝖔𝖒𝖎𝖑𝖊𝖙𝖎𝖐 𝕸𝖆𝖌𝖆𝖟𝖎𝖓, and a lengthy and scholarly defense of the use of Shang-ti.

Without warning, Arndt was gone. Obstinate and stubborn as he had been, the mission had prematurely lost its founder, father figure, publicist, scholar, and prime mover.

## Concordia Seminary's Second Location

Carrying on Arndt's determination to train a local clergy, the mission re-opened the seminary on September 16, 1929. A suitable house was rented at 14 Yun Chin Road near the Japanese concession close to the Hankow Race Club. The house was converted into two classrooms, a library, a dining room, a kitchen/cook's room, a faculty office, and ten 7ft. by 7ft. cubicles for housing students. Henry (Deke) and Frieda Theiss rented the neighboring residence.

Zschiegner, Fischer, McLaughlin and Theiss taught the standard synodical college curriculum, courses being offered on a three-year cycle. This missionary Henry W. Theiss was a cousin of earlier missionary Henry O. Theiss.

Nine students were accepted as theological students, seven younger men were

An outdoor celebration of the 400th anniversary of the Augsburg confession drew students from all Hankow Lutheran schools and congregations on May 25, 1930. Special programs were printed with an engraving of Luther's portrait.

Title Page of Hankow Quadricentennial Program.

Dr. Martin Luther.

pre-seminary, and another twelve boys attended the middle school or preparatory department for a total of 28. Twenty of those lived at the seminary, under the eye of Max Zschiegner. Both graduates of the 1926 seminary class participated in the opening service, joining in the singing of A Mighty Fortress in Chinese accompanied on a new reed melodion, played by one of the mission women.

The LCMS primary schools in Hankow continued operating for another year until pressured to close by the local Hankow soviet (tang-pu) acting under directives from the Nanking government. Across Hankow were 639 pupils in 19 Lutheran day-schools. Each local congregation was left to sort out its own situation. A very clear dictum from the Ministry of Eduction in April 1930 effectively quashed the school program, although Meyer had dealings with the Hankow government over schools until the last closing in 1934.

## Luther's Small Catechism

In late December 1929, all of the chapels and schools in Hankow held a double jubilee. In tandem with the 400th anniversary of Luther's Small Catechism, the mission published its first complete LCMS edition in Chinese, the *Lu teh Hsiao Wen Ta* (Luther's Ask-Answer Book). Since 1913, the mission had been using the catechism of the Hsien I Wei, all-the-while working on a direct Chinese translation of Luther's book from the original German. Arndt, Riedel, and others had mimeographed their partial vernacular translations to establish the confessional basis of the mission, calling it the Layman's Bible.

On May 25, 1930, the 400th anniversary of the Augsburg Confession (the "Magna Carta of the Reformation") was celebrated in festive manner with an outdoor ceremony with 300 schoolchildren and 100 adults present. Chinese translations of The Augustana, courtesy of Erik Sovik of the United Lutheran Mission, were given to all present. Boisterous glad-hearted singing of many hymns augmented sermons from Evangelist Pi and

Missionary Fischer. A choir of primary school teachers and the girls' school sang A Mighty Fortress and a second German hymn, translated into Chinese.

## Upriver Developments at Shasi and Ichang

Upriver stations revived in 1928 when Thode returned alone to Shasi. Only four Christians, all men, had remained. The chapel had become a barracks and the furniture burned for fuel. From there, he also served Ichang, which was yet too disturbed for foreign residency. E. C. Zimmermann and his wife, Anna, took up residence in Shasi in November, literally off-the-boat. The brick mission house and compound had been built in 1926 on a five-foot raised dirt foundation. That extra height had preserved the house during a recent flood. They worked with Thode and took intense language instruction for six months. The new missionary preached his first Chinese sermon the following June 1929.

Thode re-occupied Ichang in September 1929, leaving Hsu Yo-ch'in, a lay assistant, to help Zimmermann. Gertrude Simon joined the work at Shasi in 1929, to help with a new mission school, located about a 15-minute walk from the mission house. Enrollment in the primary school numbered about 50. An experienced teacher and nurse, Simon had come from St. Louis despite the troubles, doing her language work in Shanghai while awaiting upriver peace. There, she sat out the uncertain times with her brother Martin and his bride, who had been evacuated from Wanhsien. Martin was soon recalled, but Gertrude would remain in China for a 40-year career.

Simon opened a makeshift dispensary next to the mission school in the city, recording 1002 individual treatments in a four-month period. She tutored a local man, Tzen Tze-fu, in basic procedures to assist her. Townspeople contributed about 200 cash per visit (about one U.S. penny) and were told of Jesus along with their treatment. Sores and boils, the itch, run-

The mission at Shasi consisted of a large walled compound, enclosing the missionary home within sight of the Yangtze. In the city were three chapels. The masonry  Zion church would be re-built 3 times. Several schools served over 100 students who gathered for a one-time photo by the mission house.

ning ears, infections and maternity cases were most common. On Palm Sunday, 15 baptisms were celebrated. Easter worship included communion and sermons in English and Chinese.

Not all was peaceful. In September 1930 a Communist regiment bombarded the city, and the Zimmermanns and Simon took refuge on a Japanese ship on the river. Zion chapel was totally destroyed, but rebuilt within a year with local funds.

Simon was assigned in 1931 to Shihnan to run the orphanage, when Alvin and Lily Diers arrived and began their work in the Shasi mission.

Under Zimmermann's relaxed yet organized leadership and comfortable adjustment to Chinese ways, Shasi became a successful mission hub with three local congregations—Eternal Life, Zion, and Trinity. The latter two eventually combined. Mrs. Zimmermann helped with tutoring of women catechumens, taught singing in the Shasi schools, and raised three daughters.

Sixty miles downriver was Owchihkow, where the China Inland Mission (CIM) had discontinued its work. In agreement with the CIM and local Christians, Zimmermann and Diers basically picked up the CIM locations and began Fu Yin Dao Lo Deh Huei work there. In this unique situation, the LCMS missionaries experienced growth at three other former CIM stations even renting several former CIM chapels in Shihshou, Huan Ti, and Chao Chia Chang.

Three locations in the south Shasi field became self-sustaining, having their own pastors. Owchihkow and Shihsow eventually called and shared Pastor Tai Ch'iu-tao in 1937. Kuantang and Mitt'ossu, ten miles from Shasi on the Yangtze, also grew to the point of supporting their own pastor, Wei I-yun, called in 1936. Four new stations were opened in other villages, and fourteen country preaching locations grew in the following six years. The momentum of an indigenous church showed great promise. When the seminary in Hankow temporarily closed, ten students spent the 1937-38 school year doing country-work near Shasi under the supervision of E. C. Zimmermann. Reduced financial support was being planned at the time of the 1937 Japanese Occupation.

At Ichang, Thode and his Chinese laborers cleaned and restored the heavily damaged mission house in 1929. He reopened the chapel, and was soon joined by his wife, Teacher Frieda Oelschlaeger, and new missionary, Eugene Seltz. Evangelist Wei I-yun aided in opening a school, teaching about 24 students. Frieda taught singing and played the organ. Despite several skirmishes among bandits and nationalists, all scheduled worship and Bible study meetings were held for the 50 regular members. New arrival Richard Muehl assisted Thode after 1931, when Seltz left to re-open the upriver Wanhsien station.

Kweifu, in Szechwan, sustained major damage and remained inaccessible to foreigners. Elderly Mr. P'an, who had been baptized by Nagel in 1925, kept the small band of isolated Christians worshipping and maintained the reading room on a busy street. He would engage and witness to any inquirers at the former mission house, and maintained sporadic contact with missionaries Seltz and Thode at Ichang.

Shihnan, far off the beaten track, had not fared as well during the civil fracas, with communications interrupted for months. It had been impossible for missionaries to return to the Ching valley due to continued bandit activity and destruction of villages along the trails. The two chapels at Shihnan were occupied by troops until the summer of 1928. Gebhardt returned from furlough in August to find damaged facilities. Looting by bandits and scofflaws had caused damage costing $2000, but he was encouraged to see how the local Christians under Evangelist Shen had continued the chapel, school, orphanage, and dispensary. Gebhardt carried on alone, running all four programs with a Chinese staff.

Nurse Marie Oelschlaeger returned from furlough in 1929 to re-open the dispensary and orphanage that was home to 21 chil-

Work with blind orphans grew over time. Wu Bao-lo (Paul) learned to read Chinese braille and became a popular teacher with the other blind boys in Shihnan. Boys raised farm animals and learned to weave straw sandals on special benches.

Heavy flooding in 1931 extended for nearly 300 miles along the Han and Yangtze Rivers. Tidal waves breeched the Hankow dikes. Water did not receede for six months; more floods occurred in 1933 and 1935.

dren. Many wounded soldiers were brought to the clinic. Shihnan continued to be isolated by political unrest and banditry well into 1930, when in May the city's protectors repelled bandits occupying the mission compound at the Hu House. Even so, Gebhardt distributed tracts and copies of the Chinese Lutheran Witness and Gospel portions to wounded civilians and soldiers being cared for by Oelschlaeger. Intense fighting forced their temporary evacuation to the hill at Yang Wan from June 2-13.

On Christmas 1930, nine boys and eleven girls were baptized. Schools operated at two outstations, east at Chi Le-ping and south at Chin Lung-pa.

New missionaries Mike and Dorothy Mueller arrived that same year to help in the orphanage and the 158-student school, and also started work at the local prison. Mueller also took on work with blind and deaf orphans. He found most of these boys excellent at both memorization, and at music. Wu Bau-lo (Paul) was an exceptionally successful student, becoming a teacher and evangelist in adulthood. In June 1931, Gebhardt and Marie Oelschlaeger married in Hankow, prior to the tenth annual Kuling conference. They would return to Shihnan (re-named Enshih by the new government), to serve until 1937.

### The Yangtze Floods – 1931

As the Yangtze rumbles through the 120 miles of its gorge, melt water from the Himalayan Mountains can raise river levels by dozens of feet within hours. The Han River, the longest of the Yangtze tributaries, drains much of Shensi and Hupeh to the northwest. The two river systems join at Hankow, draining an area larger than Western Europe. Seasonal flooding of the Yangtze stresses—and sometimes breeches—the ancient dikes that protect fields, villages, and cities.

When the Han dikes failed on July 7 1931, floodwaters submerged the Han and Yangtze basins, and within three days created an inland sea the size of Illinois and Indiana combined. Torrential rains from a slow-moving typhoon were to blame. At the junction of the Han and Yangtze Rivers, Wuhan suffered inundations over 25 feet, three feet higher than any flood since 1870, and six feet over the stone bund. Towns and villages disappeared. An estimated two million people died and 40 million were homeless. At one Hankow pit, 16,000 matting-wrapped bodies were layered and stacked 30 feet high in two mass graves (men separated from women), hastily covered over with cement.

Ripening fields of cotton, peanuts, and rice washed away. Livestock down Wind-generated waves eroded city walls and building. Waters laden with industrial, agricultural, and human detritus threatened famine and disease. In one macabre scene hundreds of traditional wooden coffins, unearthed by floodwaters, bobbed downstream with their contents exposed. Only the tops of a few hills, ridges of the 13-foot dikes topped with railway tracks, and buildings over two stories tall were above water.

Missionary families had scarcely arrived at Kuling for their conference, when reports of the widespread damage and loss of life reached them. The men, seeking to discern the condition of their congregations and properties, returned to Hankow. Upon reaching Kiukang, they found the Yangtze in flood 30 miles beyond its banks, and few steamers to take them the 140 miles back to Hankow.

None of the Chinese Christians had perished, but many had sought shelter in the upper floors of school-chapels. Four brick faculty residences under construction on the new seminary grounds were inundated to the eaves; the other two new houses had collapsed from waves generated on the immense lake. Approaching the mission houses by sampan, the men and helpers alighted on the roofs to move salvaged materials to the attics and tiled rooftops. Any items on the lower levels were a total loss. The rented seminary and houses at Milan Terrace were also flooded.

Missionary Klein assumed a community leadership role in humanitarian operations, coordinating with the Provincial Relief Com-

Floating on water up to 25 ft deep in some areas, rescue work meant supplying food and medicine. Cholera inoculations were provided, as were first aid from a "clinic" boat. Mass graves were quickly dug, filled, and covered with lime and dirt. Missionary Klein coordinated relief efforts across the city.

mission. The local YMCA, the United Council of Hankow Churches, two Christian hospitals and Rotary Clubs throughout China gave money and services. Refugees were exposed, starving, and drinking untreated river water, inviting dysentery. Masses huddled atop any ridge or hillock, some suffering from extreme exposure. There were congregants who were stranded in the upper floors of several chapels. An estimated 100,000 Han River refugees from Hanchuan County encamped on a gentle plateau in Hanyang called Black Hill (*hei san*). About 700,000 refugees were scattered across the Wuhan area.

At Black Hill, Dr. Schneider, the mission's medical advisor, assembled a large thatched shed to be used as an emergency hospital. Klein distributed anti-cholera and anti-typhoid medicines. Four hundred sacks of flour were provided. For ten days, Klein and 30 mission helpers using a punch card system, distributed one large rice bun each to about 10,000 children, many separated from their families. Each night, the volunteer Christians scoured the city's bakeries—those that had moved their operations upstairs above the water. Buying and gathering buns in gunny sacks, the survival rations were delivered to Black Hill on a government launch.

Synod forwarded $3000 from the mission and relief boards. The Walther League appealed for and raised another $16,000. In August, the U.S. government, Red Cross, and other world relief agencies began distributing sparse allotments of uncooked rice to refugees. This was the situation until the floodwaters receded six months later.

Determined to help the children, Klein had five large thatched school buildings fabricated, each of which could hold 350 primary students and two teachers. Religion (Bible history and catechism), reading, writing, and arithmetic were taught. Loud singing of newly-learned hymns filled the camp. At Christmas, snow lay on the ground as carols were sung by several thousand refugees and visiting Chinese Lutherans from the various Hankow chapels.

Flood waters had drained sufficiently by February 1932 so that the government be-

gan dispersing the camp on the hillock. There was anxiety over homeless hoards turning red as Communist troops were marshaled within 50 miles of Hankow. Before the camp was abandoned entirely, Klein and Werling baptized 400 children and adults at a special service on the last day. Werling reported that he had to change the baptismal water numerous times as the water clouded from the unwashed heads.

For five months, the missionary wives and children had remained high and dry at Kuling, which had become a refuge for many other European expats. The seminary and its sixteen students were moved to Kuling for a semester. Young missionary children were home-schooled, while the oldest attended the British Redcroft School.

The Hankow missionaries returned and for nearly a year, rented housing above a bank in the upper floors of the Ting Kuang building. Before leaving for Kuling, the mission staff had stored or moved their libraries and other belongings into the nearly finished houses. Most of their household goods and clothing were lost in the flood.

Many sampan loads of wet furniture (including a piano) and soggy clothes were hauled from the quarters at Milan Terrace to the upper levels of the remaining four houses. Clothing and bedding were laid out on the roofs to dry. Men salvaged submerged items in the murky water amid schools of passing fish and the occasional snake.

Eight months had been focused on recovery from the flood. Six Hankow chapels and the two in Hanyang were re-established. Most reopened their schools, hoping to avoid the required government registration. Teaching religion was still prohibited.

## Concordia Seminary Number Three

Eight acres of marshy land had been purchased in 1925, anticipating a permanent seminary compound. Many missionaries at the time preferred that the seminary be located at a station more central and in a smaller

Construction resumed at the Seminary building site 6 months after the flood. Scaffolding was topped with small branches to simulate a forest. Walls of brick were 18" thick, hollow to promote dryness. Finished classrooms and the chapel resembled any Synodical building in North America.

city-Shihnan or Ichang. They were wary of the site, being about two miles out in the country off Peking Stone Road in Jardines Estates, and lying about 15 feet lower than the dikes of the Yangtze. It was at this site that the faculty houses were submerged in the 1931 flood.

As the land drained and dried over five months, restoration work began on the houses. A friend of the mission in the States pledged in 1930 to pay for the construction of a seminary building, and construction of a four-level western-style masonry structure began in March, 1932. This was to be the first phase of a complex designed to eventually serve 150 students.

Local German architect Sachse designed the symmetrical building with a raised central pedimented entrance, supported on Ionic columns. Distinguished from many local European buildings which combined Chinese and western styles, the exterior resembled the semi-Teutonic style of many stateside LCMS college campuses. The noble crisp exterior held ten large concrete Chinese characters which read By the Law is the knowledge of sin; justification is of the Gospel. A large Latin cross topped the main entrance. To some, the building represented the stability of Lutheran doctrine.

Walls were 15 to 20 inches thick, with an inner airspace, not for insulation as much as for venting in the humid climate to reduce condensation and mold. Chinese carpenters and masons reproduced the German's drawings. The hipped tile roof, pierced with shed dormers, was to be the dormitory for unmarried men. In the basement were a dining hall, kitchen, and industrial room for a print shop and press. On the main floor were two large corner classrooms, an assembly/chapel to seat 200, and offices. The second story held a library, four smaller classrooms and study spaces.

Luther's seal was fabricated into a stained glass window at the Jesuit school in Shanghai for $12. It was placed prominently above the paired main door entrance, and was to survive Japanese and PRC occupations. The window disappeared after 1982, but the solidly built seminary still stands, used as a kindergarten. Prophetically, one local Chinese official remarked. "You have built a fine building, but it will be used by others."

Opened for students and faculty on September 19, the building was formally dedicated in October 1932. The flooded faculty houses had been dried out and occupied at the same time, although water damage would cause problems for years. A duplex was built to replace the two residences destroyed by the flood.

The Hankow group functioned like a large family, living closely first at Milan Terrace, then in the bank building, and ultimately at the seminary. They were saddened by the unanticipated October death of Cornelia, Meyer's young wife. The cause of her death was a weakened heart from a bout with diphtheria, in September 1931, as the newly-weds traveled the Pacific with the large group of new missionaries. She was the third person from the mission laid to rest in the International Cemetery, adjacent to the German chapel used by the mission.

Transportation from the seminary into Hankow involved rickshaws, wagons, or walking. There was no car until Meyer was informed that the BFM would pay for a multipurpose vehicle. Using $700 from his wife's estate, he purchased a Dodge chassis In 1934 onto which the mission carpenter constructed a wood bus/station wagon, with flat benches along the sides and mica isinglass windows. He was never reimbursed.

In 1935, the congregation at the seminary opened a chapel in the compound. One side of the chapel was the perimeter wall along the Peking Road, and the other three sides were lean-to's made of wood. Thus occupants on the seminary compound had an alternative choice to the German chapel for their evening services. However, attending the onsite chapel did take away attendance at the various Chinese chapels.

## Concordia Press, Hankow

Publication of the Chinese Lutheran Witness (*Lu-teh-chiao chien-cheng*), hymnals,

The Seminary was dedicated in the fall of 1932, in time the opening of classes. Close-by was the 3-Eye bridge, one of two access routes, which also gave the name to the adjacent village.  The remote location meant that a vehicle was needed - a hand-built carriage on a Dodge Chassis. In the basement, students printed hymnals, books, newsletters, and devotional materials and books on a hand-feed press.

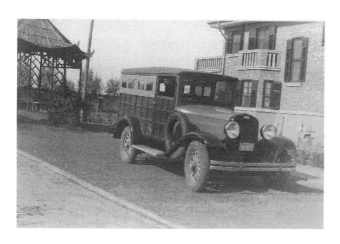

textbooks, tracts and other Christian literature took place in the basement print shop of the new seminary after 1932. The press was supervised by several missionaries; many seminary students worked there to offset some of their fees.

The 1934 hymnal project had been years in preparation, dating back to Arndt's 1914 involvement with the Hsin-I-Wei Union hymnal at Shekow. Riedel, Meyer, Gebhardt, Lillegard, and McLaughlin were among LCMS missionaries who contributed translations in Chinese from German lyrics. Included were twelve new Chinese hymns. Two thousand inch-thick copies of Spiritual Hymns to the Praise of the Lord were signature-bound with a semi-hard blue cloth cover, hinged on the right in Chinese style. Copies sold for 35 Mexican cents—about 15 American pennies. One major distinction was its poetic translations of rhyming couplets, using an intellectual vocabulary, establishing the hymnal as literature. Musical notation was not included, but the appropriate hymn tune was given, in German:

> In Dir ist Freude (In Thee is Joy);
> Ein' Feste Burg ist unser Gott
> (A Mighty Fortress is our God);
> Fang dein Werk mit Jesu an
> (With the Lord begin thy task).

In other publications, photographs were made from copper engravings, such as a portrait of Luther used for a flyer commemorating the Augsburg Confession. Wall calendars with biblical references and designs were printed annually.

A major edition of Bible History in Chinese was printed in 1936, based on the Concordia Publishing House edition of 1918. Blocks crafted by Schnorr von Carolsfeld had been used for the CPH publication and funding for a set of those blocks for the Hankow Press came from Trinity Lutheran Church in Wellsville, New York, Max Zschiegner's home congregation. The textbooks with pictures sold for about twenty cents per copy. Schnorr's designs re-appeared 75 years later in CPH's Lutheran Study Bible of 2009.

Erhardt Riedel, a typesetter in his earlier years in Illinois, headed the operation eventually to be supervised by Adolph Koehler. Funds were donated to set up a press when the seminary building was designed. Some funds earmarked for opening new street chapels were diverted to the print shop, justified both by anticipated savings and manual arts benefits to student workers. Seminary students had been fully subsidized by the mission in years past, but this had led to some abuse (see rice Christians). Students were to declare their good intentions by working for their room and board.

## Up the Han

Concurrent with the restoration and completion of the Concordia Seminary compound in 1932, the Han River basin had also dried sufficiently so that refugees from Black Hill were re-establishing their lives, still amid great poverty. Meyer, Klein, and Werling did not forget the desperation of Black Hill, the needs of the refugees, nor at least 380 baptized souls in need of spiritual nourishment. Mission manpower was limited, but Vicar Wei T'ien-nien did itinerant work reconnecting with the baptized Christians from Black Hill.

The Han overflowed its banks again in 1933, but not as severely this time. Wilbert Werling—who had directed previous clean-up efforts—accompanied by Vicar Wei and Mr. Yang from one Hankow congregation, made a visit in October 1933 to locate converts from Black Hill. A list of names had been made in 1932 for such a purpose, but it was not to be found. Pockets of these new Lutherans were found in several villages. So it was decided by the Missionary Conference, and approved by the BFM, that a missionary should be stationed in the Han Chu'an district, over 100 river miles up the Han from Hanyang.

Meyer made an exploratory trip to find and acquire a site near Hsimakow, a port city in Han Chu'an. A half-mile walk from town

## Map of LCMS 1930s preaching out-stations -
## Han River District & South Shasi District

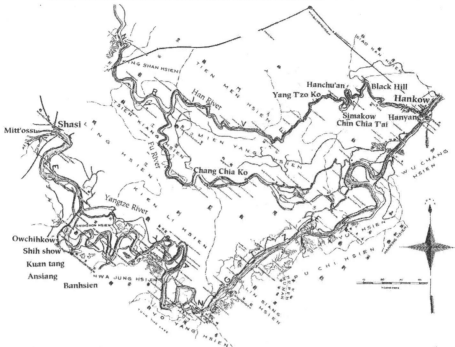

Map showing the circuit of villages of the outstations south of Shasi. To the northeast, in the Han River vicinity, Werling and two evangelists regularly visited several villages where survivors of the 1931 flood lived. Werling's home was a traditional court yard farm house.

was the village of Liao Chia P'o, where a half-acre hillock with a country house was rented in perpetuity like many Chinese-style negotiations. The traditional brick courtyard house (*shikumen*) was upgraded with locking doors, glass windows, a wooden floor, and thoroughly whitewashed. A wall around the property set it apart. Fresh water was available at a spring about a half-mile distant, but as always, it needed to be boiled.

That summer of 1934, Werling, his wife, Clara, and their two infants, were assigned to occupy the house and work in the surrounding counties (*hsien*), to establish worship groups and schools. An oil-burning scow, the *Fu Yuan*, carried them and their freight on the twelve- hour trip from Hankow. A Chinese servant fetched the water, went to market, and cooked in the local way. A pot-bellied Franklin stove could burn cakes of coal for winter heat. Cockroaches, large aggressive centipedes, and the occasional rodent kept housekeeping lively. Villagers cautiously investigated their first foreign neighbors and their tow-head babies (*hsiao mao mao*). Before long, the house became an information center, book depot, guest house, and dispensary run by Clara. She treated patients suffering from "the itch" with sulphur mixed into lard, and applications of Epsom salt for infections.

The fledgling congregation of Lutherans bargained for a worship space. They were self-supporting. Clara played the reed melodion to accompany hymn-singing. Ducks frequently waddled into the rude chapel.

By bicycle and junk, Wenger covered about a 20-mile circuit of 15 villages from Hsimakow west to Kao Lung Wan. There, a land-owning elder of the Lung clan held together a Christian group. From Kao Lung Wan, a 50-mile trail led south to Shasi and the LCMS mission there. Seminary student Shen Chiu-hai itinerated another large area north into the Cho River basin, 10 miles above its merge into the Yangtze. Another student, Tai Yu ch'en, was placed at one village on the Han.

Meanwhile, unbeknownst to the missionaries, a battle was raging at this same time between Nationalist and Communist armies in Kiangsi province, 250 miles south of their beloved Kuling. Under Mao Tse-tung, 90,000 rebels escaped the December 1934 confrontation at Juichin along with the government army and began a circuitous 6,000-mile journey ending in the northwest at Shensi. Reduced a year later to about 20,000 survivors, the trek became known as the legendary Long March. Caves at Yenan were destined to be the stronghold of red troops during the next eight years of Japanese occupation and war.

The Han flooded terribly again in 1935. Now living in Hsimakow, Werling was better able to direct relief efforts. Five Hankow students were excused to distribute food and medicine. Vaccinations to prevent cholera, and tincture of opium to cure it, were given. Several latrines were dug, and matting placed on the ground which read: "Provided by the Ev. Lutheran Mission." Free advertising to a captive audience!

Idle young refugees needed schooling. Permission was granted from the BFM to construct a large mat-shed to lodge and teach middle school boys. The word went out that any boy with a 1932 baptismal certificate from Black Hill was qualified to attend. The long-missing list of names from the Hankow flood was found, and many original Han area survivors were located. Feng, a Christian from another church, operated a school in the town. With another elderly scholar, they translated Luther's Passion of Christ into poetic couplets which were painted on hanging scrolls. About 115 boys showed up with bedrolls and a few belongings. They ate well, behaved well, and listened to the teachers.

When the emergency ended after about two months, Hankow seminarians returned, and the refugee school was disbanded, with the hopes the gospel had once again been brought to the area Chinese. Schoolboys would hopefully Influence their parents. As in many areas of China, women were held in low regard, and it was presumed that wives

In isolated Shihnan, missionary Mueller began a ministry to inmates at the local prison, serving both men and women's groups. A constant tool was his Concordia flip chart of Biblical illustrations, in addition to the Bible portions he distributed.

Missionaries continued their annual pilgrimage to Kuling for conferences around the first week of August. During this period, staff grew to its largest number. Back in America 150 seminary graduates were un-assigned, and over 300 pastors were without congregations.

would follow whatever their husbands told them, even about faith. Werling took comfort in Luther's words, "God's Word is like a passing rainstorm which does not return where it has once been. Therefore take and hold fast to the Gracious Word, whoever can,"

By 1936, Werling reported about 1000 students in 20 village schools below Hsimakow and nine schools upriver. One school was operated by seminary student Tai Yu ch'en, and another by Teacher Feng.

In mid-year, Werling contracted tuberculosis, necessitating a return to the U.S. and the sanitarium at Wheat Ridge, Colorado. No missionary was available in the area along the Han, but until the Japanese occupation, men from Hankow or Shasi visited as they could to encourage the indigenous churches. In the chaos of occupation, war, and revolution, mission contact seems never to have been re-established. Werling recovered to serve several congregations in Wisconsin, and ministered for ten years among the Menominee Indians.

## Post-diluvian Progress – 1932-1937

The city of Shihnan, renamed Enshih [Enshi] by the central government in 1932, revived. The mission entered a period of ambitious expansion under the direction of Marie Oelschlaeger and Arnold Gebhardt. Enshih blossomed as a diverse location. The town congregation called Ch'en Huai-jen as their first full time pastor. Under his leadership, True Light congregation would thrive and survive later wartime hostilities.

With the efforts of Nurse Oelschlaeger and a local doctor, medical work became a major program and eventually led to the establishment of a midwifery school and hospital. Herbert Meyer was transferred there from Hankow in February 1937. Nurse Bernice Hollrah, (Meyer's new bride after 3 years of trans-Pacific correspondence) joined the medical effort after an August wedding in Hankow.

Kweifu, renamed Fengkieh near the upper Yangtze rapids, proved the most difficult station to serve. Hostile to foreigners, land forces and gun boats prevented putting ashore there. The half-house rented from the Pao family was still leased by the mission in hopes of further work. Rev Tai Ch'iu-tao, and his father, Teacher Tai Chin-tang, had maintained a mat-shed school three miles outside the city. Their isolated work yielded surprising results in the future.

At Wanhsien, no resident missionary was ever on site after the disturbances, but Evangelist Ch'en Huai-jen was instrumental in nurturing a very small congregation and a school, before receiving his call to the city congregation at Enshih. Thode from Ichang and Gebhardt from Shihnan visited the evangelist as often as they could. There were seven baptisms. It would be a year before missionaries could re-occupy Wanhsien. Brighter days were ahead.

While Hankow was under water in August 1931, Seltz was able to establish residence in Wanhsien, relocating from Ichang and working with Evangelist Ch'en in assembling a congregation of 22 and a mission school of 41. Nurse Clara Rhodenbeck joined the Wanshien team the same year. Seltz worked alongside, and married Clara in 1933. They continued to serve Wanhsien until they took furlough with their two young children in 1937. They would return to serve in Hong Kong in the 1960s.

## Hopeh Province and North China - Pi P'ei-ying (Pastor Bee)

The saga of Rev. Pi P'ei-ying marks the most thoroughly documented success of indigenous ministry in the entire mission. The tale starts in Hankow where Pi had been brought to faith at age 40 and baptized by Edward Arndt in 1922. Rev. Pi was instrumental in converting his much younger friend, Ch'en Huai-jen, and the two joined the original evangelist school begun by Lawrence Meyer that same year. Starting with 22 men, by February 1926 ten candidates had graduated, and two became pastors. Chen and Pi became the first ordained Chinese clergy in the LCMS.

Rev.Pi (Bee) established two major congregations amongst his clansmen in Hopeh province,150 miles south of Peking.  Several young men decided to attend the Seminary. Missionaries Klein, Zschiegner, and Frillmann visited often by bicycle, but contact with these northern groups was never re-establlished after the Japanese occupation.

Missionary Conference 1935

Even though the seminary faculty had recommended all graduates for placement and ordination, the Board of Foreign Missions did not think these men were ready to assume full pastorates. Diplomas were withheld pending more experience as vicars and evangelists. Five men remained true, but one died and another proved incapable. A third man, Wei T'ien-nien, had not completed requirements, eventually graduating years later. So it was not until after the Troubles and the floods that the first two Chinese Missouri Synod pastors were actually ordained, eight years after completion of their studies. Ch'en was called in 1934 to True Light congregation in Enshih.

Pi (pronounced *Bee*) was a northerner from the Yellow River plains of Hopei. His ancestral home was the village of Hsi-ma-yang, in Shen-tse county. This was about 60 miles west of the Shih-chin-chung railway junction, on China's only north-south rail line, which linked Hankow with Peking. As a northerner, he was not trusted by the southern forces occupying Hankow in 1927. He and Teacher Li Chin-chang were the men jailed for two months during the disturbances because of their Christianity.

In April, 1931, Pi returned to his northern home by rail, locating several Lutherans who had been dispersed by the Troubles. He found two in Peking, and five more at Hsin-chi, 20 miles from his home village. Pi traveled about 160 miles (500 *li*) by foot and cart for two months, exploring several villages and towns including Yang-pei, where he found his Hankow associate, Teacher Li Chi-ch'ang.

Much encouraged, Pi returned to Hankow in June with an optimistic report. The missionaries encouraged Pi to return north, which he did in January 1932, preaching in Yang-pei and Hsin-chi. To cover territory more efficiently, Mr. Pi purchased a bicycle. Not until after a collision with a wall that resulted in several bruised ribs and shoulder bones did the 50-year old master the wheels. He pedaled 60 miles east to Tung-kuang to work with several church members, but took the train to Peking to minister to a young military officer and his wife.

Pi returned again to Hankow in May, reporting on 12 baptized members, plus five faithful wives, 15 children, and 15 catechumens. Pi's pilgrimage was inexpensive since an enthusiastic native could travel and preach among his countrymen at a fraction of the cost of a foreign missionary. His monthly salary was $30 (Chinese); the bicycle cost $35; and his rail and living expenses totaled $43. Altogether, this amounted to about the price of a pair of imported men's leather shoes.

Pi's third missionary journey began in January of 1933. After five days in Shih chin chung, he boarded a mule cart for Hsin-chi. Despite a snowstorm, he tracked down and encouraged several catechumens in the vicinity. Renting a Chinese wheelbarrow, he was taken the 30 miles to Hsi-ma-yang. After Chinese New Year observations, he began regular preaching in his home village. He also published letters in the Chinese Lutheran Witness requesting prayer and financial support for these northern missions from the other LCMS stations. Generous support came from the Chinese Lutherans of the Yangtze, including $127 from Ch'en's congregation at Enshih. The Ichang congregation held a first-ever mission festival (*pu-tao-chieh*) to support Pi. With the involvement of these other Lutheran congregations, a milestone was reached-local support for local mission outreach. Pi returned again to Hankow in June to make his report.

Missionary Max Zschiegner accompanied Pi on his return to Hankow in August 1933, despite the Yellow River floods. Bicycling to three areas, congregations were organized at a meeting in a dry-goods shop in Hsin-chi; in Hsi-ma-ying (Truth Church) at Pi's home; and in Yang-pei (Eternal Life) at the home of Teacher Li. Many other towns were also visited, as far as Tientsin and Peking. The Missionary Conference at Kuling in 1934 would enthusiastically endorse Pi's Hopei project.

So it was that Pastor Bee was called by these congregations and ordained, first in Hankow, then in both Hopeh congregations

# Proclamation of the North China
# Evangelical Lutheran Church

This congregation, wishing only to  keep the Lord's Word and follow the truth, cannot but reject the old customs and keep only useful or harmless customs. Therefore we herewith state plainly to our clans, relatives, neighbors, fathers, brothers, and sisters the following:

1. As to the worship of idols, calling (the gods) for rain, thanking the gods (with theatricals), fire-crackers, burning of paper, and anything else that has to do with idolatry, we join in none of this, nor do we contribute money for it.

2. As to ancestor-worship, we do not worship the spirit tablets of ancestors, nor do we worship them by burning paper at their graves; only at Easter and the memorial day of the departed we go and repair the graves, and a memorial address is held, treating of the history of the dead in order to stir up the love of the descendants and keep the dead in memory.

3. As to marriage, we reject the three kinds of kotow by the groom and the worship of heaven and earth by the bride. We use only the marriage service of the Church. The bride and groom may make a bow to the guests; the bridal chair and cover, fire-crackers, and the feast may be retained;

4. As to burial, the old customs are entirely rejected. Whether rich or poor, a simple burial is preferred, entirely according to the church service; a hearse is used; guests from afar are to eat (but not feast), near guests are not to bother the bereaved (expecting a feast).

May 20, 1934

The market street  and Congregation at Yang-pei, 1936

in January 1934. Within months, his field had grown to four small congregations with 20 outposts. Bee's son, Phillip Pi, left the seminary to assist his father. Student Shen Chio Hai bicycled throughout many villages in the Hopeh field with Pastor Bee. Missionaries Zschiegner, Klein, and Frillmann often visited Pi's growing ministry. Five young men from Pi's congregations enrolled in the new seminary class in Hankow. In so many ways, Pastor Pi's work promised unprecedented growth of a truly indigenous church. The disruptions of the 1937 Japanese Occupation changed that.

Concerning local Chinese folk religion, the Proclamation of the North China Evangelical Lutheran Churchclarified the distinctions which these Christians had made.

## Explorations Afield

Ever alert to new mission geographies, missionaries investigated several possible new fields in the mid-1930s, none of which materialized into on-going programs. Wenger and Meyer took a holiday trip to Peking and Tientsin, hoping to connect with some relocated Hankow Lutherans, but no further work is recorded.

A connection was briefly made with a group of Christians in Anhwei [Anhui] Province. A pocket of Chinese faithful in that province east of Hopeh were led by an evangelist named Liu Wan-yuan, whose denominational roots are unknown. Liu had passed thru Enshih while evangelizing in western Hupeh and had met Arnold Gebhardt. Liu and Gebhardt engaged in such a positive dialogue that Liu invited the LCMS man to visit Liu's Christians in the hamlets of Shih keng and Shu shih k'ow in Anhwei's Ningkuo county. When Gebhardt was able to visit, Mr. Liu had passed away, but the four Liu sons welcomed an LCMS link. From Hankow, Riedel pursued this with a visit, taking along Seminarian Li Jen-chi. Nothing firm was established, although in 1936 another seminarian, Ch'en Fu-t'ai, continued undocumented work in this region.

## Radio and The Lutheran Hour

Commercial American radio broadcasting, first begun in 1920 in Philadelphia, rapidly expanded worldwide as production of receivers proliferated, technology developed, and commercial programming matured. Reception quality was subject to weather, season, and other technical factors. By 1935 there were 48 AM stations in Shanghai, and two in Hankow. One of those was small 100kw radio station XHJA (570kc). By the 1930s even some frugal missionaries had a few receiving sets. The weak XHJA signal could be picked up throughout the Wuhan region.

Teacher Theobald Breihan, a fresh graduate from Concordia Teachers College in River Forest, Illinois, started reading English stories over XHJA. In December of 1935, his upper primary students from Concordia Evangelical School broadcast a live concert from the XHJA studio with Christmas songs and readings from Luke 2. They were hauled to the station in the mission bus, and were not very satisfied with their first performance.

The Huachung Broadcasting station began regularly airing Lutheran Hour, on March 8, 1936, with initial sermons from Missionary Adolph Koehler and music provided by Riedel's Seminary Chorus. (Radio and department stores in Hankow enhanced the quality and volume using street amplifiers, drawing crowds in front of the shop front speakers.) The English language version aired at 1:00 pm on Sundays and Chinese language broadcasts were at 5:00 pm, supervised by Riedel. Seminary student Chi Tao-an gave the Mandarin language message. At the end of the sermons, the locations of the seven Lutheran preaching places were announced. Listeners were urged to tell their friends to tune in, and to write for information via Concordia Seminary, Hankow.

How could this have come to be? How could an innovative missionary venture of a small ethnic Protestant church body using new technology during the Great Depression in America reach the air waves of the Yangtze Valley?

In 1926, Deke Theiss in Shihnan had been exploring the emerging technology of short-wave ham radio, and obtained Chinese

operating license AC9HT from the Ministry of Communications for his AC Super Wasp Receiver. From Shihnan, Theiss established radio contact with Koehler in Hankow, using equipment he had shipped with his luggage from the States. Morse code radiotelegraphy was an instantaneous communications boon, augmenting the slow surface mail and expensive cablegrams. Located in the recently completed seminary, the set was operated by recently-widowed Herb Meyer after 1932. Up country in Shihnan, R. J. Mueller (AC9RM) replaced Theiss, who had returned to the U.S. for family medical reasons. The radio link existed for several years during the turbulent build-up to the 1937 Japanese occupation. During occupation, sets were confiscated.

Just how the 1936 Hankow broadcasts came about is not on record, but surely involved these mission *radioheads*. Seminary graduates arriving in Hankow after 1930 would have been in tune with Lutheran Hour programming since the KFUO broadcasts originated on the St Louis campus.

Locally-generated Hankow programs were silenced by the 1937 Japanese occupation.

The next reference to *The Lutheran Hour* in China was in 1940 when Lutheran families in Hong Kong were able to pick up the shortwave signal from Manila over KZRM.

*The Lutheran Hour* will re-appear many times in the on-going story of Lutheran enterprise in the Chinese world. *The Lutheran Hour* continues as the flagship outreach of Lutheran Hour Ministries, broadcasting, taping, and streaming in 30 languages on Armed Forces Shortwave Services to this day.

But in 1937, war clouds were looming.

Concordia Seminary in 1936. Faculty from left to right include Maclaughlin, Riedel, Zschiegner, and Koehler . The kneeling student on the far right was still attending Eternal Life congregation in Taipei, Taiwan, in 2008.

## Significant Sources:

| | |
|---|---|
| Benge, Janet & Geoff | *Gladys Aylward:The Adventure of a Lifetime* |
| Buck, Pearl | *The Young Revolutionist* |
| Carlberg, Gustav | *Thirty Years in China* |
| Frillmann, Paul | *China: The Remembered Life* |
| Hersey, John | *A Single Pebble* |
| Moseley, George | *China Since 1911* |
| Pankow, Fred & Edith | *The Best is Yet to Come* |
| Parker, George | *The Mysterious Yangtze* |
| Parsons, David | *Wait and See: A Biography of Herman Klein* |
| Riedel, Erhardt | *From the Land of Sinim* |
| Werling, Wilbert | *Up the Han from Hankow* |

**Chapter Eight**
**Arrivals**                                                        **Origin      School**
1939 - Oct    Arr via *Empress of Russia* from Vancouver, BC:
    Martens              Paul                                        Cumberland, WI  CSL
    Voss                 Kurt                                        Saginaw, MI  CSL

1940 - April   Arr via *SS Asama Maru* from San Francisco:
    Dohrman              Clarence & Annette (nee Ehrhardt)          Brooklyn, NY  CSL

1943 - Sept 4  Arr at Calcutta via *MS Priam* from Philadelphia (accompanied by O H Schmidt):
    Egolf                Ralph                                       Perkasi, PA  CSF
    Hinz                 Herbert                                     Melrose Park, IL  CSL

1945 - Dec 5   Arr Karachi via *SS Santa Paula* from New York and Suez:
    Boss                 Martha                                      Cleveland, OH  LH-FW
    Hoeltje              Wilbert & Geraldine (nee Bierwirth)         Oak Park, IL  CSF

**Returning to China**
1936 - Aug 3   Arr via *SS President Grant* from San Francisco:
    Zimmermann           Elmer & Anna + three children

1937 - Jan 4   Arr via *SS Nanking* from San Francisco:
    Ziegler              Albert & Laura + eight children

1938 - Dec    Arr via *Empress of Canada*:
    Riedel               Erhardt, without family

1939 - April   Arr in Hong Kong via SS *President Coolidge* from San Francisco:
    Buuck                Lorenz & Ella + two children
    Mueller              Reinhold & Dorothy + daughter

     - Nov     Arr in Hong Kong via *Empress of Britain:*
    Wenger               Gilbert & Elsie

**Departures**
1937 Breihan          Theobald & Caroline                          (family health)
     Riedel           Erhardt & Carmelia + Marie, Gerhardt, Joseph, Ted, Herb    (furlough)

1938 Koehler          Adolph & Irmie + James, Marilyn              (furlough)

**Relocated to Hong Kong**
1937 McLaughlin   Wallace & Mary + Aldine, Glenn            (resigned - health 1938)

1938 Ziegler      Laura+ Howard, Everett, Eunice, Doris, Larry, Ruth, Ted, Laura Lu (POWs 1942)
     Zschiegner   Max & Helen+ Max Jr, Martin, Arthur, Carl          (health 1938)

**Death**
1940 Zschiegner       Max                    at Wanhsien  age 42 - (angina pectoris / $CO_2$ poisoning)

**Prisoners of War Repatriated to New York August 25, 1942 on *SS Gripsholm*)**
    Thode            Elmer & Frieda + Daniel, Eunice              from Ichang
    Klein            Herman & Ruth + Ray, Ruth, James, Lois       from Hankow
    Zimmermann  Elmer & Anna +Betty, Dorothy, Katherine, Christian   from Shasi
    Buuck            Lorenz & Ella + Leonard, Elaine, Robert       from Hong Kong
    Ziegler          Laura + Eunice, Doris, Larry, Ruth, Ted, Laura Lu   from Hong Kong

## Chapter Eight

# The End of an Era   1937–1945

In London, his Royal Highness Albert of York, was crowned King George VI of Great Britain on May 12, 1937, amid rumblings of war. King George and his queen, Elizabeth Bowes-Lyon, would guide the Empire, including the Crown Colony of Hong Kong and many interests in China, through dark days from 1937 to 1945 as Germany and Japan tried to rearrange their respective cultural spheres.

The approaching Pacific War (1937-1945) would forever change Asia, America, and the LCMS China mission, which disseminated missionaries into four groupings. Some remained at their posts in areas beyond Japanese control. Some carried on in occupied China until repatriated; some transferred to Hong Kong, eventually becoming prisoners of war; but over half of the mission staff returned permanently to the States and parish ministry.

## Wars and Rumors of Wars

The latter half of 1937 brought unexpected changes for the mission, and multiple disasters for China. The next eight years would bring a wartime inferno throughout China; a perfect storm of intrigue and blunders; a tapestry of political and military events and developments; and plagues of disease, death, and destruction on a scale never envisioned in modern times.

Japanese aggression in the systematic takeover of Northern China and Manchuria had already begun in 1931 with their occupation of Northern China under the pretext

of building the Manchurian Railway. Hoping to add a semblance of legitimacy to this land grab, the figurehead child emperor Pu Yi had been installed as ruler of Manchukuo by officials in Tokyo. The Tangku Truce Agreement of 1933 forced de-militarization on China north of Peiping (Northern Peace) [Beijing].

East Asian nations and western powers shared anxiety and dread that Japanese aggression could lead to an Asian war on the scale of the recent Great War of 1914-1918. Japanese presence in Shantung Province, once occupied by Germany, had precipitated the distrust and animosity of the Chinese. Civil disorder from the conflict between Central government and Communist troops kept the Chinese Republic in a state of flux. Transportation, telegraph, and telephone systems were undependable. The postal service was still administered by European powers. Cable and wireless communication was in the hands of the British.

Tension evidenced itself in the continued patrolling of the Yangtze by gunboats flying American, British, Italian, and French flags. Europeans still benefited from extrality, enforced by foreign navy craft stationed at most of the treaty ports, especially Wuhan and Shanghai. Expatriate life continued to be comfortable, glorious, consumptive, enabling business and consular families to enjoy an isolated and privileged lifestyle. Shanghai was the international city.

Christian missionary groups were on the fringe of all this, carrying out their goals

Detail of a large color map of China, published in Japan in the 1930s. Japan would occupy northern China in1931, and eastern China in late 1937. The ensuing war, with various names, would not end until 1945, with Japan's defeat. This shows the major railway from the north ending at Hankow and the major railway to the south beginning at Wuchang. Small figures show economic activities.

Two views of Canton (Kwangchow) [Guangzhou], painted in overglaze during the 19th century on porcelain vases. The buildings are on Shameen Island, in the Pearl river, where europeans were permitted to trade and live 6 months each year. Canton became the southern terminus of the railway from Wuchang in 1936, linking via and Kowloon-Canton Railway (KCR) to Hong Kong.

and operating schools, orphanages, and medical facilities with low profile. Their letters home hinted at the local discord, but projected the impression of stability and confidence in God's blessings on their work. Reports and articles in the *Lutheran Witness* and Walther League *Messenger* informed LCMS constituents of detailed skirmishes, bombings, and stories of survival and need.

## 'Twas Good, Lord, to be Here

The 1937 General Missionary Conference at Kuling convened just a few days after a seemingly unimportant skirmish in the north on July 7. That clash between Japanese and Chinese troops at the Marco Polo Bridge at Wanping, an old walled town near Peking, triggered what would become an eight-year occupation and war. It was also the same week that famed American aviatrix Amelia Earhart (a Lutheran, incidentally) disappeared over the South Pacific as she attempted global circumnavigation.

The Riedel family had already left Hankow on their scheduled furlough. Most other families were en route to Kuling for the August 6 retreat, unaware that the Japanese were concurrently attacking Shanghai.

When mission families came down the LuShan hills from their retreat, they entered a changed world. Life in China would never be the same. Months of confinement and years of warfare lay ahead. They were relieved when they found no one had been killed among the mission staff, teachers, or workers; however, two congregation members had been killed in skirmishes.

Seminary classes began as usual on September 8. Students began emergency war work in October, visiting and witnessing at military hospitals and camps. Organized as the Concordia Comfort Service and Mission Society, seminarians consoled injured men, wrote letters for the wounded, handed out tracts and Bible portions, and witnessed to the gospel.

The Hankow missionaries, fearing isolation or worse, cabled to the Board of Foreign Missions, requesting that overseas personnel willing to take their furloughs early should be permitted to do so. On September 24, the Wuhan area was bombed. More bombs fell on October 18. Lacking a full grasp of the international situation, the BFM countered with the message to stay the course, and to evacuate only when absolutely necessary to either Hong Kong or Manila. The board did send an additional $7,000 USD with the September payroll, in case evacuation was necessary.

## The Panay Incident
## December 12, 1937

Japanese troops began an attack on Nanking, the Nationalist capital 440 river miles east of Hankow. Pillage and rape continued over a six week period. By December 12, there were 300,000 casualties (as later determined by the Nanking War Crimes Tribunal). Nanking Theological Seminary, with as many students as Concordia, was destroyed and many Christians killed. Word reached Hankow by radio.

That same day, a Sunday, the American gunboat *USS Panay* left Nanking to lead a convoy of three U.S.-owned SOCONY-Vacuum Oil barges. Although clearly marked with large American flagging, the neutral ship was boarded just twelve miles upriver, and then attacked from the air by the Japanese. It sank within two hours. Survivors wandered the swamps and villages near Kaiyuan for three days. Among them were 59 crewmen, plus many diplomats, civilian refugees, and several civilian newsmen who were coincidently filming a documentary about life aboard a Yangtze patrol boat! News of three casualties and 45 wounded took days to collect and report.

Japan apologized profusely, convincing the American government it was a mistaken attack. Loathe to start another war, the U.S. did not retaliate, but American and international opinion was turned. Five months later, the Japanese government paid $2.2 million USD in reparations.

Mission staff reluctantly closed the seminary and boys' prep school within days. Nine seminary-level students were moved temporarily 300 miles upriver to Missionary Zimmermann's large compound at Shasi, but

Hong Kong, a Crown Colony since 1841, was the oldest and most stable British settlement in China. One of the twelve inhabited outlying islands is Cheung Chau, a dumbell-shaped isle, an hour ferry-ride from Central (Victoris). The view from the missionary cottage at #29 captured rice terraces and fishing village and docs. Close by was a popular-bathing beach.

younger boys returned to their homes. Before the capture of Shasi the following January, the seminary would again relocate in 1938, upriver at Wanhsien, another 290 miles west in Szechwan province, beyond the Japanese-occupied area. The closure marked the demise of the promising seminary program. There would never be another graduating class from the Chinese Concordia Seminary in Hankow.

## Evacuation to Hong Kong
## Fall 1937–Winter 1941

Hong Kong first appears in LCMS records in 1937. Until then, missionaries had traveled only through Shanghai on their way to the Yangtze interior mission stations. With the Japanese occupation of east China and the Lower Yangtze cities in 1937, several missionaries made the decision to move their families out of the path of approaching Japanese forces to the presumed protection of the British Crown Colony.

That February, Richard Muehl evacuated from Ichang, bringing his wife and two sons to Kowloon. From there, he served as the China mission treasurer, organized a school for mission kids, and held services. To use his time well, he took additional Mandarin classes from the Nanking University Extension Language School, with the intention of eventually returning to Hankow. Walter Arndt (son of the mission founder) lived in Hong Kong, working for the Dollar Steamship company (later, the American President Lines), on whose ships so many missionaries had come to China. Walter had once studied to be a medical missionary, and did what he could to be supportive of the LCMS China mission.

When Japanese bombing in October 1937 forced closure of the Hankow seminary, Herman and Edna Klein and their nine children evacuated. They passed the time in Hong Kong waiting for the SS *Thomas Jefferson* to take them to Seattle.

The Koehler, McLaughlin, Ziegler, and Zschiegner families felt they had to evacuate. In late December, the occupying Japanese allowed a 48-hour window for an International Christmas Train from Hankow to Hong Kong. The Japanese guaranteed it safe passage. Railcars were draped with flags of Sweden, Italy and the United States. Two large white crosses were painted atop the rolling stock. The McLaughlin, Ziegler, and Zschiegner families were aboard. They narrowly avoided Japanese bombing when the train was mistakenly switched onto an alternate track. The overcrowded train took hundreds of refugees south, arriving on Christmas Day at the KCR station in Kowloon.

The Koehlers arrived on a second train, and took an early furlough to Minnesota, never to return. Hankow briefly became the capital of China in 1938, affecting the only missionary still assigned there, Paul Frillmann.

The Zieglers had brought their amah, Nan Shang, and found a temporary space in Mong Kok at 295 Prince Edward Road. All three families took up residence in Kowloon, later moving to house #29 on Cheung Chau, an island in the Hong Kong anchorage. The small island is an hour ferry ride west of the harbor. Chinese residents were restricted to the fishing village, while Europeans lived on their own section of the island. Beyond the dockside village, there were so few European houses on Cheung Chau, that these were simply numbered, with no street names. The three-room lower level of #29 also had a kitchen and two bathrooms. Most importantly, there was a porch, where the families could play, exercise, and hold school. Children could explore the island and swim at the nearby beach.

Wallace McLaughlin taught catechism to the Zschiegner and Ziegler boys. Richard Muehl conducted school for the missionary children (five families with nineteen school-age children, three toddlers, and two infants).

Max Zschiegner worked on translating Luther's Large Catechism; McLoughlin translated Luther's Small Catechism into Cantonese with help from a local language teacher; and Rev. Muehl supervised its publication.

Missionary families pause before listening to
a broadcast of the Lutheran Hour from Manila
in January, 1941. The same porch doubled
as the school room for between 8 to thirteen
missionary kids, from 1939 to 1941.

Muehl and Zschiegner managed the China mission's funds.

The McLaughlins departed in July 1938 for the Philippines. Missionary Ziegler had returned to Wanhsien, in Free China, beyond Japanese control, in June, and Zschiegner followed in August, so that the re-located seminary could open with four of the students from Shasi by September. Their families remained in the British colony. Laura Ziegler and Helen Zschiegner taught the children in a one-room school on the porch. The Lorenz Buuck family had come to Hong Kong after their 15-month furlough from China in March 1939, and lived close-by at house #30. Buuck managed the finances for the mission in Free China, and helped with the schooling.

The saga of this Hong Kong remnant group was to become one of the most dramatic episodes in Missouri Synod mission history.

In January 1938, China Lutheran Church (Hsin-I-Wei) had re-located their American school for missionary children from Kikungshan (40 miles north of Hankow) to Cheung Chau on the campus of Tiger Balm Hospital. Living within a mile on the same island, LCMS missionaries could have sent their students to this school, but did not want their children to participate in the required daily chapel services, risking unionism!

The LCMS regarded Hong Kong as a temporary location, a chaotic holding tank until hostilities ended. Back home, the Board of Foreign Missions had no anticipation of opening mission work in the Colony, where so many other Christian denominations had been long-established. All families planned to return to their mainland missions. They were in wartime survival mode, and little thought was given to any permanent work in Hong Kong. Besides, LCMS missionaries had been trained in Mandarin, whereas Cantonese was the vernacular of Hong Kong. They lacked printed materials, which had been left behind in Hankow. Nor did they have the aid of any indigenous evangelists or Bible women. They had no access to a chapel or other space for assembly or worship.

McLaughlin was the official pastor to the small group of missionary families, and continued to hold weekly services. Worship was conducted on the verandah of house #29. There was even a piano in the Cheung Chau house, used for hymn singing. The adults tried to maintain as much of a normal life and routine as they could for the children. Until Buuck arrived, McLoughlin, Muehl, and Laura Ziegler taught school, with courses in German, English, mathematics, and other core curricula. When Albert Ziegler visited annually from Wanhsien, he taught the older boys as much Latin as possible. These same three boys were the ones confirmed in June 1938.

In their loyalty to the goals of the mission, Ziegler and Zschiegner left families in Hong Kong and returned to Free China to operate the re-located seminary at Wanhsien. Lorenz Buuck would continue schooling the three remaining families (10 children). When the McLaughlins left in the summer of 1938, Buuck was also designated as pastor to the isolated group. After another year, the Muehls left.

The Zschiegners had to leave Hong Kong in December 1938 due to Helen's severe illness, but Max returned to Hong Kong with new missionary Kurt Voss in late 1939, enroute to the Wanhsien station. Voss had an appendectomy in Hong Kong and stayed a month then flew to Chungking to meet up with Zschiegner and other returning missionaries, Gilbert and Elsie Wenger, and Paul Martens. It was on the final leg of that journey that Zschiegner suffered a fatal heart attack,

Across the South China Sea in Manila, LCMS chaplain J. Floyd Dreith, serving U.S. forces at Cavite Naval Station, proposed the broadcast of Lutheran Hour programs on shortwave to the manager of radio station KZRM. First airing February 1, 1940, the programs on Asia's most powerful station brought a tremendous listener response from around the Pacific, which stunned and impressed the radio officials. The missionaries in Hong Kong tuned-in regularly, maintaining a link with their Lutheran roots amid their seeming isolation. Weekly programs were

Stanley Prison became a six-month home for civilian detainees, American, British, and Dutch. The ld buildings still stand today. Laura Ziegler, ran the "diet" kitchen for the benefit of babies and sick inmates.

Missionaries sang carols on Christmas eve from their 1934 hymnal, printed at the Hankow Seminary.

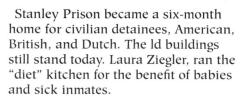

aired until the station was shut down in December 1941 with the Japanese invasion.

In April of 1940, new missionary Clarence Dohrman and his wife Annette arrived in Hong Kong but were forced to wait two months for transport into Free China. They used the time to learn basic Chinese language. When they did leave, with a load of supplies and medicines, they sailed for Hanoi, and then took the train to Kunming. There they met up with Voss and Martens. A truck was purchased so as to skirt occupied China to Chungking, and on to Enshih.

From Washington D.C. came advice for all U.S. citizens to quit the Far East, forbidding women or children to sail to the Orient. On January 14, 1941, the U.S. Secretary of State relayed the fears of the American consul at Hankow to the BFM recommending evacuation of personnel, but the St. Louis men did not heed the warning.

On December 2, 1941, the Buucks and the Zieglers were advised by the American consulate in Hong Kong to move off Cheung Chau, because of the threat of an imminent Japanese invasion. After staying in Kowloon a few days, they retreated to Hong Kong Island a basement room at 34 Kennedy Road.

## The Fall of Hong Kong

Americans, living at home or abroad, are typically positive, helpful, and resourceful problem-solvers. The expatriates in Hong Kong, although bewildered, frustrated, and confused, did their best in the deteriorating situation. Political and military leaders scrambled as news came from Europe and Asia. Signs of an inevitable two-front world confrontation became ever clearer in late1941. Another world war was imminent and seemingly unavoidable.

On December 8, Japan launched its full invasion of the Pacific and Asia, still Dec 7 In Hawaii. Americans call it Pearl Harbor Day. The garrison of British regulars, 300 recently-arrived Canadian troups, and local HVG (Hong Kong Volunteer Group) held Kowloon for five days, evacuating to Hong Kong Island on December

14. On Christmas day Governor Mark Young surrendered the colony.

Zieglers and Buucks were to become civilian prisoners of war. The two families had found refuge in the house owned by a Hong Kong Japanese business family on Kennedy Road. In hiding and despite a large shell hole in the roof, they celebrated Christmas day.

Local Chinese civilians spent the next 3 1/2 years foraging for food and existing as unobtrusively as possible under the Japanese occupiers. The food situation was desperate. There were reports of cannibalism. Some Chinese remained faithful to their colonial morals, many more resorted to looting. Carnage and death were rampant.

Four camps were established for prisoners of war. Three of these were on the Kowloon side - Shamshuipo for most British and certain Chinese; Mautauchung camp at Kai Tak airport assigned to British Indians; and the Argyle Street camp for British officers. On the Hong Kong side, Canadian and British units occupied a camp at North Point.

All civilians had to surrender to the Japanese. Most European civilians were temporarily housed in a few old hotels. On January 23 they were loaded onto an old ferry and sent around the island to the Stanley peninsula. They were put ashore at a pier on St Stephen's Beach and led to Stanley Fort, adjacent to Chek Che, a fishing village on the island's south shore. The site is hilly, at the end of a long peninsula with bays and beaches on both flanks. Stanley was also the location of Hong Kong's largest colonial prison.

Approximately 2000 British, 60 Dutch, and 300 Americans were billeted in cement flats originally built for families of prison staff. The Buucks claimed a single bedroom in a former warden's house. They had much more room than other internees who were housed 15 to a room. Mrs. Ziegler and her six children were assigned to a 12 ft. by 14 ft. upper room in a different building.

The first order of business was to bury the remaining bodies left from the Christmas

# Christmas Eve 1941 – Hong Kong

A combined account from **Rev Lorenz Buuck** and Mrs. Laura Ziegler

**What a night! Never did the Christmas message mean more to us than that night when the shells were screaming through the darkness. In the midst of the noise of war and the ever nearing machine gun fire, only one or two ridges from the city, we sang "Silent Night, Holy Night." There was really no gift exchange. We often said this was the most blessed Christmas we ever celebrated. All the earthly trimmings were cast aside as we rejoiced solely in the Babe of Bethlehem.**

Christmas day we tried to have our Christmas service three different times, but we were always disturbed by bombs or shells. There was usually a lull for about half an hour just before dark so we decided to have our service at that time. We had just taken our places and Reverend Buuck drew the quilt away from the window to read a sermon when we heard an airplane power dive above our heads. We all rushed for our places but before we reached them the bombs burst around us. We heard three distinct explosions, one closer than the next. We were quite certain that at least one had hit our house and expected the house to fall on us any second. As the little ones ran past me I took one and leaned over her thinking that if the rafters would fall they would hit me and our smallest girl wouldn't be so badly hurt. But when the dust cleared up a little, I noticed I had Reverend Buuck's little girl and not my own. Upstairs, there was such a cloud of dust. When it cleared we saw so much glass broken, plaster fallen and furniture broken that we thought our house had received a direct hit.

We then went outside to see if the enemy had used an incendiary bomb. They had been using them the last few days as we had seen several houses burning on the mountain side. We saw that our house was still standing but it was so dusty we couldn't see where the other bombs had landed.

We had just gone back into the basement when two British police came in. They said they had been on the way up to tell us there was no need to worry about any more bombs or shells because Hong Kong had surrendered at 3 o'clock. This was hard to believe because it was already 6 o'clock. **Hence the last bomb, which was dropped in the entire Hong Kong siege almost took our lives. It was indeed close.** The big British gun below us kept firing for almost half an hour more, and then everything was very quiet except for occasional machine gun or rifle fire.

**An eerie silence settled as night fell. Into this darkness and ominous silence marched the singing and victorious Japanese. This singing was bone-chilling to us adults because we knew what had happened in other captured cities. Commending ourselves to the protection of God's holy angels, we went to sleep on that memorable Christmas night.**

We expected to see the Chinese looters come in during the evening and steal our food and other things. We also expected the Japanese soldiers to come in sometime during the night. We tried to save some of our food by hiding it in different parts of the house. We also left something in the cupboard hoping that the looters would take what they found there and hurry on. It was very quiet that night. When we awoke the next morning it was light in the basement because everything had been blown out of the windows the night before. It was 8:30 in the morning and we had heard or seen no one all night. The sun was shining brightly and we could go upstairs and eat our breakfast, which was a nice change from eating in the dark basement. We went upstairs and helped clean the house. We could see now that the first bomb had blown the top floor off the house next door. The second bomb had landed in the street in front of us and the third to the left of us, demolishing the house."

massacre. Rice and miniscule portions of raw vegetables were provided daily. An entire day's ration would not fill a pint mug. Bits of unidentifiable meat were a rarity. The British lamented the lack of a good *tiffin* (lunch).

Certain goods were available at a canteen open monthly in the camp. The unit of currency was the MY (300 Military Yen=HK $1=USD .25). POWS were allotted 200 MY each month. A compradore named Cheng supplied limited items at exorbitant prices — MY400 for a 10-pack of smokes; MY 4500 for a tin of milk powder. A barter system operated among the prisoners, and many people slowly sold off whatever jewelry, clothing, or household effects they had in exchange for MY, but more often for contraband cigarettes and food. Barter and smuggling was common, and essential to survival. A clandestine radio set, well hidden, picked up occasional war news, until it was confiscated and destroyed

Each nationality organized its own communities within the barbed wire and did communal cooking with the meager rations. Creativity with inadequate food supplies was the order of the day. British cooks experimented with making bread, growing the yeast from rice. After an outbreak of beriberi, an interned British doctor, Selwyn-Clarke, was able to obtain thiamin, which was added to the internees' soup. Within three months the epidemic was stemmed.

Laura Ziegler set up a diet kitchen for infants and the seriously ill. Between her nursing experience, and the mothering of eight children, her knowledge and innovations provided more nutritious meals from the same supplies. For her work, she was later recognized in several books and articles about Stanley Camp. One of those journalists was Joseph Alsop, a stranded correspondent for the *Saturday Evening Post,* who wrote detailed accounts of Stanley Camp life after his repatriation.

The American community at Stanley Camp consisted of sailors from a stranded American ship, plus business people and missionary families. Children from all communities attended an ad hoc school, taught by a dozen well-educated volunteers from the British and American population. British exams, often written on Chinese toilet paper, were even sent by Red Cross packet to London for marking and return. An odd collection of books became a lending library. Clothing was at a premium, and the winter was damp and cold. The first spring, the Japanese sent in several sewing machines and remnant cloth. Ella Buuck and several women sewed skirts, shorts, and other necessary items.

Each Sunday, Roman Catholic, Union, and Lutheran services were conducted in the Prison Officers' Club. Rev. Buuck preached each Sunday morning. With only one hymnal among the group, hymns were handwritten on bridge score cards for the fifteen or twenty attendees. Some *Portals of Prayer* books had been brought along, and were used for daily devotions. On Easter Sunday, Rev Buuck also baptized a baby.

There were several deaths from disease and malnutrition in camp. One rough wooden box with a removable bottom was reused as a coffin. A grave would be dug and the body placed into it, briefly covered with the bottomless coffin. The dead box was then reused for the next funeral. Most burials took place in the early morning.

Internees made the best of their situation and several social groups formed. Children crawled under the perimeter fence for an occasional swim at the nearby beach. The Japanese expected the internees to cooperate within the barbed wire enclosure. Tensions sometimes developed over politics or the ever-present concern with fairness and equality of food distribution. A Red Cross shipment of parcels, one for each internee, arrived containing tinned corn beef and salmon; Bovril and Oxo (bouillon), cod liver oil and malt, chocolate, cheese, crystalized ginger, oats, biscuits (cookies), soap and highly-prized toilet paper.

## Meanwhile, In Occupied China Fall, 1937 – Spring, 1942

The skeleton mission staff, who neither returned to the U.S. nor re-located to

During the period from July 1937 to late 1941, America was not at war with Japan. To mark mission property as "neutral," missionaries Riedel and Mueller laid out a large US flag, visible from the air. An American flag was also painted on the pillars of mission houses. It was intentionally reversed.

Hong Kong, carried on at their posts under the watchful eyes of Japanese soldiers. Since America was not then at war with Japan, the missionaries were able to continue most congregational and school work at Hankow, Shasi, and Ichang, until late 1941.

Hankow was bombed on September 24, 1937, and again on October 18 with the loss of 900 lives. Two missionaries, Paul Frillmann and Gilbert Wenger, remained to watch over the seminary compound and to protect it from looting or occupation.

In May, a cholera epidemic broke out in the Yangtze valley. Frillman allowed the League of Nation's Red Cross to set up a contagious diseases isolation hospital at the seminary. A large red cross was painted on the seminary roof. A British doctor became resident for a few months and the missionaries helped as they could while bearing gospel witness, sharing the one thing needful. Other seminary houses and makeshift lean-tos were occupied by homeless Europeans seeking shelter from the chaos of the concession areas.

After thirteen months of sporadic bombing, the Japanese occupied Hankow on October 25, 1938. Max Zschiegner later reported:

"For a month at a time, the Japanese planes might not come; then sometimes twice a day the ominously droning silvery planes would appear, in groups of nine or eighteen or thirty-six, high in the sky, dropping tons of explosives or incendiary bombs and dealing out terrible destruction. The bark of anti-aircraft guns from various parts of the city, and the deep rumbling and the shocking concussion of the exploding bombs became a thing to which our people had to accustom themselves. Needless to say, prayers became more fervent, and praise too, for God's wonderful protection. But how pitiful the plight of the non-combatant Chinese people in all such cities as are subject to bombing!

Near our St. John's chapel, a deep hole and a large area of debris marked the spot where hundreds of refugees from Anh-wei lost their lives, and gruesome were the sights unearthed before our eyes by the excavators."

Wenger had to quit Hankow for medical leave in the States. Alone, Frillmann stood at the seminary gatehouse and convinced Japanese occupation troops to respect the American property, since the U.S. was still neutral. Signs were posted at the three-eye bridge and gatehouse to keep soldiers and others out. The hospital closed.

On the backside of the seminary wall was a small village, and it was not many days before the invading soldiers began molesting the village women at night. Once he learned of this, Frillmann allowed about 200 women and children of the village to sleep within the compound. They would return to the village each morning and the ruse was never discovered. An esprit d'corps developed over the next years, and a mutual appreciation grew between the Chinese and Americans, and many were the opportunities for Frillmann to live out his Christian witness.

Missionary Klein and his young family returned to Hankow in the summer of 1940, becoming caretakers of the seminary compound when Paul Frillmann took furlough in April, 1941. While on leave, Frillmann accepted a position as chaplain to the newly formed American Volunteer Group (AVG). These were the famous Flying Tigers, who kept China's back door open under General Claire Chennault's leadership. As the only Chinese-speaking member of the 100-strong unofficial group, Frillmann returned to Free China as translator, aide-de-camp, and spiritual advisor to the heroic pioneer aviators defending the Burma Road. After his wartime service with the U.S. army, major Frillmann was part of the peacetime restoration corps.

America declared a state of war with Japan on December 8. Within a month, the Kleins were interned in Hankow, but not before having to watch the contents of the seminary library and classroom being tossed through windows and burned. Klein had made arrangements for the church to continue under a possible occupation - he withdrew all mission funds from local banks, entrusting gold coin to loyal

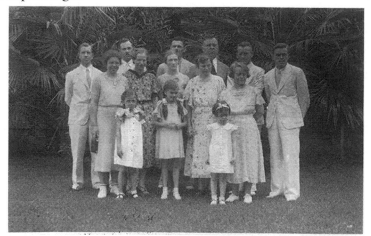

Shasi was the site of a reduced missionary conference in 1938 gathering all but one missionary. Bombing raids soon thereafter totally destroyed Zion chapel in Shasi, leaving the back room and the evangelist's family unharmed.

supporters. A German businessman and good friend of the mission, Frederick Titus, and his wife Eva, looked after the mission property and affairs as best they could throughout the war, and aided in restoring financial records after hostilities. The Kleins were repatriated in July, 1942, on the *Conte Verde* to Africa and the *Gripsholm*.

Hanyang's two congregations, Trinity and Yin Wu Chow, had jointly installed Sun Chiu Hai, one of the five 1937 seminary graduates, as their pastor on September 12. His classmate Wei T'ien-pei assisted the missionaries at Sun's ordination. A middle school in Hanyang for boys included some of the dispersed pre-seminary lads from Concordia. In the months ahead, Hanyang, the most industrial part of Wuhan, was to be heavily bombed.

In August, 1938, members of the Hankow churches evacuated to a piece of land adjacent to the French Concession. With money from one local family, and discretionary funds from the conference, a large building was hurriedly constructed and inhabited by about 300 bombed-out Chinese Lutherans. Pastor Sun Wen-en, from the damaged Grace Congregation in Hankow, took charge of the camp. When the French later barricaded their concession with coils of barbed wire, this building was also enclosed. Thus, a de facto Lutheran refugee camp was created, and left untouched by the occupying Japanese.

Northern mission fields, 150 miles south of Peking, were the first areas of the LCMS mission to be affected, and hardest, by the Japanese occupation. Hopeh province was cut off from communication by battlefields. This was where elderly Rev. Pi P'ei-ying had successfully founded two congregations at Hsi Ma Yin, and established several outstations. The Japanese commandeered Christian men and their draft animals, systematically disrupting the economy and demoralizing the populace. Evangelist Sun Chiu-hai, aiding Pastor Pi since 1934, was unable to continue his work because of chaotic and unsettled conditions, and went back to Hanyang. Pastor Pi and several Christians migrated as far south as they could. Contact with the Lu-

therans and Rev. Pi was made in March 1938, but funds sent for him from Hankow never reached the congregations. Pi's son, Philip, a seminarian in his vicar year, journeyed north to his homeland with his wife and child to locate his father, but there was no news for a year. Then a letter reached Wanhsien that Pi had been able to continue serving several of his far-flung congregations.

Several out-stations started by Pastor Pi continued after the war, but the stress of the Japanese occupation took its toll. Pi, the most effective of the mission's native pastors, served congregations via his bicycle until his death in 1948. Word reached Hankow that a seminarian, Liu Ch'iu T'sai, had started doing independent evangelism in his home region of Hopeh. Following the Communist takeover, however, all contact with the Hopeh Lutherans ceased, becoming the *lost tribes*. Remnant Lutherans re-appeared after the 1979 reforms and subsequent growth of a revitalized Chinese church.

Han River work, begun with refugees by Werlings at Hsi Ma K'ou in 1933, had been conducted by evangelist Liu Shih-chi at Han chuan after 1935. Evangelism soon diminished because of increasing incidents of banditry by rogue former soldiers separated from their Nationalist army units. They stole food and abused women as they wandered the countryside without leadership or pay. Nothing was heard from Han Chuan or Mien Yang counties during the Japanese occupation.

At Shasi, the Zimmermann family continued life and work at their compound near the Yangtze. For months, the city was bypassed as the next target of Japanese westward occupation. Zion and Eternal Life chapels were located in town, about two miles from the mission compound. Several out-stations had been started by Zimmermann and Alvin Diers, doing *wai-tang* speaking on market days. These were at Mitossu, Owchihkow, Shishow, and Kuantang. At Mi Chi T'ai, old Evangelist Wei worked with about 30 Christians. It was to these stations that the seminary students from Hankow, were assigned from September 1937 until the

Sixth-grader Dottie Zimmermann spent much of her time aboard the Gripsholm drawing life on the repatriation journey from Shanghai to New York via East Africa and Brazil.

following spring. The result was a successful cluster of ten Shasi out-stations, four of which continued throughout the war.

## 16th General Conference -Shasi

Unable to reach Kuling in occupied Kiangsi Province for the 1938 annual summer retreat, eight missionaries were able to assemble in Shasi for a reduced 16th General Conference, July 5-7. The Zimmermanns and Diers were the local hosts; Thode had come from Ichang; Olive Gruen, Gertrude Simon, and the Meyers arrived after an arduous overland journey from Enshih; Frillmann and Zschiegner represented the Wuhan operations, while Wenger stayed behind to keep a vigilant eye on the Hankow properties. There was no representation from Kweifu or Wanhsien, but several of the displaced students from the closed Hankow seminary attended.

The attendees conducted what business they could, prayed, sang, worshipped, and communed at Eternal Life Chapel. They were much in need of fellowship and renewal in the face of so many deteriorating situations, the shift to survival mode for their members, and difficulties with communication and finances. A major positive step was the decision to re-open the seminary upriver at Wanhsien, west of the Yangtze Gorges. The nine student evangelists were enthusiastic for classwork again after their time in Shasi's out-lying villages. And a group of boys with potential for middle school also lived in smaller (and safer) Wanhsien city.

Shasi seemed to be the most active and promising station, with three chapels and its four out-stations. After losing 80% of his congregation in Hankow, Pastor Wei T'ien-nien re-located to assist with the work in Shasi.

On January 10, 1939, Shasi was attacked from the air. Zion Chapel, re-built just four years earlier, was totally destroyed. A fire from an overturned brazier in the rubble was doused, and the two-day old child of evangelist Yin Chung-yuan was unharmed. The only recoverable salvage was the pulpit Bible, wrapped in a blue cloth and un-scratched. Stoically, Zimmermann had the detritus - bricks and kindling - cleared off, repairs made to the two slightly damaged school rooms in the rear, and comfort services and regular catechism sessions resumed. He wrote:

"It is the Lord who gave us the buildings and the property, and it is He who permitted the buildings to be destroyed. Nothing can happen without His knowledge and sufferance. We still praise the Lord."

Shasi did not fall to the Japanese until June 8, 1940. The Zimmermanns had freedom of movement within the city even after its fall to the Japanese. E.C.Z. established good relations with a Japanese officer named Suga, who was interested in Christianity, and later befriended the family. The Japanese also granted permission to rebuild the chapel. Evangelist Cheng Shang-wan continued to operate the Shasi outstation at Kuantang, Rev. Wei I-yun served at Mitossu, and Rev. Li Mu-ch'un served at Shihshow.

After Pearl Harbor attack, the Zimmermanns were placed under house arrest until, like the Kleins, they were moved to the Columbia Country Club grounds in Shanghai to await repatriation back to America. Work at the outstations would cease later in 1942. The second chapel was also destroyed later in an American bombing raid ferreting out Japanese officers who had holed-up in the building. Today, a third incarnation of the church stands on a large plot in another neighborhood.

At Ichang, the Thode family continued to live in the mission house and maintain a presence, and visit congregations weekly. The airfield adjacent to the Lutheran mission compound was targeted as the Japanese moved west. Refugees arrived weekly in the tens of thousands. The 120 – mile dirt road from Shasi was traversed daily by an estimated 20,000 coolies carrying salt westward, and Hunan cotton eastward on their shoulder poles. Lutherans from the surrounding area were housed in both Ichang chapel buildings. Many were desperate for money to travel somewhere ...anywhere. On December 13, 1939, an estimated 200 bombs

Civilian POWs boarded the Gripsholm in Brazil, arriving in New York City August 25, 1942. LCMS missionaries from Ichang, Hankow, Shasi, and Hong Kong had been interred since January.

After a service of thanksgiving, repatriated missionary families posed on August 25, 1942, in New York City, before completing their homeward journeys. On the left was Mission Board Director Frederick Brand; Elmer and Frieda Thode (seated children Eunice and Daniel); Eunice, mother Laura, and Doris Ziegler (seated children Ted, Laura Lou, Ruth, and Larry); Rev. A. R. Kleps from the Mission Board; Herman and Ruth Klein with daughters Dorothy and Ruth (seated children James, Raymond, and Lois); Elmer Zimmermann holding son Benjamin Christian, Betty, and wife Anna (seated children Katherine and Dorothy); Ella and Lorenz Buuck with son Robert (seated children Elaine and Leonard).

were dropped. Although several fell near St. Paul's, the chapel and two rented properties sustained surprisingly minor damage. Thode and his wife committed to stay put, but for the safety of their two children chose to sleep at the home of consular friends within the city. Several bombings of the airfield had sent shrapnel flying into their house, some being embedded in their furniture.

Thode arranged a place of refuge for his members in mountainous country about 40 miles away, the home area of two of the Ichang school teachers. On March 10, 1940, a series of four bombing raids laid waste to much of the city. Although many members and students fled to the countryside and Thode had no teachers for his two schools, he continued evening classes and Sunday worship at both Grace and St. Paul's Chapels. His family resolved to stay together in Ichang, which eventually fell to the Japanese June 12, 1940. A more strict house arrest detained the missionaries, until transferred to Shanghai for their repatriation with the Kleins and Zimmermanns aboard the *Conte Verde*. Evangelist Ts'ai Pao-lo was then in charge of the Ichang station, amid difficult conditions and harsh Japanese treatment.

## Repatriation August 1942

In April of 1942, rumors filtered throughout Hong Kong that there might be a prisoner exchange and repatriation. The war had begun to go badly for Japan by June, with a damaged fleet from the Battle of Midway. Japan withdrew from Burma, and reconsidered her plans to invade India and Australia.

The Stanley Camp Americans were in limbo. A repatriation exchange was arranged by the U.S. State Department and Japanese government through the auspices of the International Red Cross. Missionaries had hoped they could be released back into Free China but that was not an option. Payment of fare needed to be provided or guaranteed and there was much diplomatic and economic sorting-out to be done. At long last, the inmates were informed that they would be sent home. The British organized a farewell dance for the Americans on June 19. Many Americans, in turn, gave much of what they had to the British and Dutch, who held out hopes of their own repatriation. They were bound to stay in Stanley for three additional years. On just three occasions did relief parcels came through the International Red Cross (IRC) for those 2000 remaining civilian internees.

The *Asama Maru* sailed into Hong Kong a week late, already carrying repatriates from Korea and Japan. Alongside the missionary families on board the ship were several hundred other Americans. Walter Arndt, son of mission founder Edward Arndt, was also aboard. The missionaries were assigned a spot in steerage, but benefited from good and generous meals of western food.

While the children had the run of the ship and enjoyed their outing, Rev. Buuck spent several days on a project. He had retrieved the China mission's financial records in Hong Kong, but fearing confiscation by the Japanese, had torn them into small bits and hid them in the lining of several jackets. With time on his hands, he painstakingly reassembled the small bits, and upon arrival in the States was able to produce the records nearly intact, so that $12,000 USD (equivalent to the annual salary of eight missionaries) was eventually reclaimed from various banks for the mission board.

The Japanese ship sailed south toward Singapore. The rescue ship from Shanghai, the *SS Conte Verde* sailed into view July 11, carrying repatriates from North China. The Buucks and Zieglers held out hope that the ship might be bearing their fellow missionaries from Shasi, Ichang and Hankow. The two ships sailed westward in tandem through the Sunda Straits and Indian Ocean for twelve nights. Both vessels were brightly lit from bow-to-stern, marking them as neutral.

On July 23, both ships anchored at a long pier in Lorenco Marques, Portuguese East Africa. For the first time in six months, an American flag was seen, fluttering from a docked steamer. It was a Swedish passenger liner, once a queen-of-the-line luxury ship, converted into a rescue ship and troop carrier.

Japanese bombing had destroyed
the chapel at Shasi in 1939. At
Shihnan, a barge of bombing raids
pulverized the city chapel, once
filled with worshipping families. The
Hu house was damaged and splintered lumber salvaged, but most of
the city lay in ruin

*MS Gripsholm* was loaded with an exact number of Japanese equal to the American repatriates. The birth of a baby on the *Asama* confused the count, creating a two-day bureaucratic tither. On the day of exchange, a row of rail box cars separated the two groups as they filed along the dock from rescue boat to homeward bound ship. The freed prisoners only saw each other's feet, never having eye contact.

Once on the gangplank, the Buucks and Zieglers spotted all three Missouri Synod families who had arrived on the *Conte Verde* from Shanghai. It was an emotional reunion with the Kleins, Zimmermanns, and Thodes - six adults and eleven more children to share the westward voyage past Cape Town; stopping at Rio de Janiero; and sailing past the Statue of Liberty on August 26, 1942. Three months later, another repatriation ship the *Lisbon Maru*, loaded with British military POWS, was torpedoed in the south Pacific with the loss of 800 men. Thus ends the first installment of LCMS history with Hong Kong. But the best was yet to come (chapters 10-14).

Meanwhile, missionaries at Enshih and Wanhsien would spend the war years at their stations beyond enemy penetration.

## Wartime in Free China

At **Enshih** in Free China, Herb Meyer could listen to fifteen minutes of world news each day. Powered by a gas generator, or from a windmill at the mission, his Telefunken receiver picked up signals from KZRM in Manila and XMHA (*The Call of the Orient*) from Shanghai, telling of Japanese movements, conquests and defeats. Limited clipper mail brought overseas letters as far as Ichang. The letters were then transported by junk and bus to Enshih. A gravel road from Patung to Enshih was graded in 1936 shortening the seven-day hike to just one dusty day. Hankow could thus be reached within a week.

Meyer assumed the same *can do* attitude in Enshih that Herman Klein and Wilbert Werling had taken during the downriver flood disasters of 1931 and 1935. At the Hu house, near the eastern city gate, the school, the or-

phanage, and dispensary continued operations under the leadership of Gertrude Simon. Pastor Chen served the city chapel and congregation. Two miles across the river and up the hill at Yang Wan were the two stone missionary residences, and four-bed hospital. Money was tight, pressure was constant, and medications in short supply. Japanese planes made westward bombing runs from Ichang toward Chungking, the newly established capital of Free China. An airfield had been carved out at Enshih, which facilitated allied defenses. The city teemed with transients fleeing embattled areas to the east. It was often the target of air raids, and the old walled city was essentially destroyed after two years of salvos.

Bypassing the peacetime protocol of obtaining permission from the Board for nearly any decision, Meyer made several important choices, for which he would later be censured. He condoned the establishment and growth of a midwifery school first proposed by Marie Gebhardt and Gertrude Simon years earlier. When Dr. Chuan, a medical doctor (and refugee) came to Enshih, Bernice Meyer and nursing student Ching An sought her help with the pitiful and unsanitary birthing situation for local and refugee mothers. Filth was accepted as common in childbirth. Several unhealthy superstitions and folk medicine complicated survival. Rusty knives were used to cut umbilical cords, and mud was frequently packed over the cord to staunch the bleeding.

The school set out to train local women in western techniques and sterilization practices. The three women started with 23 students. A small upper room at the Hu house became a four-bed maternity hospital. Months later, when a letter from the St. Louis board withheld permission and financial support, it was too late to stop the momentum. When Dr. Chuan died suddenly, Meyer and Simon committed to continuing the school and hospital operations.

On July 3, 1938, a refugee medical doctor arrived in Enshih to run the government's military hospital. Dr. Y. C. Ch'en, a Christian, had spent the previous three months escaping with his wife and five children from his former

Keeping the hospital and orphanage running during wartime meant special efforts and innovations while maintaining and growing both facilities. Supplies, and new staff, were brought in by truck from Kunming

Max Zschiegner and his family shortly before his untimely death at Wanhsien. He had served the mission for 20 years

home and successful practice in Hangchow, near Shanghai. Finding the LCMS Christians in Enshih, he soon became involved with the mission, and was persuaded to teach two classes per week at the midwifery school. His life story merits a separate book.

The Ch'en family was offered living space at Yang Wan and the midwifery school moved there. Simon, Meyer, and Ch'en's wife, all trained midwives, taught courses. Three classes of student midwifes were graduated. The doctor helped with difficult deliveries, assisted by a refugee nurse, Ms. Hu, and one of the midwives.

After the near total destruction of the city on July 7, 1939, mission operations were moved out of the Hu house, relocating the dispensary, maternity hospital and midwifery school, and orphanage up into the hills at Yang Wan. Meyer wrote:

"Enshih as a city is no more . . . the heart of the city has been laid waste the Lord has been with us hitherto, protected us, and we are confident He will do so in the future. Sufficient unto the day is the evil thereof."

Meyer led salvage efforts to reclaim lumber from the destroyed city chapel. His plans to rebuild a chapel at Yang Wan went up in smoke as the wood was chopped up for much-needed cooking fuel. Rev. Ch'en Huai-jen lost his worship space.

## Max Zschiegner (1899-1940)

In a complicated effort to bring medical supplies to Enshih, and seminary materials to Wanhsien, a plan was developed in late 1939. Normal transportation on the Yangtze had been stopped by the Japanese blockade. Returning from sick leave in the U.S., Max Zschiegner and new missionaries Kurt Voss and Paul Martens sailed to Hong Kong aboard a camouflaged ship. Voss and Zschiegner then packed all the medications and books possible, and sailed to Vietnam. By taking the new railroad from Haiphong and Hanoi to Kunming, they avoided occupied China. The men purchased a flatbed truck in Kunming, loaded it with even more

medical supplies, and drove five days on part of the Burma Road to Chungking. Gilbert and Elsie Wenger flew in from Hong Kong, joining them in the wartime capital for Christmas.

Wenger and Martens drove the truck of medical supplies to Enshih in three days. Meanwhile, the library books and seminary equipment destined for Wanhsien were loaded aboard the decrepit coal-burning *Mien Yu*. Fumes from improper combustion nearly asphyxiated Missionary Zschiegner, and a half hour after reaching Wanhsien, he died of an apparent heart attack on the boat at the pier. The nineteen-year veteran and recognized leader of the China mission died at age 42, on January 23, 1940. His fellow missionaries Mueller, Riedel, and Voss, conducted funeral services the next day. Mourning students sang Beautiful Savior. Laid to rest beneath a memorial stone in the Wanhsien mission compound, his family has never been able to locate the gravesite.

Increasing numbers of wounded and ailing soldiers came to the twelve-bed hospital at Yang Wan. His military hospital closed in 1940, leaving Dr. Ch'en available for fulltime work with the Lutherans. Meyer and the medical team erected a small hospital that same year, with an operating room in memory of his first wife, Cornelia. The Meyers, Gertrude Simon, and Nurse Hu all coincidentally took furloughs within a year. This left experienced missionary Gilbert Wenger and his wife Elsie, a nurse, in charge of the operation that soon occupied four buildings with twenty-five beds for adults, ten spaces for infants, and housing for several nurses.

Disagreement over support and finances of the midwife school and hospital operation plagued its progress. Meyer had not obtained initial approval from the St. Louis Board, which now fretted over his ability to run the Enshih compound, while serving outstations at Hanfeng and Laifeng.

Meyer reported he worked on hospital business only after hours and never on mission time. Medical supplies were always in short supply. Meyer worked with the International Red Cross, and any other resource, to obtain basic drugs. The most sophisticated piece of

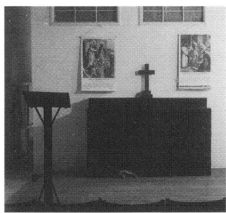

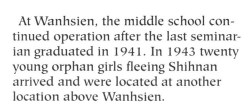

At Wanhsien, the middle school continued operation after the last seminarian graduated in 1941. In 1943 twenty young orphan girls fleeing Shihnan arrived and were located at another location above Wanhsien.

equipment was Bernice's home pressure cooker, used to sterilize implements. One hypodermic needle was available, sharpened with an emery board until after three years it was only one-half inch long. Meyer's letters to family, congregations, and Synod full of news and pleading for support were not published in their entirety, and donations were often delayed or misdirected. Yet the hospital was self-supporting, with fees paying over 90% of operational costs.

Back in Missouri, the Board of Foreign Missions installed an executive secretary on April 14, 1940, to aid aging Director Brand. Rev. O. H. Schmidt departed just four days later on a four-month tour to visit all stations in Free China. Schmidt's compassion and energy during the coming war years would hasten the 1942 evacuation and facilitate repatriation of the other 25 stranded missionaries.

**Wanhsien**, perched at a sharp bend on the Yangtze 80 miles above Kweifu, developed into a major mission station during the war. Isolated in Szechwan province, on the river route to the capital at Chungking, it was a major port for produce and valuable tung oil from the agriculturally productive Red Basin. The mission, first opened in 1923, operated at a chapel in the city and at its walled compound in the hills beyond town.

About an hour uphill trek from the ancient walled city, Concordia Seminary re-opened on the mission's six-acre plot on September 19, 1938. The 32 students in the theology and prep schools included ten evangelists, the seminarians who had spent a year at Shasi. Five men came from Rev. Pi's Hopeh churches, including Pi's son. Missionaries Riedel, Ziegler, and Zschiegner taught classes, while their families remained in the relative safety of Hong Kong or America. Pastor Wei Tien Mien and another Chinese teacher completed the staff. One of the student vicars taught organ-playing. About 90 bombs dropped on the city on February 4, 1939, killing hundreds of civilians, but no members of the Lutheran community were harmed. Seminary students volunteered at various hospitals, mostly letter-writing and witnessing to the wounded.

While on leave in the U.S., seminary president Max Zschiegner had made great efforts to assemble a new library and to bring additional supplies to the seminary. His untimely death was a huge setback. At the time, he was the longest-serving missionary, embodying a stability and continuity needed by the fragile mission enterprises in Free China.

The seminary was now run by Ziegler and the greater mission was led by Herbert Meyer from Enshih. Twenty-eight students remained at the school that year. Chang Tung-chin graduated in 1946 and served until the 1990s despite persecution and the Cultural Revolution.

Missionaries Reidel, Mueller, and Ziegler became aware of a great need for a middle school to serve the many older children roaming the Wanhsien streets. Pooling their resources, Concordia (*Hsieh tong*) Middle School opened in Wanhsien in 1940. Mr. Wong Hin Ju was called from Enshih to be principal. In no time, students from surrounding areas enrolled.

They returned to Enshih after the war. The mission school at Wanhsien enrolled 180 pupils. Hundreds of applicants had to be turned down. Olive Gruen ran the girls' school and managed the Sunday school.

Missionary Paul Martens sent occasional messages to the U.S. via a radio service offered over Chungking station XCOY. Every Sunday, broadcasts were picked up by the Columbia Broadcasting System (CBS) in the US; messages were put onto postcards and mailed to their destinations.

## One Cup of Water

In 1943, Gertrude Simon arrived with twenty-one young orphan girls after an eleven day trek from Enshih; they were housed for two years in a country house at a place called I Wan Shui, near Wan Shien. The orphanage at Enshih first opened in 1921, when the city was still called Shihnan. Refugees and orphans from the internecine battles between the north and south were found among ruins, in the countryside, abandoned on doorsteps, or wandering aimless and starving.

Shihnan, under leadership of
Herbert and Bernice Meyer,
boasted a major medical operation, with clinic, hospital, and
nurses school under conditions
of isolation, lack of funding, and
few medical supplies.

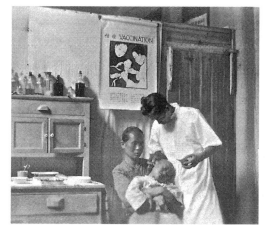

Originally set up at the Hu House, after the *troubles* it bcame apparent the city was not a place for the orphanage, and the children were moved into rooms in the two stone missionary houses out at Yang Wan. After several weeks, a better location for housing and schooling was found at Chi Shue Tong (place where water comes out of a cave). Orphan boys learned to grow and harvest rice, raise chickens, and weave straw into shoes. One pair of baggy pants and a shirt made of homespun blue cotton was their annual clothing allotment. A group of about six blind boys had their own blind teacher, Wu Bao-lo. Girls were in a separate section. They had nicer uniforms, and were taught to read and write, to sing, to memorize Bible passages, and to train as potential Bible women.

In the summer of 1943, Japanese forces advanced westward from Ichang and Tung Ting Lake towards Enshih. It was decided that the orphanage must be moved to a safer location, -over 100 miles west at Wanhsien. The Japanese forces were notorious in their foul treatment of women and children. Gertrude Simon directed the evacuation plans for the twenty-one youngest girls. Unique two-pole sedans were built supporting two crib-like enclosures each, designed for two children per crib. These were to be carried by the coolies or porters. Food and bedding for the ten-day trek was carried on shoulder poles. The entourage snaked its way across five mountain ranges and valleys, stopping at waysides and in villages. The girls, all under five years of age, arrived in good condition, without a mishap. A plan to bring the older children later did not materialize.

At I Wan Shui, the female orphans were housed in an old farmstead and courtyard house provided by the supportive local magistrate. The name means "one cup of water," referring to Christ's encouragement "to do this unto the least of these." All orphaned girls returned to Enshih when the war ended. This event parallels a similar odyssey by well-known missionary Gladys Aylward, who later befriended LCMS missionaries in Hong Kong. That event is documented in the book, *The Small Woman* by Alan Burgess, and in the 1958 film, *Inn of the Sixth Happiness*.

**Kweifu** Lutherans, although without a resident foreign missionary since 1927, and deep inside territory hostile to Christianity, maintained a reading room in the city. Meyer and other missionaries supervised and visited as they could. Aged teacher Tai Chin-tang erected two primitive houses and a chapel-school at the cost of about five U.S. dollars. In the school were 33 children, and worship was conducted by Pastor Tai Ch'iu-tao, son of the teacher. After visiting Kweifu, Executive Secretary Schmidt pushed to expand the work there, and to rent a building for worship. After a few months, an old building was purchased and a second teacher, Mr. Yin Tzu-liang, conducted a school in that space.

**Chungking** was China's wartime capital, isolated in Szechwan 1400 miles west of Shanghai. Paul Martens in Wanhsien encouraged Li Mu-ch'un to begin work in the teaming and chaotic city. Luther Li tried unsuccessfully to find venues for worship, and although many Americans and refugee Chinese passed thru the city, there was little permanence. Cut off from occupied China, access required weeks on the Burma Road or scarce air passage with war cargo. It required three months' travel via India for O. H. Schmidt and two new missionaries, Herb Hinz and Ralph Egolf, to arrive from New York in 1943. Opportunities to reach civilian and military souls improved somewhat after *V-J Day* until the Communist liberation of 1949.

**Kunming**, in southern Yunnan province, was the second hub in occupied China. Rev. Paul Frillmann, after furlough from the BFM in 1941, was recruited by the AVG as chaplain liaison to the Flying Tigers, based in Kunming. Several mission personnel also passed through Kunming enroute to Chungking, Wanhsien, or Enshih. Chiang Kai-shek and the 14th Army Air Force of about 20,000 troops under General Claire Chennault headquartered at Kunming, a jumping-off point for air attacks on Changsha and Wuhan.

In an effort to protect their 20 youngest girls, Olive and Gertrude organized a ten -day caravan to take the orphans overland to Wanhsien. Wartime produced a constant source of the homeless and injured.

Gateway entrances guarded both mission compounds - at Shihnan (Enshih) in Hupeh and at Wanhsien in Szechwan.

The LCMS began chaplaincy work in Kunming in 1944. Paul Martens transferred there from Wanhsien and opened the Lutheran Service Center late that year. Another chaplain, Reuben Langhanz from Minnesota, had already made contacts there with a German Christian group, the Sisters of the Vandesburger Mission. The nuns offered the use of the upper floors of their building, which also contained residences and Sister Kunigunde's dental office. Martens set up a chapel, conducting regular English worship services open to all. A recreation room and some small parlors were used for group discussions. Many servicemen also became involved in the Vandesburger activities in several local orphanages, the school for the blind, and clinics.

With the Allied victory in 1945, troops moved out, the center closed. Yunnan work was not re-started, and was inaccessible after 1949. A half century later, Kunming would again become a significant focus of synodical outreach.

## Other Perspectives: 1937-1945

The Board of Foreign Missions of the LCMS found itself in an unenviable position during wartime, jockeying responsibilities far beyond the experience or insight of eleven stateside pastors.

Director of the board was the dedicated, but aging, Frederick Brand, part-time administrator since 1895, fulltime after 1920. He knew the China field well, having made long personal visits in 1921, 1926, and 1935. Dr. Brand had participated at several Kuling conferences. Brand could be compassionate and personal, adventurous and enthusiastic, but more often autocratic, paternalistic, patronizing, and headstrong - a micro-manager and fiduciary judge. He could be generous in some situations, or a hard-line interpreter of procedures. Most of his decisions were conservative, often cutting corners and creatively re-allocating funds to finance what he saw as the most expedient needs. He did not treat all personnel with equanimity, and several missionaries were not well supported upon return.

In April of 1938, Madam Chiang Kai-Shek announced at a meeting of many missionaries in Hankow that the Generalissimo had rescinded the government prohibitions on the teaching of religion in schools. This lifted the ban imposed by the Nationalist government in 1928, but because of wartime chaos, the Lutherans were able to open only one school, and the gesture was inconsequentil. Too little, too late.

Author Pearl Buck wrote stories and novels about the lives of common Chinese, rural and cosmopolitan, as their traditions encountered western thought and practices. Her first novel, *The Good Earth* about the life of a rural Chinese family, won her the Pulitzer Prize in 1932. Readers began to grasp the debacle between opposing forces in China, as well as in overseas Chinese communities. Herself the daughter of Presbyterian missionary Absalom Sydenstricker (*Fighting Angel*), she spoke sympathetically about the Chinese people. She depicted the plight and life style of isolated up-country mission families (*The Exile*). Her *Young Revolutionist* was read and highly recommended by several LCMS missionaries. In a well-publicized speech and article, she mused that mission boards had not always sent their best men and women. Needless to say, this ruffled feathers in many churches, and contributed to ill feelings towards Buck, questioning her Christianity and, by extension, her patriotism.

Many correspondents filed reports from Free China reporting on the refugee situation and the hoards of Chinese fleeing west. Chungking became the capital of Free China and headquarters of American and international forces defending thenarrow Burma Road, last backdoor link with western powers. Large overloaded trucks kept up a constant parade, powered with fumes from charcoal converters when petrol ran out. Nearly all supplies for Free China were airlifted over the hump from India. The poverty and displacement seemed overwhelming. Food was in short supply. The rice basket of Szechuan's Red Basin was fallow. Many Chinese resorted to eating *Kuan Yin* rice, a subsis-

## Responsibilities of a wartime mission board

- Overall responsibility for the welfare of families;
- Oversight of theological and social ministries;
- Supplying overseas staff with regular salaries and financial support;
- Approving unbudgeted expenditures for transportation and supplies;
- Support of missionary children—their schooling, health, and spirits;
- Correspondence with six mission stations using sea mail; clipper mail; radiograms or cables;
- Answering the concerns of stateside relatives;
- Producing or editing articles and reports for church and secular press;
- Giving personal council and advice in collegial and administrative ways.

At Wanhsien the orphanage continued and workers prepared to construct additions to the thriving middle school

tence gruel of yellow clay and poor rice. Chinese civilization seemed to be at its ebb.

Back home in the States, confusion and consternation were rife among families, supporting congregations, Walther League and *Lutheran Hour* contributors, the Lutheran Women's Missionary League (LWML) newly formed in 1942, and the general public. The debate over what to do about China missions included staunch supporters of the mission at any cost to skeptics on the importation of western commerce and religion onto a classic civilization of ancient wisdom and independence.

With the atomic bombing of Hiroshima and Nagasaki, and the surrender ceremonies in Tokyo Bay on September 2, 1945 (V-J Day), China and the world looked to a new, hopeful, and uncharted future.

Winnowing rice at Shihnan

## Significant Sources

| | |
|---|---|
| Brauer, Janice, ed, | One Cup of Water |
| Buuch, Lorenz & Ella | I am with you always |
| Darnell, Laura Ziegler | Send Me, Send Me |
| Frillmann, Paul | China, The Remembered Life |
| Gilkey, Langdon | Shantung Compound |
| Gittins, Jean Stanley: | Behind Barbed Wire |
| Harrop, Phyllis | Hong Kong Incident |
| Meyer, Herbert & Bernice | Wartime Diaries (unpublished) |
| Proulx, Benjamin | Underground from Hong Kong |
| Wright-Nooth, George | Prisoner of the Turnip |

**Chapter Nine**
**Arrivals**

| | | Origin | School |
|---|---|---|---|
| 1946 - March 28 | Dep from New York via Panama Canal: | | |
| Kretzmann | Herbert | Hillsdale, MN | CSL |
| | | | |
| - Oct 16 | Arr via *SS Marine Lynx* from San Francisco: | | |
| Bringewatt | Ralph & Martha | Tobias, NB | CSL |
| Buntrock | Orville & Cecilia | Columbia, SD | CSL |
| Hafner | Victor & Adeline | Marten Co, MN | CSL |
| Kreyling | Paul | Fords, NJ | CSL |
| Suelflow | Roy & Wanda | Germantown, WI | CSL |
| Wilenius | John | Ironwood, MI | CSF |
| | | | |
| 1947 - Nov 20 | Arr via *SS Maiden Creek* from Brooklyn: | | |
| Hass | LeRoy & Ruth | Manning, IA | CSF |
| Schalow | Frederick & Sarah | New York City, NY | CSF |
| | | | |
| 1948 - Mar 30 | Arr via *SS General Meiggs* from San Francisco: | | |
| Martens | Paul & Dorothy (returning) | | |
| Meier | Dorothy (secretary) | Loraine, TX | |
| | | | |
| - Sept 22 | Arr via *SS General Gordon* from San Francisco | | |
| Behling | Lorraine (teacher) | Boyne City, MI | CTC-RF |
| Lenschow | Norma (nurse) | Burlington, IL | LH-SL |
| Meyer | Richard ("Pedo") & Lois | Cullman, AL | CSL |
| Mueller | Adelheid (nurse) | Worden, IL | Colq. |

**Marriages**

| | | |
|---|---|---|
| 1947 Martens | Paul | to Dorothy Sohn (on furlough) |
| | | |
| 1948 Kretzmann | Herb | to Dorothy Meier (in Hankow) |
| Kreyling | Paul | to Carol Suttmeier (in Hankow) |
| Wilenius | John | to Tellervo Korpivaara (on furlough) |

**Departures**

| | | |
|---|---|---|
| 1948 Gruen | Olive | on furlough (to Taiwan 1951-60) |
| 1948 Hinz | Herb | on furlough (to Hong Kong 1950-d.1981 |

**Evacuated**

| | | |
|---|---|---|
| 1948 Hass | LeRoy & Ruth+David | to Japan (until 1965) |
| | | |
| 1949 Behling | Lorraine | to Hong Kong (until 1959) |
| Boss | Martha | to Hong Kong (until 1973) |
| Bringewatt | Ralph & Martha+Margaret,Marlene | to Japan (1954); Taiwan (1969) |
| Egolf | Ralph & Barbara | to Japan (until 1955) |
| Holtje | Wilbert | to Hong Kong (until 1962) |
| Kretzmann | Herb & Dorothy | to Philippines (until 1972) |
| Kreyling | Paul & Carol+Peter | to Japan (until 1971) |
| `Lenschow | Norma | to Japan (1954); New Guinea (1956) |
| Meyer | Richard & Lois | to Japan (until 1971) |
| Mueller | Adelheid | to Japan (until 1954) |
| Simon | Gertrude | to Hong Kong (until 1966) |
| Suelflow | Roy & Wanda | to Japan (1952); Taiwan (1960) |
| Willenius | John & Tellervo | to Philippines (1953); Taiwan (1956) |
| | | |
| 1951 Schalow | Frederick | to Hong Kong (Taiwan 1953-55) |
| | | |
| 1952 Thode | Elmer & Frieda | to Hong Kong (until d.1965) |

*Beloved, I urge you as sojourners and exiles to keep your conduct among the Gentiles honorable, so that when they speak against you as evildoers, they may see your good deeds and glorify God on the day of visitation.*                                   Peter 2:11,12  (ESV)

## Chapter Nine

# The Brief Return  1945 –1949

Missionary Kurt Voss was the first American civilian to enter Hankow in 1945, twelve days after the September 2 formality of Japanese surrender aboard the USS Missouri in Tokyo Bay.

The extent of the atomic devastation of Hiroshima and Nagasaki was still unknown. Reports of imminent peace prompted Voss and Pastor Wei T'ien-nien to investigate the reportedly-liberated downriver operations at Ichang, Shasi, and Hankow. On September 12, through connections with two Lutherans in the American military, they were permitted space aboard the steamer *Hua Yuan*. Heading east from Wanhsien, they briefly visited Pastor Tai Ch'iu-tao at Kweifu, convinced Pastor Wei I-Yun at Patung to join them, changed steamers at Ichang, and arrived at Shasi on September 13. In his brief two hours there, Voss contacted Evangelist Wei Chang-yung who had carried on at the chapel and school throughout the war. By late that afternoon, the *Mingshi* was steaming alone in wide shallow waters. The river pilot navigated using a mine chart, but the customs buoys had been removed. Passing 70,000 surrendered Japanese troops and several bands of red soldiers encamped along the shore, they dropped anchor at Hankow the next afternoon, September 14, coincidently the same day that the Chinese army re-occupied the Wuhan cities.

Their afternoon arrival at the seminary compound was fortuitous. With the departure of the Japanese occupants of the seminary buildings, civilians were about to begin loot ing the buildings for anything salvageable. Voss and Pastor Wei were able to dissuade the crowd. Within days Voss inveigled a number of the arriving American forces afflicted with dengue fever to encamp in the seminary buildings as a temporary hospital, thus providing vigilance and protection from would-be looters.

Hankow itself had been severely damaged by American bombings the previous December 18. The former German and Japanese concessions were destroyed as was the older inner city where Arndt had established his first chapel at Wha Ching Kai. Thousands of stick bombs had incinerated the Russian Concession, St. Paul's Cathedral, and most other sturdy European buildings and *godowns* (warehouses). The seminary building and faculty houses were intact, although the student dormitory and kitchen buildings were gone. Pastor Wei took charge of restoring the buildings and grounds. Wei also immediately began seeking out former members of the various city congregations.

With clean-up begun and  reconnection with Chinese Lutherans in process, Voss was able to hitchhike aboard a C-47 aircraft, to inspect most other LCMS mission locations. This is what he discovered:

**Ichang**: Most of the city was destroyed, but the rented chapel was intact, complete with benches and altar. The mission compound and residence of the Thode family was in good condition, although all original furniture was gone. Mr. Ts'ai had kept both properties well maintained and used.

**Shasi**: The city itself was barely damaged, although Zion Chapel had been bombed

At the dock in San Francisco on Sept 29, 1946 were missionaries bound for China: Back row from left - LeRoy and Dorothy Buuck; Orville and Annettee Buntrock, Martha and Ralph Bringewatt; Gloria, Dorothy, and R.J. Mueller (returning); Roy and Wanda Suelflow.  Front row - F.H.Menzel of San Francisco; bachelors Paul Kreyling and John Wilenius.

The first LCMS mission group to sail for China after WW2 arrive aboard the Marine Lynx in 1947. It was the third return for "Mike" Mueller, his wife and daughter.

At the first opportunity, missionaries returned to Kuling to evaluate and restore the mission hous-es. Built of local stone, they had survived Japanese occupation.

at the onset of the Japanese occupation on January 10, 1939, and the missionary house had collapsed under bombing the following December. What had been the first major building of the Lutheran mission was debris, with no remnants of pulpit, altar, or the prized ornate reed organ. Evangelist Wei Chang Yung was conducting services regularly for about 20 members at Eternal Life and Trinity Chapels. The out-stations at Owchihkow and Mitossu, first started in 1934, were intact and requesting pastors. Seminary graduate Tai Ch'iu-tao, a former cobbler, was soon called to pastor the rural village congregations at Owchihkow and Shihsow.

**Enshih:** (Shihnan) - This ancient city on the Ch'ing Kiang River had been annihilated by Japanese air raids in 1941, its airstrip being the primary target. Most foreign-owned structures were rubble. Amazingly, the Hu House was protected from incineration by a thick wall. Lumber from the church building eventually was carried up to the Yang Wan mission compound, about two miles east up steep trails. Missionaries and staff there had often resorted to hillside bomb shelter tunnels, so were untouched by the bombing. Mi ssionaries Martens, Voss, Egolf, the Dohrmans, and the Wengers had continued work under frequent air raids. Gertrude Simon had continued the middle school. News of the orphanage, hospital, school, chapel, and residences was incomplete .

Local magistrates had allocated a cluster of buildings at Ch'u Hsui Tung, about a 45-minute walk from the city, for a refugee camp and temporary site for the girls' orphanage.

**Kweifu:** Pastor Tai Ch'iu-tao operated out of a bomb shelter within the city wall. The congregation had grown large enough to erect a small crude chapel next to the shelter. The pastor's father, Tai Chin-tang, taught 33 children at an out-station a few miles uphill from the city. No missionary had resided in Kweifu since 1927, but an isolated and stalwart Lutheran group had survived.

**Wanhsien:** Never occupied by the invading Japanese, the walled city on the upper Yangtze remained intact. Mission operations had continued in Free China from Wanhsien. Concordia Seminary had moved there from Hankow in 1938, and the last student was graduated in 1942. *Hsieh tong* Middle School, founded in 1940, was still operating with almost 600 students under the direction of Evangelist Liu and principal Wong Him Ju. Boarding students came from Szechwan, Hankow and Chungking.

The recruitment of qualified Christian teachers was very difficult. On furlough in 1945, Olive Gruen had tried to enlist teachers from Concordia Teachers College at River Forest, Illinois. Four students accepted the challenge and began learning Chinese language from former LCMS Missionary Louis Schwartzkopf, who had left China 20 years earlier. The only student to prepare seriously and actually come to China was Lorraine Behling, in 1948. She worked in Wanhsien with Olive Gruen for about a year, before they had to evacuate.

About 50 youngsters were resident in the orphanage. Twenty of those were the girl foundlings brought overland from Enshih in 1943. The hospital-clinic served patients and included a nursing-midwifery school. Missionaries who had stayed on during the war were Herb Hinz, Voss, and Olive Gruen. President Albert Ziegler had returned to the U.S. via the Burma Road to India, joining his repatriated family in Minnesota in 1944.

**North China:** Work at several Hopei stations started by Pastor Pi continued after the war, but the stress of the Japanese occupation would take its toll. Pi, the most effective of the mission's native pastors, served congregations until his death in 1948. Another evangelist in Hopeh, Sun Chiu-hai, was unable to continue his work because of chaotic and unsettled conditions leading to the Communist victory; he relocated to the south in Hanyang. Contact with the Hopeh Lutherans ceased.

**Chungking:** An upriver terminus for major shipping, this city on a sharp bend of the Yangtze had become the wartime capital of Free

Missionary Paul Frillmann had spent a term as missionary in Hankow, taking responsibility to oversee the Seminary compound during the years of Japanese occupation.  After furlough, he returned as part of the Flying Tigers, based in Chungking. P-40 aircraft with tiger-shark faces kept the Burma Road open while reinforcements camr from British India.

At isolated Kweifu, teacher Tai continued operating his rustic school about 2 miles beyond the city walls, while his son Tai Hh'iu-tao ministered to a small but faithful congregation.

China. The town grew into a major city during the Japanese hostilities, overcrowded with refugees from all parts of occupied China. The location was essential to the Flying Tigers (AVG) as the eventual terminus of the overland route via Burma and India. Their chaplain was former missionary Paul Frillmann, the only speaker of Chinese in the AVG. Another LCMS chaplain, independent of the mission, was placed with American forces at the capital during the war.

The remnant LCMS missionaries in Free China had assembled in Enshih August 2-7, 1943, for a conference. In spite of their wartime despondency, they determined to begin an operation in Chungking. Evangelist Tai Kuang-ming (son of the Kweifu teacher) was selected by the mission to begin work at Chungking. He attempted holding services in a hotel room, unsuccessfully. Tai worked for the national government after the war, later in Japan and Africa, and then came to America. He was eventually ordained into LCMS ministry in California. Thirty years later he visited post Cultural Revolution China sparking LCMS interest.

Rev. Li Mu-ch'un replaced Tai, establishing a presence in Chungking, but apparently making little headway with evangelism.

**Kuling**: Although not a part of the mission's system of chapels and schools, was as important to the missionaries as any other location. The mountain retreat had been occupied and overrun by Japanese troops and officers for eight years. Contents and furnishings of most foreign houses were long gone, but the stone villas were intact. The stone Walther League retreat houses were still usable, requiring minor repairs and major scrubbing.

**Kunming**: Paul Martens served until late 1945 as the service center pastor for military personnel in this Yunnan city so essential on the overland supply route to Chungking. He worked under the Armed Services Commission, while seeking mission opportunities in southwest China. Martens took furlough in September 1946, sailing home with his father, who had served as a post-war chaplain in Manila. Sixty years later, Kunming would again become a focus of LCMS efforts.

## Reactivation In Hankow

Albert Ziegler returned to Wanhsien in November of 1945. He was determined to reactivate the original Concordia Seminary at Hankow. With Voss, Mrs. Wei, Evangelist Pi and their families, a junk was hired to carry books, supplies, and furniture on the 20-day down-river return to the seminary compound in Hankow. Stopping at Shasi, Evangelist Yang Pei and family joined them.

Fierce winds delayed their journey. On Christmas Eve, they tied up to hold services, attracting a local crowd of about 300 with hymns played on Voss's accordion and Ziegler's violin. Pi, Yang, and Ziegler did the preaching. The junk tied up at Hankow on January 1, 1946. Infrastructure and staff for a restored seminary was being slowly reassembled.

Evangelist Yang organized Chinese worship services in a rude shelter on the seminary grounds. His addresses and instruction drew up to 60 listeners each night. Eager to rebuild, work was also started in a new section of Hankow by Evangelist Phillip Pi, who operated a school of about 25 pupils. Government limitations on primary schools had been lifted by the victors, so Christianity could be taught, and students could learn hymns. Across the Yangtze, Ziegler and Voss helped Evangelist Yin dedicate the Son of Man Chapel at Yin Wuchow by late 1946. Pastor Sun established a congregation across the Han River in Hanyang, where a new chapel was built with a loan from the mission.

Throughout the winter of 1945 - 46, Pastor Wei T'ien-nien reconnected with dispersed members of the Hankow chapels. With the former chapels and schools destroyed, Wei obtained permission from the local consul to begin conducting worship in the historic chapel in the International Cemetery. Founder Edward Arndt's large stone crypt still occupied a prominent place on the grounds. The graves of Cornelia Meyer, Norbert Nero, and young Dickie Theiss lay nearby. Rev. Wei became ill at Christmastime, passed away, and was laid alongside them.

Language school was held at Concordia Seminary, entered via the undamaged gatehouse and bridge. A bearded President Ziegler posed on the steps with the 1947 group. New arrivals from several American and european groups spent full days in group and individual instruction. taking relief in basketball skirmishes often including sailors from visiting ships

The first post-war General Conference of the Mission met from August 20-29, 1946, at the restored Concordia Seminary compound. Board of Missions Executive Secretary Otto H. Schmidt had arrived three days earlier having obtained passage on the *SS General Meigs*. Several Christians from the northern field attended, except Rev. Pi P'ei-ying. An executive committee consisted of two Americans and two Chinese members. Twenty-eight Chinese attended, and lay delegates took a prominent role. Eight laymen from as many parishes were taking steps to form an indigenous Chinese church. One conference highlight was the installation of the remaining Wanhsien seminarian, Chang Tung-chin, originally in the class of 1942. Acting seminary president Ziegler did the honors.

In Hong Kong, other Hsin I Wei Lutheran missions were working among the refugees and ruins of the British Crown Colony. They published the very informative English language China News Letter. The monthly 20-page publication featured articles about programs and individuals involved in restoring Christianity to Chinese-speaking Asia and provided Lutherans with current news of progress.

## In Saint Louis

Meanwhile, anticipating the end of hostilities, the LCMS Board of Foreign Missions had set a course for restoring the China mission. With the motto The World is Our Field, a dozen graduating seminarians in the classes of 1944 and 1945 were called to serve in the Asia-Pacific, waiting until the actual end of the war in September 1945. Civilian passage to China being scarce, men and their wives still had more than a year to wait.

On furlough in 1942, Herb Meyer had written several recommendations for more clarification in presenting salvation to the Chinese. Several missionaries in the field, especially Kurt Voss and Paul Martens, had also made positive suggestions the same year regarding changes in the mission's internal structure, oversight, and revised goals in helping establish a truly local Chinese church. The war tested the mettle of congregations and evangelists. It was realized that many congregations had functioned well, without daily involvement of missionaries.

Seminary graduates, with newly received overseas calls, attended Synod's first Missionary School, operated by the mission board and initially taught by veteran China missionary Adolph Koehler. Soon after his 1942 repatriation, E. C. Zimmermann replaced Koehler as head of the school. His anecdotal tales of China and Christianity infused the neophytes with basic language instruction, missionary practices, local St. Louis service opportunities, and a diverse reading list that included works by noted Christian China historian K. S. Latourette and philosopher Lin Yu Tang. The program improved cultural awareness, but could not provide an understanding of the changing Chinese world view. New concrete insights on specific methods to break down barriers between Christianity and Oriental theologies were few. More than 100 workers trained at the school before it was incorporated into the seminary program.

Recommendations from Martens, Meyer, and Voss were apparently unknown to the fledgling missionaries, only to surface years later in dusty files. Their constructive suggestions were not utilized until the next generation of mission workers.

## Reinforcements and Restoration

The largest team of new LCMS missionaries for China sailed from San Francisco aboard a converted troop carrier, the *Marine Lynx*, arriving in Shanghai October 16, 1946. Still configured for military use, men and women were assigned to separate dormitories, and assigned to separate hatches. The eight men and five women were on the first civilian sailing to China since the end of the war. The majority of fellow-passengers were also China-bound Protestant missionaries.

Within days of arrival, the new people were immersed in Mandarin study. A full-time language school was conducted on the seminary grounds, under the auspices of Hua Chung (Central Christian) College across the Yangtze,

Re-occupying mission properties included raising the flag daily, gathering to honor the memory of fallen Americans on Memorial Day, and even pasturing two Russian cows in an unsuccessful attempt to be self-sufficient in milk.

in Wuchang. Several other new arrivals from other churches were part of the class. Frequently, these fresh young linguists would invite visiting American sailors to join them in volleyball contests, baseball games, and holiday feasts.

Life at the Concordia compound assumed a collegial atmosphere. Repair work and restoration of the main seminary buildings was completed by local Chinese workers, with some less-than-code electrical wiring at the hands of Paul Kreyling. "Prez" Ziegler took to raising a few goats in addition to recruiting and educating students. A Russian occupation group sold the seminary two dairy cows - promptly named Pravda and Izvestia. A dilapidated Japanese staff car, smaller than a Volkswagen, provided basic transportation, but had to be push-started. In January 1947, new recruits Vic and Adeline Hafner arrived, bringing with them the mission's first refrigerator.

With freshman confidence, the energized missionaries began work in the community. These were the first class of LCMS graduates to put into practice knowledge gained at the St. Louis Seminary Mission School. Worship services and most mission activities were conducted at the old German church in Hankow, near the six remaining Chinese chapels. The seminary had no prep students, and it would have taken some years before enough local Christian men could have been recruited to form a class, yet a two-year program for evangelists was begun by Ziegler, with teaching help from the other veterans.

There seems to have been less emphasis about re-opening former out-stations. Scrambling to make sense of post-war China and the developing civil war, new mission staffers were still in the basic language stage, while trying to support meaningful projects to advance the gospel. Returning veterans attempted to restore what they could of the programs and locations they had in place before the war. The seminary compound became a de facto rest and relaxation post for several upriver Chinese pastors and evangelists, war-weary and lacking back pay. Remuneration for up to four years of service caused some stress as mission funds were allocated. Most Chinese staff did not return to their former stations, and promising pre-war work at Lichuan, Laifeng, Patung, and other outstations was not restored.

## Wuchang

The large cultural and educational city across the Yangtze became a focus of new work. The elegant Hupei capital city was home to six universities and thirty middle schools. The hope of a better China lay with its promising students. Voss and Ziegler, with several Chinese evangelists, dedicated a rented chapel on Christmas Day 1946. Evangelist Yin Chung-yuan was placed in charge of the new small congregation at Son of Man Chapel.

Roy Suelflow, commuting via sampan and bicycle, began an English Bible class for secondary and university students in spring 1947. The post-war government had set a requirement that all students study English, so when English Bible classes were offered, interest grew rapidly. Held twice each week, attendance grew to standing-room-only, well over 100 students. Missionaries Orville Buntrock and Herb Kretzmann continued the classes at the chapel during the summer. Students asked meaningful questions about Christianity as well as English grammar. A Chinese language catechism class grew from that start.

Stateside interest in the Chinese had mushroomed after the Nationalist victory. Local WL societies held China Nights to increase awareness and raise funds.

In 1947, Paul Kreyling was assigned leadership of a new project in Wuchang. The Walther League had donated $5,000 for a Chinese youth center in the Wuhan area. Envisioned as an all-Christian facility in co-operation with other Protestant churches, the center was to have social rooms, a library, chapel, and residences. The mission found a promising location in the university neighborhood of Wuchang. Kreyling signed for the traditional house with open rafters on good property. As in most empty properties, rats had taken up quarters and much cleanup was needed. Ralph

Lutheran Hour operations were moved from Hankow to Shanghai, initially supervised by Mueller, who operated the Lutheran Hour office from a house which tripled as office, worship space, and residence .Among many visitore were LCMS chaplain Ernie Wolfram (in cap). Paul Kreyling directed operations from a small office with a staff who answered mail generated by the broadcasts originating in Chungking. A small space was also rented in a large modern building in the International Concession.

Egolf was scheduled to reside there, and a student steering committee began to form. The Kreylings and the other foreigners would end up evacuating from all of Wuhan before the Wuchang student center could become a reality.

## Shanghai

LCMS missionaries had been passing through S'hai for 33 years, but only after the war was any consideration given to doing work there. Among the 1946 *Marine Lynx* group were Reinhold and Dorothy Mueller, and their teenage daughter Gloria. It was Mike's third term of China service, with mission experience since 1929. The family was to reside in Shanghai as Mueller started a local congregation; preached in English, German, and Chinese; and became treasurer for the mission. His role included greeting military and civilian visitors and facilitating missionary travel as the political situation deteriorated.

More significantly, Mueller represented the *Lutheran Hour*. The evangelistic radio broadcasts had resumed in 1946, via shortwave from KZRM Manila. It was decided to also begin Lutheran Hour broadcasting in China. From Shanghai, Mueller arranged for rebroadcasts of Walter A. Maier's recorded programs on 16-Inch red plastic vinyl discs, from St. Louis. Listeners were encouraged to write to the Shanghai office (Mueller's home) with inquiries, and to enroll in a correspondence course. A Lutheran Hour Far East office was set up at Concordia Seminary in 1947, managed by Paul Kreyling, although actual broadcasts would not be transmitted from Hankow. Impossible to mail them to Hankow through the postal system, the *St. Paul* airplane delivered the discs directly.

Kreylings evacuated to Shanghai in January 1949 to expand Lutheran Hour work. *Bringing Christ to the Nations* was broadcast on Sundays over station XORA. Listeners were invited to attend 10:00 am Sunday services at The Lutheran Hour Church at 112-6 Changshu-Satzoong Road. The location was actually the residence of the Kreylings

and the Muellers. Attendance at one time reached fifty.

The Thode family, LCMS missionaries since 1923, also returned to China on a later 1946 sailing of the *Marine Lynx*. Thode's assignment was to teach in the Hankow seminary. Frieda Thode home-schooled their two adolescent children, taught music anywhere needed, and mentored the newer missionary families.

Newly married, Paul and Dorothy Martens arrived in early 1948. His primary assignment was teaching in the two-year evangelist program at the Hankow seminary. He also assisted with the Lutheran Hour. In September, he and new missionary Roy Suelflow drove the mission-owned flatbed truck from Hankow west on new roads to Enshih, Chungking, and south to Kunming to reestablish the work that Martens had begun there in 1944 with Sister Kuni and the Vandesburger Mission. They hauled a load of tea, which they sold to help pay for fuel. In Kunming, Suelflow and Martens were again aided by the German nuns, spending six weeks doing country work and visiting isolated Chinese Lutherans in several rural villages. The truck, nicknamed "Happy," remained in Kunming and the men flew back to Hankow on the *St. Paul*.

## Up Country Developments

The congregations at Shasi and Ichang re-established themselves after the war under guidance of their own pastors and evangelists. Only Gertrude Simon was available to provide missionary assistance, which she did at Ichang with vacation Bible school and a regular middle school. Missionaries at Enshih and Wanhsien continued services and programs with less hardship than they had during the war years, waiting for relief from newly arriving recruits.

.Enshih supported the most extensive of the China mission's medical facilities. The progression of nurses and doctors starting in 1923 evidenced God's blessings on the unanticipated shoestring operation, led by tenacious and determined but under-trained staff. Initially built to provide clinical and maternity services, the in-

By 1947, the congregation at Ichang had rehabilitated itself to the point that land was obtained and plans begun for a new church and school, using funds advanced by the Mission. Gertrude Simon helped the pastor organize a sizeable vacation Bible school, and establish a middle school. She is shown here with faculty and student groups in 1949. Bottom picture is of teachers and students at the opening of the regular school in 1950.

creasing number of casualties from the Japanese and civil wars changed those plans. Emphasis shifted from midwifery to emergency wound treatment and surgery, in addition to ever-present disease control.

Dr. Y. C. Ch'en, who was instrumental in starting the clinic/hospital, returned in 1946 from his hometown of Hangchow, convinced that serving God through medicine was his calling. His family soon joined him. Deaconess Martha Boss arrived in 1946, traversing overland from Karachi across India and the Burma Road. Her nursing experience dovetailed with the work of missionary wives Elsie Wenger and Geraldine Holt. Boss, originally a German-American deaconess from Cleveland, tutored the nursing staff in the English language and conducted daily devotions. Two additional nurses, trained in midwifery, Norma Lenschow and Adelheid Mueller, joined the team in November 1948.

True Light, the thriving Enshih congregation, included about 300 members. Rev Ch'en Huai-jen had pastored the church since 1934.

Gilbert and Elsie Wenger with three young children, returned from furlough in April 1947. In contrast to their hasty overland evacuation via India in 1944, they were the first missionaries to fly into Enshih. They were aboard the *St. Paul*, a surplus C-47 transport airplane operated by three German pilots with the Lutheran World Federation. The Wengers resumed their work at the isolated orphanage, preaching stations, and hospital.

Wanhsien missionaries continued operating the primary and middle schools, using a staff of refugee Christian teachers, displaced by the war. Olive returned from India in 1946, after a year of teaching at the school for LCMS missionary children at Kodikanal. She trained Sunday school teachers, conducted classes for women, and taught in the middle school. Ziegler returned, alone, determined to re-activate the seminary. Hinz transferred from Enshih and also worked with American servicemen from the Chinese American Composite wing. Voss and his Norwegian bride returned briefly in 1948 to re-

place Hinz who was unable to return due to visa problems. Teacher Lorraine Behling, still learning Mandarin, joined the group in early November.

The only Walther League chapter in China was chartered at Wanhsien, guided by Gruen and Behling. The club was composed of about 40 Christian students, who had worked together as a choir and drama group. A dedication festival on November 23, 1948 heard messages from Missionary Herb Hinz and from Mr. Wong. Students planned the event, highlighted by a movie and slide show, using kerosene projectors.

Wanhsien fell to Communist forces late 1949. Gruen and Holtjie were in Chungking at the time, and never returned. Lorraine Behling flew on the *St. Paul* to Chengdu, joining Martha Boss there for advanced language work at the Methodist West China Union University. But within weeks, a midnight evacuation brought them to Hong Kong.

## An Indigenous Church

Conditions in China rekindled the concept among the Chinese of an indigenous church, rather than a missionary-centered enterprise from abroad. Paul Martens was a primary proponent, organizing conferences in Enshih, Wanhsien, and in Hankow. Growing from these meetings, plans were outlined for a greater representation from Chinese pastors and congregations, allowing greater self-rule. Lack of local and mission board funding undercut this progress, and it ceased with the Communist takeover.

BFM Director Otto H. Schmidt visited Hankow on his 1948 Asian inspection trip. Ever the adventurer, Schmidt had negotiated scarce post-war passage to visit Japan, the Philippines, and India. He prepared an extensive report for several Lutheran Witness articles, and the 1949 Synodical Convention.

By 1948, other fledgling mission start-ups began down river at nearby Chang Chin Chiao, in the Yangtze port of Wushih, and in Nanking. These embryonic efforts were all thwarted by the Chinese war of liberation.

St. Paul, a converted C-47, flew missions of mercy and rescue for three years throughout China, serving mostly the needs of Lutheran Missions from Chungking to Shanghai and Hong Kong. Through innovative planning, hauling freight supplemented all the airplane's expenses. On its last flight into Chengdu, pilots rescued Martha Boss, Lorraine Behling, and a derelict Volkswagen.

Upon arrival in Hong Kong, Gertrude Simon (far right), Martha Boss, Lorraine Behling and Wilbert Holtje quickly established work among refugees, eventually centering work at Rennie's Mill Refugee Camp.  By the time of this photo in 1950, another evacuated China missionary, Herb Hinz (on the left) had joined the effort, which would lead to an eventual church body of about 10,000 believers in Hong Kong (See Chapters 10-14).

## Exodus

Like many hopeful westerners, the LCMS missionaries held optimistic goals for the New China, and underestimated the seriousness of the developing civil war. Their missionary schooling had prepared them more for the rural up-country aspects of a tranquil China than for the revolutionary bloodshed as the nationalists fell before the onslaught of the once-oppressed Communist forces.

Throughout the second half of 1948, deliberation was brisk concerning probable evacuation in the face of the Communist advance. As victorious troops neared Hankow, safety concerns forced the Kreylings and Martens to consider evacuating to Shanghai by the end of summer, 1948. The *St. Paul*, now a rescue plane, ferried the Kreylings, Wengers, Martens, and Buucks to the safety of Shanghai in January 1949. There, Kreyling worked as a Lutheran Hour representative, re-working Walter A. Maier's published sermons, so that they were relevant to the times and culture of Shanghai. His messages were translated and broadcast to Chinese listeners. The two missionaries and a small local staff answered large quantities of mail generated by the programs, and monitored the correspondence courses headquartered in the upstairs of Mueller's residence.

The Kreylings, with a week-old baby boy, were finally able to get steamer tickets and their exit visa, sailing on the *General Gordon*. After a brief stop September 27 at Hong Kong, the ship laid over for twenty-four hours, at Yokohama. LCMS missionary Bill Danker had secured visas so the young family could disembark to work in Japan. Thus began the Kreylings' twenty-five years of work in Hanno, Niigata and Tokyo. Other evacuees, Bringewatt, Hass, and Meyer were similarly recruited for the growing Japan mission.

Never completely at peace since 1911, China was experiencing the finale of civil war between Nationalist and Communist armies. In Peking, on October 1, 1949, Mao Tse-tung would declare the Peoples Republic in Tien An Mien Square. Martha Boss and Lorraine Behling had gone west to Chengdu, hoping to take language courses until the kerfuffle blew over, but Szechwan and the last remote areas of mainland China would be taken by the end of 1949.

On its final flight Into Chengdu, the Hong Kong-based *St. Paul* flew under cover of darkness to airlift the stranded women. A telegram informing them of their eminent rescue was never delivered, so they were awakened by telephone about mid-night from the pilots waiting at the airstrip. Within a half-hour, they reached the plane. In the meantime, the pilots had bought a Volkswagen from a fleeing officer, dismantled it to fit into the C-47, and still had room for the two LCMS women plus a last-minute evacuee, Methodist missionary Mary Shearer. Escaping just after midnight December 8, they flew for four hours back to Hong Kong, without instruments, jammed against the disassembled car. Communist forces entered Chengdu with the morning light.

The phenomenal work of these two women in Hong Kong is detailed in the following chapters. To complete the story, *St. Paul* carried freight to destinations throughout the South China Sea for a few years. It then sat idle for a decade, since private aircraft were not allowed over China. When *St. Paul* was sold, the proceeds financed the construction of Truth Lutheran Church on Hong Kong's Waterloo Road in 1964 an Hsin I Wei congregation.

## Living under the PRC - Thode, Mueller, and Schalow

When the *Bamboo Curtain* fell in the winter of 1949, Mueller remained in Shanghai, facilitating *Lutheran Hour* broadcasts until the family departed in April 1951. Two other missionary families were still living in Hankow, tending what they could of the seminary compound. Missionary Schalow's wife and family obtained exit permits in January 1951 and departed for Iowa. Schalow, detained and on trial for disturbing the economic stability of China, was later deported, leaving in May 1951. He spent several months with the fledgling Hong Kong mission while in travel limbo.

Interest in the Chinese grew in America during and after the War years. In New York City, True Light Lutheran churchestablished in 1936, opened a new building in a refurbished 4-story shoe factory in the heart of Chinatown. Walther League groups throughout the country held "China Night"s to raiseawareness and funds supporting overseas work.

CHINESE YOUTH NIGHT

JUNE, 1949

In Shasi and Jingzhou, the former Zion congregation would become a 3-Self (TSPM) church under the normalization reforms of the 1980s.  See Chapter 19)

Thodes remained in the vain hope the regime would somehow permit the Christian religion in the New China. Thode was able to conduct a survey of the remaining mission outposts, filing his report in May, 1950. His two high school-age children returned at that time to the U.S. When it became apparent in May 1951 that non-Chinese religious activity of any kind was impossible, the couple decided to apply for exit visas, but were delayed by several legal issues until July 1952. Frieda had served in China since 1923; this was her third evacuation. There is more to come on this couple in the Hong Kong chapters.

"Let us not give up meeting together" (Hebrews 10:25) said the apostle Paul to the first- century Hebrews. This became increasingly difficult to fulfill in the New China. The apostle's admonition was to not lose touch with new converts who needed visits and instruction. This reinforced belief in the saving grace of Christ, the creation by the Father, and the indwelling source of strength given by the Holy Spirit. Continuation of any form of foreign involvement with Christians in China appeared impossible.

The PRCS intent to purge counterrevolutionary elements within the country turned into an indiscriminate campaign to banish all forms of political dissent. An estimated two million Chinese were eliminated during the Terror. In May of 1952, Premier Chou En Lai [Zhou Enlai] declared that while religion was permitted in the People's Republic, all worship groups (churches, mosques, or temples) must be self-supporting, self-governing, and self-propagating— the Three-self vision proposed already in the mid-1850s by two mission administrators, Briton Henry Venn and American Rufus Anderson, and echoed in national terms by Sun Yat Sen. Thode analyzed the situation, and realized that the role of the mission was terminated. He applied for release, but was held up several months. Foreigners wanting to leave China had to post their intentions in a newspaper ad for three days. During this period, several former church workers brought claims that they were owed back-pay. A hold was placed on the missionary couple when some pastors demanded their money. Other Chinese pastors came forward to defend Thode, revealing that all staff had agreed to take a reduction in salary when funding from the States was cut off. The government granted the required exit visas to Hong Kong for the Thodes in July.

Apparently all national pastors and leaders of LCMS Chinese churche remained behind the *Bamboo Curtain*. Thode's report in 1950 numbered identifiable believers at less than 500, down from a pre-war census of over 2,000. At the same time, a tally of Hsin I Wei members in China was 83,126. Refugees from the Hsin I Wei had already established their mission in Hong Kong, even operating a Lutheran Community Center in Kowloon with work among Cantonese and Hakka-speakers.

Very few Chinese from any LLCMS mission station were present or active in Hong Kong or Taiwan. A few Christians from other churches were among the flotsam who became Lutherans in Hong Kong. Two of them would become LCMS pastors in the early 1950s.

Of the 65 missionaries who had served the China mission during its 35-year history, several would stay involved in Asia long after 1949. Postwar China missionaries Bringewatt, Egolf, Hass, Kreyling, Suelflow, and Meyer would serve in Japan, as would nurses Lenschow and Mueller. Norma Lenschow later served in New Guinea. Holt, Simon, Boss, Behling, Thode, Hinz, and Seltz worked long years in Hong Kong. Olive Gruen, with help from Herb Hinz, established the Taiwan mission, followed by, Hafner, Riedel, Schalow, Suelflow, and Wilenius in Taiwan. Bringewatt was called to Taiwan, thus joining Suelflow as the only LCMS missionaries to serve three different fields. The Kretzmanns and the Buucks went to the Philippines; and Kurt Voss was called out of stateside congregational service to begin work in Korea in 1957.

Hence, each of Synod's post-war East Asian missions would be salted with experienced *China hands* from the Yangtze years. Some continued their careers overseas for decades. Herb Hinz served China, Hong Kong, Tai-

## Significant locations in the LCMS Mainland

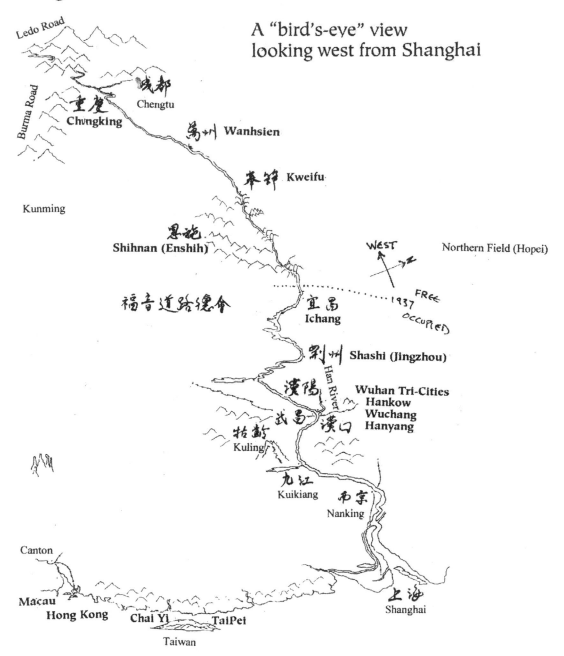

A "bird's-eye" view
looking west from Shanghai

A bird's-eye view of the areas touched by the China enterprise of the Lutheran Church Missouri Synod; the Yangtze drainage, Hong Kong & Macau, and the historic island of Formosa (Taiwan).

wan and Macau nearly 40 years. Riedel's career, interspersed with several periods in the U.S, had stretched 56 years. Olive Gruen and Gertrude Simon each dedicated almost 40 years.

I'm blessed to know the last two surviving true China hands, LeRoy Hass and Richard Meyer. Lorraine Behling was the first Mainland missionary I Interviewed. We prayed together for the Chinese people. Paul Kreyling was a great source of materials, photographs, letters, memorabilia, stories, experiences and humor the last three years of his life. "Iggy," this chapter is for you.

By most accounts, members of Synod declared the China mission closed, moribund, unsuccessful in numbers of conversions, and with very little to show for a massive financial investment over 36 chaotic years.

Thirty years would pass before any significant news came from the mainland as to the existence or practice of Christianity. Surprising revelations about Chinese believers and their experiences of striving and thriving have amazed Sinologists and Christians In the post-Mao world.

Christianity in China did not end with events In 1949.

## Significant Sources

| | |
|---|---|
| Brauer, Janice, ed, | One Cup of Water |
| Danker, William | Two Worlds or None |
| Fairbank, John | The Great Chinese Revolution |
| Pankow, Fred & Edith | The Best is Yet to Come |
| Springweiler, Max | Pioneer Aviator in China |

# Centennial Resolution - 65th Synodical Convention, St. Louis, 2013

**Whereas**, *One hundred years ago, in 1913, Edward L. Arndt founded the Lutheran Church-Missouri Synod efforts in Central China; and*

*Whereas, Sixty-five LCMS missionaries served in mainland China prior to the revolution of 1949; and*

*Whereas, Over two hundred LCMS missionary personnel have served in Hong Kong, Macau, and Taiwan; and*

*Whereas, Partner churches have been established in Hong Kong and Taiwan; therefore be it*

**Resolved**, That the LCMS in convention acknowledge and give thanks for the efforts of these missionaries and their supporters, and the fruit borne of those efforts by the power of the Holy Spirit; and be it further

Resolved, That the LCMS give thanks for renewed opportunities for mission work throughout the Chinese-speaking world today; and be it finally

Resolved, That the congregations of the LCMS fervently pray the Lord of the harvest to continue to send workers into Asia and throughout the earth, and to bless the harvest of life and salvation in the Chinese-speaking world.

*unanimously approved July 24, 2013*

---

### The Call of Abraham

*O Lord God,*
*who has called us they servants*
>    *to ventures of which we cannot see the ending*
>    *by paths as yet untrodden*
>    *and through perils unknown:*
*Give us faith*
>    *to go out with good courage,*
>    *not knowing whither we go,*
>    *but only that they hand is leading us*
>    *and they love supporting us*
*through Jesus Christ our Lord. Amen.*

# Acknowledgements

Acknowledgments and credits can sometimes sound gratuitous, but I make no apologies for honoring many wonderful fellow Christians (several coincidentally related in the Missouri Synod extended family) without whose help and support this project would never have reached fruition.

I accept full responsibility for errors in form or content, for any perceived insensitivities, and lack of detail or completeness. My caveat is that this is an account, not a systematic history, nor an exhaustive scholarly study. In the future, I would like to follow up with an anthology of some of the fine original historical, descriptive, and narrative writings of gifted missionaries and their families.

From my vague desire in 2007 to report the 40th anniversary of Hong Kong International School where I taught from 1973-80, interviews, discussions, e-mails, and research have led to the volume you now hold. It could easily be twice as long. It's been a joy to receive remarkable help through hours of conversation with co-workers in the States and in Asia. Every gathering, *dim sum* lunch, Chevanurch reunion, and convention brings renewal, and I could not possibly list everyone…but you know who you are. The bonus has been new acquaintances, friends in the faith. That started with finding Dorothy Riedel Hartle, the first baby born in the mission (1916) living right here in Portland, Oregon. Her pre-alzheimer memories were detailed and colorful, solving so many mysteries (and creating a few others). This introduced me to her brothers Joe and Gary, which led to the Richard Klein connection, to Felicitas Titus, scholar and friend of the mission from Hankow days. Lorraine Behling Sonnenberg, Ruth Proft Dannehl, Len & Ruth Galster, Ron Halamka, Roy & Betty Karner, Paul & Carol Kreyling, and Karl & LaVerne Boehmke have become close friends. Digging through their boxes of papers, letters, reports, and photos is a researcher's dream.

The incredible collection of authentic photographs in this book is the result of gracious loans of original photos and "snaps" garnered from several sources, particularly the contributions and efforts of several missionaries and their children. Many photos are duplicate prints. Thus it is difficult to credit any single photo to a particular photographer or collection. This also includes material from the  Lutheran Hour Ministries archives and Concordia Historical Institute, using a grant from the Northwest District of the LCMS. I would like to acknowledge the invaluable friendships and generosity of the following families:

Behling-Sonnenberg
Bringewatt
Boss-Doellinger
Buuck-Schramm
Christian
Fischer
Galster
Holt
Kieschnick
Klein
Koehler
Kreyling
Riedel-Hartle

Hu
Halter
Martens
Proft-Dannehl
Rodenbeck-Seltz
Simon
Theiss-Hille
Westrick
Ziegler-Darnell
Zimmermann-Wood
Zschiegner

# Acknowledgments

The gift of time, skill, and enthusiasm from Ellen Lewis goes far beyond what any acknowledgment or thank you can convey. The grand daughter of Erhardt Riedel, she has dedicated hours of painstaking editorial work with over 4000 original photographs and negatives Lois & Fritz Voeltz, co-workers of seven years in Hong Kong, supported, chided, questioned, researched and networked with me in the early stages of this project. When I needed perspective, I've counted on Bob Christian, Len Galster, Paul & Carol Kreyling, Dorothy Martens, Dotty Zimmermann Wood, and Dusty Reinbrecht Knisely.

Many families generously provided copies of personal correspondence, which brought me to understand the intense and/or subtle issues facing these expatriate men, women, and children:

| | |
|---|---|
| Edward Arndt | Paul Martens |
| Ralph Bringewatt | Lenchen Meyer |
| Lorenz Buuck | Carmelia Riedel |
| Arnold Cloeter | Gertrude Simon |
| John Fischer | Frieda Thiess |
| Arnold Gebhardt | Frieda Oelschlaeger Thode |
| Joe & Geri Holt | Eva Titus |
| Herman & Edna Klein | Albert & Laura Ziegler |
| Adolph & Irmie Koehler | Elmer Zimmermann |
| Paul & Carol Kreyling | Max Zschiegner |

Several missionaries, their children, and students have produced diaries, autobiographies, scholarly papers, and books about their China days. I am grateful for the personal loan or gift of copies of the following non-commercial (and hard to find) writings:

Albrecht, Ardon — "The CELC in Persective," Taipei, 1966

Buuck, Lorenz & Ella — I Am With You Alway", Ft. Wayne, IN, no date

Carroll, John — "Edward Arndt," St. Louis, MO, 1991

Cloeter, Arnold & Lola — "Memoirs," typescript, 1977

Darncll, Laura Ziegler — "Send Me Send Me," Henderson, NV, 2005

Gebhardt, Marie — "May 4 Movement and Its Effect," Omaha, NE, 1963

Lindner, John T. — "The Lutheran Church in Hong Kong1949-1980, Ft.Wayne, 1981

Meyer, Richard, — "The Missouri Ev. Lutheran China Mission, St. Louis, 1948

Mueller, Adelheid — "For Such as Time as This," typescript, no date

Nesse, H. M. — "Under Nippon's New Order," Augsburg, MN, 1947

Nesse, Art — "Growing Up in China," typescript, Ann Arbor, MI 2000

Parsons, David — "Wait and See" - Autobiography of Herman Klein 2009

Riedel, Erhardt — "From the Land of Sinim, A Memoir," Germantown, Maryland,edited by his daughter Schwennesen, Marie Riedel, 1993

Riedel, Libby & Gary — "Riedel Reminiscences", Murphys, CA, 2005

Stuewer, Clara Simon — "Lorchen, my Mother," Shawano, WI, 1979

Suelflow, Roy — "The Mission Enterprise of the Lutheran Church - Missouri" Synod in Mainland China," St. Louis,

Thode, Daniel — Memories of my Childhood in China, Farmington, MI

Thode, Frieda — "In China and Hong Kong with Deth," typescript

Werling, Wilbert. — "Up the Han from Hankow," 1930-36, Chico, CA, 1989

Wood, Dorothy C Z — "Memories of Kuling," unpublished, Washington, M0

# Acknowledgements

In addition, well over 200 interviews with missionaries or their progeny have enriched my research beyond my wildest hopes. These are legion, and I hesitate to attempt a listing, lest someone is left out, but I would be remiss if I did not acknowledge the incredible experience of tapping the memories of Lorraine Behling-Sonnenberg, Karl & LaVerne Boehmke, Bob Christian, Len Galster, Roy & Betty Karner, Mel & Jane Kieschnick, Paul and Carol Kreyling, Dottie Mache, Ruth Proft-Dennehl, Dorothy Riedel, Laura Ziegler-Darnell, and Dottie Zimmermann-Wood.

I have sat at the feet of some wonderful churchworkers in this process - Paul Strege, Warren Schumacher, Erhard Bauer, Carl Hanson, Hank Rowold, Dean Lueking, James Koehler and Nathan Brandt, my pastor. For rides to the St Louis Amtrak station at unreasonable hours, I thank Randy Fauser.

Research involved several languages which I neither read or speak. Dennis Rathert of Old Trinity, St. Louis, unwittingly got involved in translating several long writings from German; Li Jian Min suffered through many attempts in conveying meaning from Chinese characters; and Rev. Andrew Yong of Portland provided helpful Chinese language context. Christine Mark kindly and patiently translated many pages of printed material. Adam Gawel has proven remarkable in sleuthing out remnants of the China Mission still extant in Hankow. I am grateful for the patience and friendship of many Chinese friends, especially Andrew Chiu and Daniel Lee. For the beautiful Chinese calligraphy, I am indebted to Dan Huynh of Portland.

I am in awe of the patience and acuity of several kind readers of the manuscript as it has evolved. For their ability to tackle the vocabulary and grammar of clear communication, I thank Inez Bauer, Carl & Jo Brandhorst, Frank Inberg, Bruce Richards, Hank Rowold, and Walt Schmidt.

Concordia Seminary libarian Eric Stancliffe, Tavis Scholl of Concordia Seminary Press, and their staffs, have provided friendship and professionalism. Laura Marrs of Concordia Historical Institute has been marvelous. I owe immense kudus to Suzanne Deakins and Spirit Press for faciiitating and formatting.

Suggestions for a forthcoming study guide have come from Nathan Brandt, Richard Bringewatt, Jeff Daley, Paul Doellinger, Herb Hoeffer, Warren Schumacher, and Christian Zimmermann.

Reproduction of the unique Japanese wartime map of China is through the generosity and permission of www.oldimprints.com and www.asianbookroom.com.

For healthy perspective and comic relief, I have 6-year old Elliott Arthur Kohl and his 2-year old sister, Greta, to thank. Without realizing their roles, they have diverted my intensity, refreshed my energy, and given me cause to tell the story behind my fixation with China and their dad's birth in Hong Kong.

This story continues to unfold. Please visit www.lutheransontheyangtze.com

# Glossary

abacus - a rectangular frame with clusters of wooden beads on parallel rods, used for calculating

*aiyah* (aieeh, etc) - an exclamation of understanding, comprehension, wonder, astonishment, disgust or anger, depending on the inflection of the voice

*amah* - general term for all female servants, i.e. baby amah (often a wet          nurse), cook amah, sew-sew amah, wash amah, weed amah, etc

*baiwah* - popular simplified vernacular printed language promoted with the 1911 Revolution. Bible Societies printed the 1919 Union Version in this new lingua franca,; see *wen-li*

billet - assigned living quarters

boy - male employee or servant, regardless of age, i.e., house boy, rickshaw boy, or simply "boy"; like *coolie*, not originally a classicist or derisive term

bully beef – tinned corned beef

Bund - raised riverbank quay or promenade with vertical or canted walls

catechism - summary and explanation of fundamental Christian beliefs, presented in a question-and-answer  format, historically favored by Lutherans

catechumen - person being taught the principles of Christianity; a neophyte

catty *(kati)* - measure of weight; the Chinese pound = 20 ounces avoirdupois; has 16 divisions

chatty - small clay cooker, or clay-lined tin can with a grate; used by folk Chinese,and by internees in POW camps

China Coast pidgin - localized language in colonial areas of China, for which there are no other equivalent  words having the same exactly meaning or usage

China General Conference (Missionary Conference); known in China as Missouri Evangelical Lutheran China Mission; all the called LCMS missionaries, exclusive of local workers, laity or delegates

chit - a memorandum of indebtedness; also a brief note or receipt. In every business there were chit-coolies whose sole occupation is the handling of these Notes. Petty cash never changes hands in business dealings. Rather, chits are tabulated, and the resulting invoice delivered weekly or monthly

*ch'i tao* - (eat the doctrine - foreigners religion)

chop - unique trade mark, graphic, or brand, often a unique combination of ideogramatic characters or symbols for an individual or business; an official's seal; a carved stamp to leave such an impression

clipper mail – postal air mail; initiated to China in 1934 via Pan American Airlines amphibious propeller aircraft ("China Clipper"); very costly, once regarded as extravagant

colporteur -an itinerant agent who carries and distributes Bibles, publications, books or religious tracts from place to place; the verb is colportage. Although printing cost about 3d (three pence or pennies) per Bible portion, copies were sold to the Chinese for 1d. If they had been free, the Chinese were known to use the booklets to line the soles of cloth shoes.

comity - the legal principle that one jurisdiction will extend certain courtesies to other nations or jurisdictions. Most Christian missions in China had established respect for each other's territories by 1907

compound - a walled enclosure surrounding foreign business or dwellings; often including an open court yard

# Glossary

compradore *(mai-pan)* - the Chinese manager of a business; general contractor; a bi-lingual agent, middleman, or negotiator between local providers and foreigners for supplies (tea, silk, rice, opium, alcohol, foodstuffs, chandlery, etc) and/or services

compradore shop - equivalent to a grocery store selling boxed or tinned foodstuffs, usually for foreigners, not to be confused with a greengrocer

Concession - geographic zone within a city for commerce or residence granted by treaty for the exclusive foreign use, with no Chinese jurisdiction

Concordia; concord - of the same mind; harmony or agreement; hence the name Concordia is derived from adherence to the Book of Concord; name given to nearly every Missouri Synod institution of higher learning; Concordia University System

*coolie* – can be derogatory or commonplace reference to any menial or physical laborer; a wage earner; chair coolies are more politely called "carriers"; baggage coolies transport luggage and freight; horse coolies are liverymen; those pulling boats upriver are "trackers", etc.

"Coolie Chinese"; pidgin language- distorted and simple spoken colonial language, variously combining elements of English, Chinese, Malay, Tamil or Portuguese

copper (or "cash") - small brass coin with a square hole in the center; basic unit of currency; 800 cash = 1 Mexican silver dollar = 1/3 US gold dollar, on a fluctuating exchange rate

cumshaw *(kan hsieh)* (lycee; "tea money," baksheesh) - a tip, gratuity, bribe or payoff ;"squeeze"; a "consideration" or gift under the table

*dai yat* [ding hao] - "number one" or "best quality" Chinese equivalent of "the best possible;" thumbs up!

Delegate conference – general convention of LCMS that meets triennially.

deputation work - the process through which missionaries lecture, present at mission festivals, and raise moral and financial support in the home country

dispensationalism - protestant evangelical tradition; a series of chronologically successive periods in history in which God relates to humans under different Biblical covenants

Divine call - assignment to specific service of ministers, teachers, and deaconesses issued by LCMS Call Board (composed of seminary and college representatives and Synodical officials;

electric feet - tingling sensation as a result of malnutrition; also called dry beriberi (wet beriberi is swelling)

electric letter or "lightning" letter – telegram or "cable" (Cable & Wireless)

escape & evasion maps – U.S. government printed silk maps carried by military to aid them in emergencies with communication in wartime

expatriate ("expat") - one who resides outside their country of citizenship,

extraterritoriality ("extrality") - not under the jurisdiction of local courts; shortened to" extrality;" status of being exempt from local law;

"face" - pride; prestige, outward appearances. A person loses "face" or honor when embarrassed, outwitted or loses status

# Glossary

factory - residence of the factors (managers) of the East India Company in an Asian city; may also include clerical and warehousing areas (godowns)

fan; *faan* – rice, or by extension, food (in Cantonese: *sic fan* = eat rice= meal; *noh maai faan* sticky rice; *chau fan* = fried rice)

*fankwei-tzu; fanqui (gweilo)* - foreigner; distasteful stranger, "foreign devil;" "round-eye"; *Yeh-soo Kwai* = Jesus devils

Fu Yin Dao Lo Deh Wei – Good News (happy sound) Doctrine Lutheran Society – the Missouri Synod Chinese Evangelical Lutheran Church (so-named n 1923)

*fungalo* – small 3-legged clay brazier, used for cooking, supporting a pan over a charcoal fire

galantine - jellied meat product; as in SPAM

godown - a warehouse, originally below street level, hence the term

griffin - a trained but inexperienced bachelor working for a foreign firm; a freshman; average annual salary US$ 2500, twice the salary of a missionary family (in 1930)

*guan shi* = good friend; *pang yau; [peng you]*

*gweilo* –. non-Chinese person; literally "old devil." often derogatory or common reference to a foreigner

hong - any large mercantile establishment or business; not a retail shop.

hoover – to vacuum, to clean, to use any vacuum cleaner; or the brand name

*hsieh tong* – with harmony; term chosen to repreent "Concordia"

Hsin I Wei *(Hsin Yi Huei)* – Faith-Righteousness Church (Lutheran Church of China)

*hwa ga* - a basket chair of wicker, with footrest and straw mat shade, affixed to two carrying poles, carried by coolies to transport a passenger; a type of sedan chair

indigenation - process of returning to native or natural state; living in a natural way; not introduced; process of transferring control to native or local leadership

itineration - governing or administration whereby an governor or ruler travels around his jurisdiction; traveling to inspect progress or compliance of converts or underlings

Joss - a corruption of the Latin or Portuguese term for god - dios, deus;; meaning either god, but more likely, luck. a joss house is a temple; a joss stick is incense; Joss soldiers are troops fighting for a spiritual benefit; joss paper is imitation money burnt to assuage various gods; bad joss is no luck, misfortune; no-joss is the equivalent of "no deal."

*kang* - flat-topped hollow or vented masonry platform with an imbedded flue, which transfers heat from a fire into a surface for sleeping; a brick bed

Kellogg's - breakfast food of grain; brand name, but also generic for cold cereal

*kung-tze (gang* or *kang)* stout wood or bamboo shoulder pole, used to carry a balanced or cantilevered load usually suspended at each end; a yard-arm or cross-bar

"Larn pidgin" - to be an apprentice; literally "learn-business"

# Glossary

li - a measurement of distance (3 li equals about 1 mile); the Great Wall is the 'ten-thousand-li rampart

lightning letter – telegram; see electric letter

likin – one-thousandth of a tael; one "cash"(see copper) ; also a transit tax levied on goods between points in China; a fee to use a trail, road, bridge, or stretch of river

lilong – tenement row house, facing a common alley

lysol - disinfectant; brand name but also generic; verb or noun

mafoo - a Chinese equestrian groom or stable boy; horse-boy

ma ma hoo hoo – common expression: everything is all mixed up; literally "horse horse-tiger tiger" (when a horse and tiger get together, the outcome is a terrible uproar); "a royal mess;" a "snafu"

maskee - an ubiquitous pidgin term meaning "all right, never mind, however, but, forget it, no matter, and nevertheless"; "whatever!"

matshed - a portable or temporary structure, single room or an entire theater framed by bamboo poles covered with sheets of woven rattan or palm fronds

Mei Foo - cheap efficient kerosene lamp marketed by Standard Oil (Socony); burned 240 hours on 1 gallon of kerosene (paraffin)

Mei Foo man - shopkeeper who sold kerosene, usually by the gill (1/4 pint)

mince - ground beef or other meat; hamburger

"Missie" - term of respect used by all Chinese servants when addressing their mistresses, regardless of marital status

modernism - extrapolation of Christian doctrine into social service; contemporary application of Christianity to community needs; the social gospel

monger - a specialized dealer or seller; a ship monger sells nautical supplies and hardware; a fish monger markets seafood

mow (mu) - a Chinese land measurement equal to one sixth of an acre

muh-si – pastor

outport - any place in the interior where foreigners were allowed to reside and carry on business; not necessarily a Concession area

oxo – bullion, brand name but also generic for broth

picul - a measure of weight, especially for rice; 133 pounds; a Chinese bushel

pidgin – business of any kind; lingua franca patoise used to conduct business between asian and westerner; pidgin-Chinese; pidgin-English ("Macao talk")

poo bah - an official of unlimited authority; someone important

# Glossary

premillenialism (Chiliasm) - belief that Christ will literally and physically be on the earth for a 1000-years before the end of time

*pusa* - a god or idol (i.e. Kuan Yin Pusa)

*pu-tao-chieh* - a mission festival

rice bowl - livelihood; how a person earns wages or basic payment of some sort; iron rice bowl; "soft rice" = income or benefits earned without effort

Rice Christian – an opportunist; one who joins a group for side benefits; some Chinese were thought to convert for financial benefit or gain; individual professing Christian faith for ulterior motivations or benefit

*sampan* - a small Chinese boat, three boards wide, traditionally propelled by the use of a single oar *(yuloh)*

savvy - knowledge or understanding

separatism - see Unionism

*shen* - a god; a spirit; each departed person has three shen, one residing in the remains, one in the ancestral tablet, and one in the ether

*shen-fu* - priests or holy fathers

Shanghailander – any expatriate who ever lived in Shanghai

*shikumen* - traditional courtyard house, granite-framed entrance, no windows to the street

shroff -a clerk or collector; a cashier; one who tests the purity of silver or gold coins; used as a verb for "to audit", as in "schroff an account"

*siheyuan* – a low tradesman's house, with lightwell, but not courtyard

synod – meeting or conference, when capitalized in this book, refers to the Lutheran Church Missouri Synod; "St. Louis", location of church headquarter, is synonymous with LCMS

Synodical Conference – Conference of the Lutheran Church Missouri Synod, Wisconsin Synod, and Evangelical Lutheran Synod, formed for common ministry in 1872, dissolved 1963

tael - a measure of weight, about one ounce, 579.84 grams, usually applied to silver or gold, divisible into 10 "mace"; cast in ingots or hat-shaped bars

*taifoo* – great assistant; chief officer on a China coastal ship

*taipan* - foreign manager or owner of a large business concern or *hong*

*taotai* -a circuit or county official who deals with foreigners on local affairs

tiffin - originally a Persian word for the mid-day meal; a late leisurely lunch

Up country (or up river) - distant or remote inland areas; primitive; less urban; hinterland

unionism – perceived or real co-ordination, co-operation, collaboration or worship between religious groups, despite creedal or spiritual differences; fear that such non-Biblical association will dilute truth or purity in doctrine

# Glossary

"V'er" –a Volunteer Youth Ministry participant, usually in Taiwan or Japan for 1-2 years

Vitagraph - early British talking movies - "talkies"; brand name, like "Movietone"

*wai-t'ang* - preaching in the streets; evening services conducted in a hall or shopfront open to the street, attracting casual passers-by

walla walla - garrulous and useless conversation; a small slow boat with a very small small engine, once commonly used in Hong Kong harbor

*wenli* - traditional language and ideograph style of educated Chinese; "easy" wenli develops in the 1800's as concession to less classically educated Chinese; replaced after May 4 Movement with *baihua* (cf. *baihua; baihwa)*

Yamun - an official Chinese office or magistrate's headquarters and house; a building for same

*yuloh* - the single oar by which smaller Chinese watercraft are propelled and steered

# Index

# Bibliography
## ** Items authored by, or of special interest to, LCMS Lutherans

Aandahl, Elliot C, **In Those Days** - *Growing up as a Missionary Kid In China, 1910-24*, n.p. 1960

Abbe Huc, **High Road in Tartary**, abridged and edited by Julie Bedier, Charles Schribner's Sons, New York, 1948

Ahern, Emily, **The Cult of the Dead in a Chinese Village**, Stanford University Press, Stanford, 1973

**Aid Association for Lutherans, ed, **A Week in the Life of the Lutheran Church, Missouri Synod**, Concordia Publishing House, St. Louis, 1996

Albrecht, Ardon, **The CELC in Perspective**,n.p. Taipei, 1965

Alcorn, Randy, **Safely Home**, Tyndale, Wheaton, 2001

Allen, Roland, **Missionary Methods** - *St. Paul's or Ours?*, Moody Press, Chicago, 1912

Anderson, Johan, **The Dragon and the Foreign Devils**, Little, Brown & Co, Boston, 1928

Angus, Fay, **The White Pagoda**, Tydale, Wheaton, 1978

**Armentrout, Fred, Ed, **Hong Kong International School**: *Celebrating 40 Years of Learning and Service,* AmCham Hong Kong and HKIS, 2007

**Arndt, Edward H, **A History of the Evangelical Lutheran Mission for China**, n.p., n.d.

____**The beginnings of Our Work in China**, CHQ, St. Louis, 1932-3 (4 parts)

**Arndt, Edward Louis, **Green Pastures**, Danish Lutheran Publishing, Blair, NB, 1911

**____**Is Shang-ti Wrong?**, Hankow, unpublished, 1926

**____**Our Task in China**, Concordia Publishing House St. Louis, 1926

Austin, Alvyn, **Saving China**: *Canadian Missionaries in the Middle Kingdom,* 1888-1959, University of Toronto Press, Toronto, 1986

Ayscough, Florence, **A Chinese Mirror** - *Being Reflections of the Reality Behind Appearance,* Houghton Mifflin, Boston, 1925


Bacon, Bessie Blanchard, **With Heaps O' Love** - *The Story of Four Years in China,* Nichols Book and Travel Co, Des Moines, IA, 1925

Bacon, Ursula, **Shanghai Diary**, M Press, Milwaukee, 2004

**Baepler, Walter, **A Century of Grace** - *A History of the Missouri Synod 1847-1947,* Concordia Publishing House, St. Louis, 1947

Bailey, Steven, **Strolling in Macau**, Things Asian Press, San Francisco, 2007

Baker, Hugh, **Chinese Family and Kinship**, MacMillan, London, 1979

Banham, Tony, **Not the Slightest Chance** - *The Defense of Hong Kong, 1941,* UBC Press,Vancouver BC, Hong Kong University Press, H , 2003

____**We Shall Suffer There** - *Hong Kong's Defenders Imprisoned, 1942-45*, Hong Kong University Press, 2009

Barnes, Lemuel Call, **Two Thousand Years of Missions Before Carey**, Christian Culture Press, Chicago, 1902

Barondes, R. de Rohan, **China: Lore, Legend and Lyrics**, Peter Owen Ltd, London, 1959

Barr, Pat, **Foreign Devils** - *Westerners in the Far East*, Penguin, Baltimore, 1970

Baum, Vicki, **Shanghai '37**, Book League of America, New York, 1940

Bays, Daniel, ed, **Christianity in China** - *From the 18th Century to the Present,* Stanford University Stanford, 1996

Beach, Harlan, **Dawn on the Hills of T'ang** or *Missions in China*, Student Volunteer Movement for Foreign Missions, New York, 1898

Bechtel, John, **The Mystery of East Mountain Temple**, Bible Institute Colportage Association Press, Chicago, 1939

Becker, Jasper, **Hungry Ghosts**: *Mao's Secret Famine,* Henry Holt & Co. NY 1996

Benge, Janet & Geoff, **Gladys Aylward: The Adventure of a Lifetime**, Youth With A Mission, Seattle, 1998

Bennett, Adrian, **Missionary Journalist in China** - *Young J. Allen*, University of Georgia Press, Athens, 1983

Beth Hatefutsoth (Museum of the Jewish Diaspora), **The Jews of Kaifeng**, *Chinese Jews on the Banks of the Yellow River,* Nahum Goldmann Museum, Tel Aviv, 1984

Bickers Robert, and Seton, Rosemary, ed, **Missionary Encounters** - *Sources and Issues,* Curzon Press, Richmond, Surry (UK), 1996

Bianco, Lucien, **Origins of the Chinese Revolution 1915-1949**, Stanford University Press, Stanford, 1974

**Blumer, Deborah, **Called According to His Purpose** – Missionary Letters of George Lillegard, Amazon, ISBN: #978-0-578-01454-8

**Board of Control, **Exodus from Concordia**: *A Report on the 1974 Walkout,* Concordia Seminary, St Louis, 1977

Board of Foreign Missions, **Our Second Decade in China, 1915-1925**, Augustana, 1925

Bodde, Derk, **Peking Diary** - *A Year of Revolution,* Henry Schuman, New York, 1950

# Bibliography

Bonavia, Judy, & Hayman, Richard, **Yangzi** - *The Yangtze River and the Three Gorges*,  Odyssey Books, Hong Kong, 2004

Booker, Edna, **Flight from China**, MacMillan, New York, 1946

Braga, J. M., **China Landfall 1513**, Imprensa Nacional, Macau,  1955

**Brauer, Janice, ed, **One Cup of Water** - *Five true stories of missionary women in China*, International Lutheran Women's Missionary League, St.Louis, 1997

Briner, Bob, **The Management Methods of Jesus**, Thomas Nelson, Nashville, 1996

Broomhall, Marshall, **The Bible in China**, China Inland Mission, London, 1934

Brown, Arthur J., **The Foreign Missionary**, Fleming H Revell, New York, 1932

Buck, Pearl, **The Chinese Children Next Door**,

_____**Fighting Angel**, 1936, Giant Cardinal Edition, New York. 1964

_____**My Several Worlds**, Cardinal Giant Pocket books, New York, 1956

_____**The Exile**, Triangle Books, New York, 1936

_____**The Young Revolutionist**, Friendship Press, NY, 1932

_____**YuLan – The Flying Boy of China**, Friendship Press, NY, 1945

**Burkee, James, **Power, Politics, and the Missouri Synod** - *A Conflict That changed American Christianity*, Fortress Press, Minneapolis, 201

**Buuck, Lorenz, *I Am With You Always*, self-published, Ft. Wayne, 1977(?)


Caldwell, John C, **China Coast Family**, Henry Regnery Co, Chicago, 1953

Campbell, Persia Crawford, **Chinese Coolie Emigration**(*to Countries within the British Empire*), P. S. King & Son, Westminster, 1923; reprinted by Ch'eng Wen Publishing, Taipei, 1970

Cameron, Nigel, **An Illustrated History of Hong Kong**, Oxford U Press, Hong Kong, 1991

_____**Barbarians & Mandarins**, Walker/Weatherhill, New York, 1970

Candlin, Enid Saunders, **The Breach in the Wall** - *A Memoir of the Old China*, Macmillan New York, 1973

Cannon, Terry, & Jenkins, Alan, **The Geography of Contemporary China**: *The Impact of Deng Xiaoping's Decade*, Routledge, London, 1990

Carew, Tim, **The Fall of Hong Kong**,  Pan Books, London, 1963

Carlberg, Gustav,  **Thirty Years in China**: *Augustana Synod Missions in Honan Province*, Board for Missions, Augustana, 1937

Carpenter, Francis Ross, **The Old China Trade**, Coward, McCann & Geoghegan, NewYork, 1976

Carroll, John M. **A Concise History of Hong Kong**, Rowman & Littlefield, Lanham, MD, 2007

_____**Edward Arndt**, graduate paper, Washington University, St. Louis, unpublished,  1991

Cary-Elwes, Columba, **China and the Cross**: *A Survey of Missionary History*, P.J.Kennedy & Sons, New York, 1957

Caughey, Ellen, **Eric Liddell** - *Gold Medal Missionary*, Barbour, Uhrichsville, OH, 2000

Chamberlain, W. I., **Fifty Years in Foreign Fields, 1875-1925**, Woman's Board of Foreign Missions, Reformed Church in America, New York, 1925

Chan Kfei Thong, **Faith of Our Fathers** - *God in Ancient China*, 345 Xianxialu, Shanghai, 2006

Chen, Jack, **A Year in Upper Felicity** - *Life in a Chinese Village During the Cultural Revolution*, Macmillan, New York 1973

Chen Wei Ping, *Autobiography*, n.p. (Hong Kong?), 1965

Chesneaux, Jean, **Peasant Revolts in China 1840-1949**, Thames & Hudson, London, 1973

Chang, Leslie, **Factory Girls** -*From Village to City in a Changing China*, Spiegel & Grau, NewYork, 2008

Chiang Kai-Shek, **All We Are and All We Have**, John Day Co, New York, 1943

Chiang Yee, **A Chinese Childhood**, John Day, New York, 1940, 1952

Ching, Julia, **Confucianism and Christianity**, Kodasha, Tokyo, 1977

**Chiu, Andrew**, *A History of the Research of Exodus 18:1-12*, unpublished ThD thesis, Concordia Theological Seminary, St. Louis, 1973

**  _____*Short Historical Notes on Concordia Theological Seminary in Hong Kong.* unpublished, n.d.

Chodron, Thuben, **Buddhism for Beginners**, Snow Lion Publications, ithaca, NY, 2001

Chow, Tse-Tsung, **The May 4th Movement**, Harvard University Press, Cambridge, 1960

Chrisemer, Edgar, **The Werner Wedel Story**: *The Adventures of a Lutheran Missionary in China*, Branden Press, Boston, 1966

Christie, Vance, **Hudson Taylor - Founder, China Inland Mission**, Barbour Books, Uhrichsville, OH, 1999

Chu, Cindy Yik-Yi, **Foreign Communities in Hong Kong, 1840s-1950s**, Palgrave Macmillan, New York, 2005

Chun, T'ien, **Village in August**, Smith & Durrell, New York, 1942

Clark, Elmer, **The Chiangs of China**, Abingdon-Cokesbury Press, New York, 1943

# Bibliography

_____**What's the Matter in China?**, Methodist Episcopal Church, Nashville, 1927

**Cloeter, Arnold & Lola, *Memoirs*, typescript, 1977

Clubb, O. Edmund, **Twentieth Century China**, Columbia University Press, New York, 1964

Clyde, Paul, and Beers, Burton, **The Far East** - *A History of the Western Impact and the Eastern Response 1830-1965*, Prentice-Hall, Englewood Cliffs, 1966

Cohen, Paula, **China and Christianity:** *The Missionary Movement and the Growth of Chinese Antiforeignism 1860-1870,* Harvard University, Cambridge, 1963

Colquhoun, Archibald, **Overland to China**, Harper, New York, 1900

Cordell, Bessie, **Precious Pearl**, Light and Life Press, Winona Lake, IN, 1948

Coulson, Gail, **The Enduring Church** - *Christians in Hong Kong and China,* Friendship Press, New York, 1996

Covell, Ralph, **Confucious, The Buddha, and Christ** - *A History of the Gospel in Chinese,* Orbis Books, Maryknoll, NY, 1986

Cressey, George, **China's Geographic Foundations**, *A Survey of Its Land and Its People,* McGraw-Hill, New York, 1934

_____**Land of the 500 Million** - *A Geography of China,* McGraw-Hill, New York, 1955

Criveller, Gianni, **From Milan to Hong Kong** - *150 Years of Mission,* PIME House, Hong Kong, 2008

Crofts, Daniel, **Upstream Odyssey**: *An American in China, 1895-1944,* Signature Books, Norwalk, CT, 2008

Crow, Carl, **Foreign Devils in the Flowery Kingdom**, Harper & Brothers, New York, 1940

_____**Four Hundred Million Customers**, Hamish Hamilton, London, 1937

_____**Handbook for China**, Kelly & Walsh, Shanghai, 1933

_____**The Chinese Are Like That**, World Publishing Co, Cleveland, OH, 1943

Curtis, Claude, **My Cup of Tea**, Gospel Missions Inc, Wahiawa HI, 1979


**Danker, William, **Two worlds or none** - *Rediscovering Mission in the 20th Century,* Concordia, St. Louis, 1964

**Darnell, Laura Lou, *Send Me, Send me!* - *The Story of Laura and Albert Ziegler's Missions to China,* Self-published, Henderson, NV, 2005

**Dau, W.H.T., **Ebenezer** - *Reviews of the Work of the Missouri Synod during Three Quarters of a Century* 1847-1922, Concordia, St. Louis, 1922

Davin, Della, **Woman-Work** - *Women and the Party in Revolutionary China,* Clarendon Press, Oxford, 1976

DeFrancis, John, **The Chinese Language:** *Fact and Fantasy,* University of Hawaii Press, Honolulu, 1984

Denham, G.T., **Shen or Shangti?**, Christian Book Room, Shanghai, nd (c1930?)

DePree, Gladis, **The Spring Wind**, Harper and Row, New York, 1970

**Deterding, John, **Living with Jesus** - *A History of the Evangelical Lutheran Church of Saint Lorenz, Frankenmuth, Michigan,* Frankenmuth, 1995

Dew, Gwen, **Prisoner of the Japs**, Alfred A. Knopf, New York, 1943

Dhammika, Ven, **Good Question Good Answer**, np., Singapore, 1991

**Dickenson, Richard, **Roses and Thorns** - *The Centennial Edition of Black Lutheran Mission and Ministry in the LCMS,* Concordia Publishing, St. Louis, 1977

Dong, Stella, **Shanghai 1842-1949:** *The Rise and Fall of a Decadent City,* Harper Collins, New York, 2000

Donovan, John, **The Pagoda and the Cross** - *The Life of Bishop Ford of Maryknoll,* Charles Scribner's Sons, New York, 1967

Drummnd, Ellen, **Queen of the Dark Chamber** - *The Story of Christiana Tsai,* Mood, Chicago, 1953

DuBose, Francis de, **Classics of Christian Missions**, Broadman Press, Nashville, 1979

Dunn, George H, S.J., **The Missionary in China** - *Past, Present, Future,* Lutheran World Federation, Geneva, 1973

Dutton, Michael, **Streetlife China**, Cambridge University Press, Cambridge, 1998


Edkins, Joseph, **The Religious Condition of the Chinese**, Routledge, Warnes & Routledge, New York, 1859

Effler, Donald, **Experiences in China and Saudi Arabia**, Limited Ed, Chester, Devenow, 1975

Eggleston, Margaret, **Forty Missionary Stories**, Harper Bros, New York, 1934

Emerson, Geoffrey, **Hong Kong Internment**, 1973

Espey, John, **Minor Heresies** - *Reminiscences of a Shanghai childhood,* Alfred Knopf, New York, 1945

_____**Tales out of School** - *Stories of a boyhood in China,* Knopf, New York, 1947


Fairbank, John K., **ChinaBound** - *A Fifty-Year Memoir,* Harper & Row, New York, 1982

_____**The Great Chinese Revolution 1800-1985**, Harper Perennial, NY 1987

Farquharson, Ronald, **Confessions of a China-Hand**, Hodder and Stoughton, London, 1950

Fitzgerald, C. P., **Flood Tide in China**, The Cresset Press, London, 1958

# Bibliography

Fleming, Daniel, **Living as Comrades**, Foreign Missions Conference of North America, Agricultural Mission Press, NY, 1950

Flynt, Wayne, & Berkley, Gerald, **Taking Christianity to China** - *Alabama Missionaries in the Middle Kingdom, 1850-1950,* University of Alabama Press, Tuscaloosa, 1997

Forman, Harrison, **Report from Red China**, Book Find Club, New York, 1945

**Forster, Walter, **Zion on the Mississippi**, Concordia, St. Louis, 1953

Forsythe, Irene, **Cheng's Mother**, Friendship Press, New York, 1948

Fortosis, Stephen, and Reid, Mary Graham, **Boxers to Bandits,** Billy Graham Ev. Assn, 2006

Foster, Mrs. Arnold, **In the Valley of the Yangtse**, London Missionary Society, 1899.

Franck, Harry, **China - A Geographical Reader**, F. A Owen Publishing Co, Dansville, NY, 1927

_____ **Roving Through Southern China**, Grosset & Dunlap, New York, 1925

_____ **Wandering in Northern China**, The Century Co, New York, 1923

Fremantle, Anne, **Mao Tse-tung: An anthology,** Mentor, NY 1962

Friberg, H. Daniel, **West China and the Burma Road**, Augustana, Rock Island, IL, 1941

**Frillmann, Paul, and Peck, Graham, **China: The Remembered Life**, Houghton Mifflin, Boston, 1968

**Fuerbringer, Ludwig, ed., **Our China Mission**, Concordia, St. Louis, 1926

Galster, Leonard, **The Lutheran Church in Hong Kong**, booklet, Hong Kong, n.d.

Gannes, Harry, **When China Unites**, Knopf, New York, 1937

Gardner, Charles, ed, **A Union List of Selected Western Books on China in American Libraries**, American Council of Learned Societies, Washington DC, 1938

**Gebhardt, Marie-Louise, *The May 4 Movement*, unpublished thesis, Omaha, 1963

_____ **The Foolish Old Man Who Moved Mountains,** Friendship Press, NY, 1963

Gemmels, D. W., and Walter, N F., **Christianity vs Paganism**, Taiwan Missionaries' Conference of the Lutheran Church, Missouri Synod, Taipei, Free China, 1958

Gibson, J. Campbell, **Mission Problems and Mission Methods in South China**, Oliphant, London, 1901,

Gibson, Rowland, **Forces Mining and Undermining China**, Andrew Melrose, London, 1914

Giles, Herbert, **A Glossary of Reference** *on Subjects Connected with the Far East,* London, 1878

Gilkey, Langdon, **Shantung Compound**, Harper, San Francisco, 1966, 1975

Gittings, John, **China Changes Face**-*the Road from Revolution*, Oxford, New York, 1989

Gittins, Jean, **Stanley: Behind Barbed Wire**, Hong Kong University Press, 1982

Glasser, Arthur, Ed, **Crossroads in Missions**, William Carey, So Pasadena, n.d.

Gleason, Gene, **Hong Kong**, John Day Co, New York, 1963

_____, **Joy to My Heart:** *The true story of nurse Annie Skau*, McGraw-Hill, New York, 1966

Glover, Archibald, **A Thousand Miles of Miracle in China**, Pickering & Inglis, London, 1904

**Gockel, Herman, **The Cross and the Common Man**, Concordia, St. Louis, 1955

Goddard, W. G., **Formosa** - *A Study in Chinese History*, Macmillan, London, 1966

Gowen, Vincent, **Village by the Yangtze**, Douglas-West, Los Angeles, 1975

**Graebner, Theodore, **Concordia Seminary**, *Its History, Architecture, and, Symbolism,* Concordia Publishing House, St. Louis, 1926

** _____ **The Problem of Lutheran Union**, Concordia, St. Louis, 1935

** _____ **Tidings of Great Joy to All People** - *Stories from Mission Fields in Many Lands,* Concordia, St. Louis, n.d. (c 1918)

Green, Michael, **Evangelism in the Early Church**, Erdmanns, Grand Rapids, 1970

Gregory, John S., **The West and China since 1500**, Palgrave MacMillan, NY, 2003

_____ **Great Britain and the Taipings,** Praeger, New York, 1969

**Grindal, Gracia, **Thea Ronning:** Young Woman on a Mission, Lutheran University Press, St. Paul, 2012

Grouch, Archie, **Christianity in China** - *A scholar's Guide to Resources and Archives,* M.E.Sharpe, Inc, Armonk, NY, 1989

Guest, Kenneth J., **God In Chinatown** -*Religion and Survival in New York's Evolving Immigrant Community,* New York University Press, New York, 2003

Han, Dongping, **The Unknown Cultural Revolution** - *Life and Change in a Chinese Village,* Monthly Review Press, NY, 2008

Hao Yen-P'ing, **The Comprador in Nineteenth Century China** - *Bridge between East and West,* Harvard University, Cambridge, 1970

Harrop, Phyllis, **Hong Kong Incident**, Eyre & Spottiswoode, London, 1942

# Bibliography

Hattaway, Paul, **Operation China** - *Introducing all the Peoples of China*, William Carey Library, Piquant, Pasadena, CA, 2000

Hayes, James, **The Hong Kong Region 1850-1911**, Archon, Hamden CT, 1977

Hersey, John, **A Single Pebble**, Knopf, New York, 1956

_____**The Call** - *An American Missionary in China*, Knopf, New York, 1985

Hiebert, P, **Anthropological Insights for Missionaries**, Baker, Grand Rapids, 1985

Hiney, Tom, **On the Missionary Trail**...*with the London Missionary Society*, Atlantic Monthly Press, New York, 2000

Hoke, Donald, ed., **The Church in Asia**, Moody Press, Chicago, 1975

Hollister, Mary Brewster, **South China Folk**, Fleming H. Revell Co, New York, 1935

Holm, Frits, **My Nestorian Adventure in China**, Hutchinson & co, London, 1924;

Hommel, Rudolf, **China at Work**, John Day Co, New York, 1937

Hong Ying, **Daughter of the River**, Grove Press, New York, 1997

Houghton, Frank, **The Two Hundred**, China Inland Mission, Philadelphia, 1932

**Hsiao, Andrew, **A Brief History of the Chinese Lutheran Church**, Taosheng Publishing House, Hong Kong, 1999

Hunter, Jane, **The Gospel of Gentility**: *American Women Missionaries in Turn-of-the-Century China*, Yale University Press, New Haven, 1984

Huping Ling, **Chinese St. Louis**, Temple University Press, Philadelphia, 2004

Hutchinson, Paul, **China's Real Revolution**, Missionary Education Movement, New York, 1924


Ingrams, Harold, **Hong Kong**, Her Majesty's Stationery Office, London, 1952

Isaacs, Harold, **The Tragedy of the Chinese Revolution**, Athenem, New York, 1951


Jenkins, John Edward, **The Coolie - His Rights and Wrongs** Routledge, New York, 1871

Jespersen, T. Christopher, **American Images of China:1931-1949**, Stanford, Palo Alto, 1996

Johnson, Tess, and Erh, Deke, **Near to Heaven** - *Western Architecture in China's Old Summer Resorts*, Old China Hands Press, Hong Kong 1994

Jordan, David, **Gods, Ghosts & Ancestors** - *Folk Religion in a Taiwanese Village*, University of California Press, Berkeley, 1972


Karsen, Wendell, **The Church Under the Cross** - *Mission in Asia in Times of Turmoil*, Vol I & II, Erdmanns, Grand Rapids, 2010

**Kang, C. H. & Nelson, Ethel, **The Discovery of Genesis**, Concordia, St. Louis, 1979

**Keinath, H.O.A., **My Church** - *A History of the Missouri Synod for Young People*, Concordia, St. Louis, 1947

Kilbourne, Edwin, **Bridge Across the Century**, Vol 1 & 2, Oriental Mission Society International, Greenwood, IN, 2001

**King, Robert H, ed, **8 Models of Ethnic Ministry**, Concordia, St. Louis, 2006

Kinnear, Angus, **Against the Tide**: *The Watchman Nee Story*, Tyndall, Wheaton, 1987

**Kohl, David, **Chinese Architecture in the Straits Settlements**, Heinemann, Kuala Lumpur, 1984,

___ _**Dragon Taels**: *Memories of the Golden Age at Hong Kong International School*, One Spirit Press, Portland, 2007

Krarup-Nielsen, A, **The Dragon Awakes**, The Bodley Head, London, 1928

**Kruse, W.H., and Koehler, E.W., **Report on the Term Question**, Christian Book Room, Shanghai, n.d. 1933(?)

Kunos, Eugene, **That I May Tell of Your Marvelous Works**: *Our Life and Missionary Activity in War-Torn China, 1939-1947*, n.p.,Hot Springs AR, 1995

Kwok Pui-Lan, **Chinese Women and Christianity 1860-1927**, Scholars Press, Atlanta, 1992


Lacy, Walter, **A Hundred Years of China Methodism**, Abingdon, New York, 1948

LaFargue, Thomas, **China's First Hundred**, Washington State College, Pullman, 1942

Lang, Olga, **Chinese Family and Society**, Yale University Press, New Haven, 1946

**Lankenau, F. J., **The World Is Our Field**, Concordia, St. Louis, 1928

Latourette, Kenneth, **A History of Christian Missions in China**, London 1929, New York 1932

_____**A History of Christianity**, Harper, New York, 1953

_____**Advance Through Storm (AD 1914 and After)**, History of the Expansion of Christianity Vol 7, Harper & Brothers, New York, 1945

_____**Beyond the Ranges**: *An Autobiography*, Erdmans, Grand Rapids, 1967

# Bibliography

_____ **The Chinese:** *Their History and Culture*, MacMillan, New York, 4th ed ,1962

_____ **The China That Is To Be** - *The Condon Lectures,* Oregon State System of Higher Education, Eugene, 1949

Laury, Preston, **A History of Lutheran Missions**, Pilger Publishing, Reading, PA, 1905

Leck, Greg, **Captives of Empire:** *The Japanese Internment of Allied Civilians in China,1941-1945,* Shandy Press, 2006

Lee, Daniel W., ed, **Lorraine Behling Sonnenberg** - *Handmaid of the Lord*, The Lutheran Church-
Hong Kong Synod, Hong Kong, 2012

**Lee, Vangina (Jean) E., **Bringing Christ to the Chinese** - *China. Hong Kong. San Francisco,*
One Spirit Press, Portland, 2011

Lenker, J.N., **Lutherans in All Lands**, Lutherans in All Lands Co, Milwaukee, 1896

Lewis, Elizabeth Foreman, **Portraits from a Chinese Scroll**, John C Winston, Chicago, 1938

Li, Charles N., **The Bitter Sea** - *Coming of Age in China Before Mao*, Harper, New York, 2008

Li Cheng, **Wanderer** - *Beckoned by Eternity,* Ambassadors for Christ Fnd, Paradise, PA, 2002

**Lillegard, Geo. O, **The Chinese Term Question**, The Christian Book Room, Shanghai, 1935

** _____ *A History of the Term Controversy in Our China Mission*, self-published, Jamaica Plain, MA, 1930

Lin YuTang, **Between Tears and Laughter**, Blue Ribbon Books, Garden City, 1943

_____ **From Pagan to Christian**, The World Publishing Co, Cleveland, 1959

Llewellyn, Bernard, **I Left My Roots in China**, Oxford U Press, New York, 1953

_____ **With my Back to the East**, Travel Book Club, London WC 2, 1958

**Loest, Mark, **How the Missouri Synod was Born**, Concordia Historical Institute, St. Louis, 2001

Lodwick, Kathleen, **Crusaders Against Opium** - *Protestant Missionaries in China, 1874-1917*,
University Press of Kentucky, Lexington, 1996

_____ and Cheng, WK, **The Missionary Kaleidoscope** - *Portraits of Six China Missionaries,*
East Bridge, Norwalk, CT, 2005

Lovett, Richard, **A Primer of Modern Missions**, Religious Tract Society, London, 1896

**Lueker, Erwin, ed, **Lutheran Cyclopedia**, Concordia Publishing House, St. Louis, 1954

**Lueking, F. Dean, **Mission in the Making** -*The Missionary Enterprise Among Missouri Synod Lutherans 1846-1963*,
Concordia, St. Louis, 1964

Luff, John, **The Hidden Years:** *Hong Kong 1941-1945,* South China Morning Post, Ltd, Hong Kong, 1967

Lutheran United Mission, **White Unto Harvest** - *The China Mission of the Norwegian Lutheran Church of America*,
Board of Foreign Missions, Minneapolis, 1919

Lutz, Jessie, **Christian Missions in China** - *Evangelists of What?,* Heath & Co, Boston, 1965


Mabie, Henry, **In Brightest Asia**, 4th edition, W G Corthell, Boston, 1892

Mackay, George Leslie, **From Far Formosa**, Fleming H. Revell, New York, 1895

**Maier, Paul L, **A Man Spoke, A World Listened**, McGraw-Hill, New York, 1963

**Maier, Walter A, **The Lutheran Hour**, Concordia Publishing, St. Louis, 1931

Malcolm, Kari Torgesen, **We Signed Away Our Lives**, Wm Carey Library, Pasadena, CA, 2004

**Manthei, Ben, **In His Majesty's Service**, Creative Cottage Publishing, Charlevoix, MI, 2002

Marsh, James Reid, **The Charm of the Middle Kingdom**, Little, Brown, & Co, Boston,1922

Marsman, Jan Henrik, **I Escaped from Hong Kong**, Reynal & Hitchcock, New York, 1942

Martin, W. A. P. **A Cycle of Cathay**, Oliphant, Anderson, & Ferrier, Edinburgh, 1900

Mateer, C.W., **The Meaning of the Word**, Commercial Press, Shanghai, 1913

McNair, Harley, **The Chinese Abroad**, *Their Position and Protection*, Commercial Press, Shanghai, 1933

**Meinzen, Luther, **A Church in Mission** - *Identity and Purpose in India,* Concordia Seminary,
Nagercoil, Tamilnadu, India, 1981

**Meyer, Carl S, ed., **Moving Frontiers** - *Readings in the History of the Lutheran Church - Missouri Synod,*
Concordia Publishing, St. Louis, 1964

**Meyer, Richard, *The Missouri Evangelical Lutheran Mission in China,*MA thesis,
Washington University, St. Louis, 1948

Michael, Franz, **The TaiPing Rebellion**, University of Washington, Seattle, 1966

Michalson, Carl, **Japanese Contributions to Christian Theology**, Westminster Press, Philadelphia, 1960

Min, Anchee, **Pearl of China**, Bloomsbury, New York, 2010

Mitchison, Lois, **The Overseas Chinese**, The Bodley Head,London, 1961

Moennich, Martha, **On the China Road**, Zondervan, Grand Rapids, 194

Molloy, Robert, **Colossus Unsung** (E.S..Little), Xlibris Corp, print-on-demand, 2012

Moseley, George, **China Since 1911**, Harper & Row, New York, 1969

Mousheng, Lin, **Chungking Dialogues**, John Day Co, New York, 1945

# Bibliography

**Mueller, Adelheid, *For Such a Time as This*, typescript, c1948

**Mueller, J. Theodore, **Great Missionaries to China**, Zondervan, Grand Rapids, 1947

**_____; with Laetsch, Theodore, and Maier, Walter A, **A Reply to the Report of the Term Question Committee**, Concordia Seminary, St. Louis, 1933

Murphey, Rhoads, **The Treaty Ports and China's Modernization: What Went Wrong?**, University of Michigan Center for Asian Studies, Ann Arbor, 1970

Murray, Andrew, **Key to the Missionary Problem**, reprinted by Christian Literature Crusade, Ft. Washington, Penn., 1979


**Naumann, Cheryl, **In the Footsteps of Phoebe** - *A Complete History of the Deaconess Movement in the LC-MS*, Concordia, St. Louis, 2009

Nee, Watchman, **Watchman Nee's Testimony**, Living Stream, Anaheim, 1991

Neill, Stephen, **A History of Christian Missions**, Pelican 1964, Penguin London, 1990

_____, **Colonialism and Christian Missions**, McGraw-Hill, New York, 1966

Nelson, Daniel, **The Apostle to the Chinese Communists**, Augsburg, Minneapolis, 1935

**Nelson, Ethel, **Genesis and the Mystery Confucius Couldn't Solve**, Concordia St.Louis,1994

Nesse, Art, *Growing Up in China*, typescript, Ann Arbor, 2000

Newell, Gordon, **Ocean Liners of the 20th Century**, Superior Publishing, Seattle, 1963

Nida, Eugene, **Customs and Cultures** - *Anthropology for Christian Missions,* reprinted Wm Carey Library, Pasadena, CA, 1986

Nolan, Liam, **Small Man of Nanataki** - *The true story of a Japanese who risked his life to provide comfort for his enemies,* E.P. Dutton & Co, New York, 1966

Northcott, Cecil, **Glorious Company**: *150 years Life and Work of the London Missionary Society 1795-1945,* Livingstone Press (LMS), Westminster, 1945

Nourse, Mary, **A Short History of The Chinese**, New Home Library, NY 1942


**Pahl, Jon, **Hopes and Dreams of All** - *The International Walther League, 1893-1993,* Wheat Ridge Ministries, Chicago, 1993

**Pankow, Fred & Edith, **The Best is Yet to Come**, International Lutheran Laymen's League, St. Louis, 1992

Parker, George, **The Mysterious Yangtze**, Privately Printed, Janesville, WI, 1937

**Parsons, David, **Wait and See**: *A Biography of Herman Klein*, unpublished, 2010

Payne, Robert, **Forever China**, Dodd. Mead, & Co, New York, 1945

Phillips, J. B., **The Young Church in Action**, McMillan, New York, 1955

**Polack, W. G., **Into All the World**: *The Story of Lutheran Foreign Missions,* Concordia, St. Louis, 1930

Pollock, David, **Third Culture Kids**: *The Experience of Growing Up Among Worlds,* Intercultural Press, Yarmouth, ME, 1999

Pollock, John, **A Foreign Devil in China**, Zondervan, Grand Rapids, 1971

_____ **Hudson Taylor and Maria** - *Pioneers in China*, McGraw-Hill, New York, 1962

Porter, Andrew, **Religion versus Empire?** - *British Protestant missionaries and overseas expansion, 1700-1914,* University of Manchester, UK, 2004

Porter, Jonathan, **Macau** - *The Imaginary City*, Westview Press, Boulder, 2000

Porter, Lucius, **China's Challenge to Christianity**, Missionary Education Movement, 1924

Powell, John B, **My Twenty-Five Years in China**, MacMillan, New York, 1945

Priestwood, Gwen, **Through Japanese Barbed Wire**, D. appleton-Century, New York, 1943

Proulx, Benjamin, **Underground from Hong Kong**, Dutton, New York, 1943


Redwood, Mabel Winefred, **It Was LikeThis...**, Anslow, Sheffield, UK, 2001

Reed, James, **The Missionary Mind and American East Asia Policy, 1911-1915,** Harvard University Press, Cambridge, 1983

Reichelt, Karl, **Religion in Chinese Garment**, Philosophical Library, New York, 1931

Reinders, Eric, **Borrowed Gods and Foreign Bodies** - *Christian Missionaries Imagine Chinese Religion,* University of California Press, Berkeley, 2004

**Riedel, Erhardt, A. H. and Schwennesen, Marie, **From the Land of Sinam**, *A biography of my life in Lutheran China Missions,* desktop publishing, Virginia, 1991

Ross, Edward Alsworth, **The Changing Chinese**, Century, New York, 1911

Rowe, William, **Hankow** - *Conflict and Community in a Chinese City, 1796-1895,* Stanford University, 1989

**Rowold, Hank, *Christianity In China* - *class notes*, n.p, Concordia Seminary, St. Louis, 2007

# Bibliography

Schaller, Michael, **The U.S. Crusade in China, 1938-1945,** Columbia U, New York, 197

Scharfstein, Ben-Ami, **The Mind of China,** Basic Books, New York, 1974

Schell, Orville, **Mandate of Heaven,** Simon & Schuster, New York,1994

_____**To Get Rich is Glorious,** Pantheon/Random House, New York, 1984

_____**Watch Out for the Foreign Guests,** Pantheon, New York,1980

Scherer, France Schlosser, **Ambassadors for Christ in China,** Light and Life Press, Winona Lake, MN, 1976

**Schmidt, Otto H, **Globe-Trotting for the Gospel,** Vantage Press, New York, 1962

Schwarcz, Vera, **The Long Road Home** - _A China Journal,_ Yale, New Haven, 1984

Scidmore, Eliza Ruhamah, **China: The Long-Lived Empire,** Century, New York, 1900

Scott, Charles E., **China From Within**: _Impressions and Experiences,_ Revell, London, 1917,

Scott, Robert, **God Is My Co-Pilot,** Random House / Ballantine, New York, 1943

Scovel, Myra, **The Chinese Ginger Jars,** Harper, New York, 1962

Sharlpe, Eric, **Karl Ludvig Reichelt,** Tao Fung Shan, Hong Kong, 1984

Sewell, William, **The Land and Life of China,** Edinburgh House Press, London, 1933

Shanghai Cultural Publishing House, **Anecdotes of Old Shanghai,** Xinhua, Shanghai, 1985

Shapiro, Sidney, _An American in China:_ Thirty years in the People's Republic, Meridian (New American Library),
    New York, 1980

Sherertz, Paul, Ed, _**Lushan Memories**_ - _Stories of Kuling American Schoo,_l n.p., San Diego, 1988

Slyke, Lyman, **Yangtze** - _Nature, History, and the River_, Addison-Wesley, Reading, MA, 1988

Smith, Arthur H., **Chinese Characteristics,** Fleming H. Revell, New York, 1899

_____**The Uplift of China,** _Forward Mission Study Courses,_ General Conference of Free Baptists, Hiillsdale, MI, 1907

Smith, Carl T, **Chinese Christians:** _Elites, Middlemen, and the Church in Hong Kong,_
    Hong Kong University Press, Hong Kong 2005

Snow, Edgar, **Red Star Over China,** Bantam Books, NY, 1978; Random House, 1938

Snow, Lois Wheeler, **Edgar Snow's China,** Random House, NY, 1981

Spence, Jonathan, **To Change China** - _Western Advisors in China 1620-1960._ Penguin Books, New York, 1980

Springweiler, Max, **Pioneer Aviator in China,** _Air America Association,_ Dallas, 1998, translated by Larry D. Sall, PhD,
    from the original German **Flugpioneer in China,** Hamburg, 1996

Spurling, Hilary, **Pearl Buck in China**: _Journey to the Good Earth,_ Simon & Schuster, New York, 2010

Stanley, C.A., **The Word for God in Chinese,** Methodist Publishing House, Shanghai, 1909

Stauffer, Milton, **The Christian Occupation of China,** China Continuation Committee, Shanghai, 1922

Stewart, James L, **Chinese Culture and Christianity,** Fleming H. Revell Co, New York, 1926

Stockwell, F. Olin, **With God in Red China** - _The Story of Two Years in Chinese Communist Prisons,_
    Harper & Brothers, New York, 1953

**Strege, Paul, **How Small is Small?** _From Ludell to Beirut in Christ's Global Mission,_
    Chipmunk Chapel Books, St. Louis, 2002

Strong, Anna Louise, **China Fights for Freedom,** Lindsay Drummond, Ltd, London, 1939

**Suelflow, August, ed, **Heritage in Motion:** _Readings in the History of the Lutheran Church-Missouri Synod,_
    Concordia, St. Louis,1998

**Suelflow, Roy A .**Challenge in China:** _the Mission Enterprise of the Lutheran Church-Missouri Synod in Mainland
    China 1913-1952,_ unpublished thesis manuscript, University of Wisconsin, Madison, 1971

Sunquist, Scott, ed, **A Dictionary of Asian Christianity,** Erdmanns, Grand Rapids, 2001

Suyin, Han, **A Mortal Flower,** Mayflower paperback, London, 1970

_____**Wind In the Tower,** _Mao Tse Tung 1949-1976_, Triad Panther, England, 1978

Swift, Catherine, **Gladys Aylward,** Bethany House, Minneapolis, 1984


**Taege, Marlys, **WINGS - Women In God's Service,** Lutheran Women's Missionary League, St. Louis, 1991

Taylor, Howard, **Hudson Taylor's Spiritual Secret,** Moody Press, Chicago, 1932

Teague, Dennis, **Culture: The Missing Link in Missions,** OMF Literature, Manilla, 1996

Tharp, Robert, **They Called Us White Chinese,** Eva E. Tharp, Charlotte, NC, 1994

**Thode, Frieda Oelschlaeger, _**"In China and Hong Kong with Deth"**_ unpublished

Thompson, Laurence, **The Chinese Way in Religion,** Wadsworth, Belmont, CA, 1973

Thurin, Susan Schoenbauer, **Victorian Travelers and the Opening of China, 1842-1907,**
    Ohio University Press, Athens, 1999

**Todd, Mary, **Authority Vested,** _A Story of Identity and Change in the Lutheran Church - Missouri Synod,_
    Erdmann's, Grand Rapids, 2000

Tolley, Kemp, **Yangtze Patrol** - _The US Navy in China,_ Naval Institute, Annapolis, 1971

# Bibliography

Tong, John, **Challenges and Hopes**: *Stories from the Catholic Church in China*,
      Holy Spirit Study Center, Hong Kong , 2002
Townsend, W. J., **Robert Morrison- Pioneer of Missions to China**, Pickering & Inglis, London, n.d.
Tsou, Tang, **America's failure in China**, **1941-50**, University of Chicago, 1963
Tuchman, Barbara, **Notes from China**, Collier Books, New York, 1972
_____**Stillwell and the American Experience in China 1911-1945**, Macmillan,New York, 1971
Tucker, Ruth, **Daughters of the Church** - *Women and Ministry from New Testament times to the present*,
      Acadamie Books, Grand Rapids, 1987

Varg, Paul, **Missionaries, Chinese, and Diplomats** - *The American Protestant Missionary Movement in China,
      1890-1952*, Princeton U Press, Princeton, 1958
Verstappen, Stefan, **The Thirty-Six Strategies of Ancient China**, China Books and Periodicals, San Francisco, 1999
**Vickner, David W, "The Role of Christian Mission in the Establishment of Hong Kong's
      Education System**,*"* Ed D dissertation, Columbia University, NY, 1987

Walker, Caroline, **On Leaving Bai Di Cheng** - *The Culture of China's Yangzi Gorges*,  NC Press Ltd, Toronto, 1993
Walther, Carl Ferdinand Wilhelm, **The Proper Distinction between Law and Gospel**, Concordia, St. Louis, 1929
Wang, Gung-Hsing, **The Chinese Mind**, John Day, New York, 1946
Wang Ming-dao, **A Call to the Church**, Christian Literature Crusade, Ft Washington, PA, 1983
Warneck, Gustav, **Outline of a History of Protestant Missions**, Fleming Revell Co, New York, 1901
**Werling, Wilbert*, Up The Han from Hankow*, 1930-36, typescript, Chico, CA, 1989
White, Theodore, **Thunder Out of China**, Wm Sloane, New York, 1946
**Wiesenauer, Stephen, **The Missouri Synod in China**, Christian Friends Of China, Minneapolis, unpublished, 2007
Wildman, Rounsevelle, **China's Open Door** - *A sketch of Chinese Life and History*, Lothrop Publishing, Boston, 1900
Williams, C.A.S., **Outlines of Chinese Symbolism and Art Motives**, Kelly and Walsh, Shanghai, 1941
Wilson, Kenneth, **Angel at Her Shoulder** - *The Story of"Typhoon" Lil Dickson*, Harper & Row,New York, 1964
Wintle, Justin, **The Timeline History of China**, Barnes & Noble, New York, 2005
Wolf, Arthur. ed. **Religion and Ritual in Chinese Society**, Stanford University, Stanford, 1974
Wood, Dorothy Zimmermann*, Memories of Kuling*, unpublished, Washington, MO
Worcester, G.R.G., **The Junks and Sampans of the Yangtze**, Naval Institute, Annapolis, MD, 1971
Wright-Nooth, **Prisoner of the Turnip Heads**, Leo Cooper, London, 1994

Xinran, **China Witness** – *Voices from a Silent Generation*, Pantheon, New York, 2008

Yang Sen-Fu, **A History of Nestorian Christianity in China**, www.booksurge.com, 2007
**Yee, Edmond, **The Soaring Crane** - *Stories of Asian Lutherans in North America*,
      Augsburg Fortress, Minneapois, 2002

**Ziegler, Albert *, Biographies of Missouri Synod Missionaries in China, 1913-52,* unpublished 1981
**Zimmer, Robert, **Dreams Come True** - *Memories of a Prairie Boy*, Sorrels Printing, Ocala, FL, 2006
**Zimmermann, B. Christian, **Hostage in a Hostage World** - *Hope aboard Hijacked TWA 847*,
      Concordia, St.Louis,1985
**Zimmermann, Elmer C*, Ancestor Worship*: *A Dissertation*, Concordia Seminary, St. Louis, 1943, unpublished

# Bibliography

**Periodicals:**
China's Millions (China Inland Mission)
Concordia Historical Institute Quarterly
Concordia Theological Monthly
**Der Lutheraner**
*Lu-teh-chiao chien-cheng* (Chinese Lutheran Witness)
LWML Quarterly (Lutheran Women's Missionary League)
Walther League Messenger
The Lutheran Witness
The Lutheran Layman

**Films:**
*In the Wild Mountains
*Balzac and the Little Chinese Seamstress
*Eat Drink Man Woman
*Raise the Red Lantern
*TaiPan
*Joy Luck Club
*Empire of the Sun
*The Sand Pebbles
*The Painted Veil
*Postmen in the Mountains
*Made in China (documentary)
*Inn of the Sixth Happiness
*The Road Home

**Television:**
" "From Pew to Pulpit" NBC c1980 (B. Chr. Zimmermann)

**Websites:**
www.lutheransontheyangtze.com
www.bdcconline.net/en/ - Biographical Dictionary of Chinese Christianity
www.gospelherald.net - Gospel Herald news service
www.clswebblog.blogspot.tw    hsinshen@cls.org
www.molife.hk - Messengers of Life
www.orientalarchitecture.com
www.vatican2voice.org
www.cwef.org.hk - ConcordiaWelfare and Education Foundation
www.lcms.org - Lutheran Church MissouriSynod
www.missioncentral.us - MissionCentral
www. gwulo.com (Stanley Camp Surviors)

Colophon

Titles and Text set in Hiroshige
using Adobe Indesign

History

Hiroshige was designed in 1986 by Cynthia Hollandsworth of AlphaOmega Typography, Inc. The typeface was originally commissioned for a book of woodblock prints by the great nineteenth-century Japanese artist Ando Hiroshige, whose work influenced many Impressionist artists. The typeface has a gentle calligraphic flair that creates an interesting page of text as well as elegant headlines.

**onespiritpress.com**
**onespiritpress@gmail.com**

Made in the USA
Charleston, SC
23 November 2013